The Metaphysics of the *Tractatus*

The Metaphysics of
the *Tractatus*

PETER CARRUTHERS

Senior Lecturer, Department of Philosophy,
University of Essex

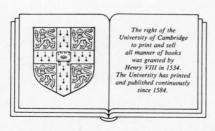

The right of the
University of Cambridge
to print and sell
all manner of books
was granted by
Henry VIII in 1534.
The University has printed
and published continuously
since 1584.

CAMBRIDGE UNIVERSITY PRESS

Cambridge
New York   Port Chester
Melbourne   Sydney

Published by the Press Syndicate of the University of Cambridge
The Pitt Building, Trumpington Street, Cambridge CB2 1RP
40 West 20th Street, New York, NY 10011, USA
10 Stamford Road, Oakleigh, Melbourne 3166, Australia

First published 1990

Printed in Great Britain at the University Press, Cambridge

British Library cataloguing in publication data

Carruthers, Peter
The metaphysics of the Tractatus.
1. Philosophical logic. Wittgenstein, Ludwig, 1889–1951.
Tractatus logico-philosophicus
I. Title
160

Library of Congress cataloguing in publication data

Carruthers, Peter, 1952–
The metaphysics of the Tractatus / Peter Carruthers.
    p.   cm.
Includes bibliographical references.
ISBN 0 521 39131 8
1. Wittgenstein, Ludwig, 1889–1951. Tractatus logico-
philosophicus. 2. Logic, Symbolic and mathematical. 3. Languages –
Philosophy. 4. Metaphysics. I. Title.
B3376.W563T73224 1990
192 – dc20   89–77289   CIP

WD

for Susan
music and meaning

Contents

Abbreviations

TS   Carruthers *Tractarian Semantics* (1989b). References by chapter number.

FA   Frege *The Foundations of Arithmetic* (1968). References by section number.

NB   Wittgenstein *Notebooks 1914–16* (1961b). References by page number.

PTLP   Wittgenstein *Prototractatus* (1971). References by section number.

TLP   Wittgenstein *Tractatus Logico-Philosophicus* (1922) and (1961a). References by section number.

PR   Wittgenstein *Philosophical Remarks* (1975). References by section number.

PI   Wittgenstein *Philosophical Investigations* (1953). References by section number.

Preface

This work brings to completion my project of defending what can be defended in Wittgenstein's *Tractatus Logico-Philosophicus*. His main semantic doctrines were dealt with in an earlier book, *Tractarian Semantics*, where I argued that they are not only defensible but mostly true. Here I consider his views on metaphysics and their relationship to his conception of logic. What I shall show is that this aspect of *TLP* is at least a good deal more plausible than is generally recognised.

(A) Aims and scope

The main aims of this work are two-fold: firstly, to make sense of the metaphysical doctrines of *TLP* by showing how powerful arguments may be deployed in their support; and secondly, to locate the crux of the disagreements between *TLP* and *Philosophical Investigations*. Most interpreters of *TLP* set it up as an Aunt Sally, attributing to Wittgenstein doctrines and arguments which are both implausible in themselves and easily knocked over by points made in the early sections of *PI*.[1] I shall argue, on the contrary, that when *TLP* is properly interpreted it turns out to contain a powerful set of doctrines, in contrast with which many of the *PI* criticisms may be seen to be facile. But this is not to say that the two works simply pass one another by. Indeed, the major premiss behind much of the metaphysics of *TLP* and its associated programme of analysis is a certain conception of the objectivity of logic and of logical relations, which I entitle 'logical objectivism'. In Chapter 15 I shall show how this same conception is the direct target of attack of the later Wittgenstein's discussions of rule-following. So *PI* does indeed contain a critique of his early thought, which goes to its very foundations. But that critique is quite other than what most commentators have believed.

Having outlined some of the main semantic doctrines of *TLP* in Chapter 1, the discussion thereafter will centre around four general themes:

1   The early Wittgenstein's view of the relationship between metaphysics, on the one hand, and semantical and logical investigations on the other; together with the question whether certain sorts of metaphysics are possible at all. This will form the topic of Chapters 2 and 3.

2   The question of the objectivity, or otherwise, of logical relations and of the principles of logic. This will form the topic of Chapters 4, 11 and 15.

3   The nature and purpose of the *TLP* programme of analysis for ordinary language, together with the various constraints which Wittgenstein imposes on the nature of elementary propositions. This will form the topic of Chapters 5–8, 13 and 14.

4   The various possible arguments for the existence of the simple objects of *TLP* ('Simples'), concluding with the one which constitutes my preferred interpretation, which is very powerful. This will form the topic of Chapters 9, 10 and 12.

Finally, in Chapter 16 I shall draw together the main strands of my discussion, to locate the fundamental point of conflict between *TLP* and *PI*.

These themes are linked together by the doctrine of logical objectivism, which is initially outlined in Chapter 3 and then defended in Chapter 4. I shall show that it is this which ultimately makes metaphysics possible, on the *TLP* view. It is also what underlies and provides the rationale for the *TLP* programme of analysis, which is to show how our ordinary propositions are really truth-functional compounds of elementary propositions. Furthermore, it will emerge that it is logical objectivism which provides the major premiss of the argument to Simples. So if the critique of logical objectivism mounted in *PI* is effective, as I shall argue that it is, then all of these aspects of *TLP* will be undermined. Yet in so far as logical objectivism may be seen as a plausible doctrine, the metaphysics of *TLP* will have been shown to be defensible in its turn. Moreover, since the underlying semantic system of *TLP* (outlined in Chapter 1 and defended at length in *TS*) is independent of any commitment to logical objectivism, this aspect of Wittgenstein's early thought will turn out to be largely unscathed by his own later criticisms. So my overall verdict on the semantical and metaphysical doctrines of *TLP* will be, respectively: controversial-and-true; and defensible-but-false.

Aside from leading to a better appreciation of one of the classic texts of our subject, my hope is that this book will contribute to contemporary discussion in at least two ways. In the first place, there are many philosophers who still endorse something like the idea I call 'logical objectivism', but without dreaming that they may thereby be committed to *TLP*'s metaphysics. So if I can succeed in showing that there are sound arguments from the one to the other, I may give these philosophers pause for thought. At the very least they will be presented with a challenge: to show how they can remain logical objectivists without embracing Wittgenstein's metaphysics. Secondly, many contemporary philosophers are currently wrestling with Wittgenstein's later writings, particularly on rule-following. But there is little unity of interpretation, or agreement about the significance of his arguments.[2] This partly results from failure to understand *TLP* properly.[3] So if I can succeed in setting these later remarks in their proper perspective, contrasting with the very basis of his earlier way of thinking, we may ourselves get closer to the truth. For the more accurate our interpretation of one of the great philosophers of the past, the more likely it is that our own engagement with their ideas will prove fruitful.

While this book makes no attempt at completeness, even when taken together with its predecessor *TS*, there are a number of respects in which the resulting view of *TLP* may strike many as not only incomplete but positively distorted. For example, I shall pay scant attention to Wittgenstein's official doctrine that all philosophical and metaphysical statements are nonsensical. This is because that doctrine merely results, in my view, from an over-extension of the *TLP* account of the semantic content of factual statements to cover all forms of discourse, as I shall show briefly in Chapter 1. The mistake is easily corrected, consistent with *TLP*'s other doctrines. And of course the official doctrine is, in any case, violated systematically throughout *TLP* itself.

Another omission is any detailed discussion of the formal apparatus involved in Wittgenstein's treatment of logic. It is easy to justify the lack of discussion of truth-tables, in that they have long since passed into the canon of logic orthodoxy; and what is still controversial about them – namely the commitment to a two-valued logic – can be considered separately, as I do in Chapter 11. As for the N-operator, which occupies such a prominent place in Wittgenstein's text, it is in fact both technically flawed[4] and insufficiently motivated. Or rather, while the aim of using just a single operator adequate for the whole of logic may have made sense given the state of logic at the time (namely in order to avoid piecemeal definitions),[5] the problem may equally be overcome, as we now know, through the use of definitions which are *recursive*. So this aspect of *TLP* is no longer of any contemporary interest.

I shall also say nothing about Wittgenstein's remarks on value and on mysticism, which have attracted so much attention in certain quarters, although it seems likely that Wittgenstein himself believed in a connection between his work on logic and his views on value.[6] Nevertheless, since it is, in my view, clearly unnecessary to take any particular stance on the *TLP* doctrine of the Ethical in order to interpret and assess the semantic and metaphysical doctrines which make up the body of the work, and since my own assessment of the former is less than flattering, I have thought it best to follow Mother Rabbit's excellent advice: 'If you can't say something nice, don't say nothing at all.'[7]

(B) Interpreting *TLP*

There are a number of principles which should be mentioned, which will need to be employed in interpreting *TLP*.[8] Two general ones are Textual Fidelity (which enjoins us to choose the interpretation which most naturally fits the text) and Charity (according to which we should select the interpretation which maximises the interest of the text). These principles can sometimes pull against one another, the process of interpretation best being seen as a search for a sort of reflective equilibrium between them. For on the one hand, there is a presumption that authors will mean what they say. But on the other, if we respect their intelligence, we should hesitate to attribute to them doctrines which are either trivial or foolish. In the case of *TLP*, whose doctrines are not only obscure but given very little explicit argumentative support, the role of Charity becomes maximal. The main task of an interpreter of *TLP* is to make sense of Wittgenstein's ideas, extraordinary as some of them are.[9]

There are a number of more specific principles relating to the secondary sources which might be appealed to in support of an interpretation of *TLP*. Firstly, very considerable weight may be attached to remarks in *Proto-tractatus*, since it is so close in time to the composition of *TLP* itself, probably having been written during the same two-month leave from the army in the summer of 1918.[10] But differences between the two texts need to be handled with caution, since they admit of a variety of possible explanations, ranging from the stylistic to substantial changes of mind. Secondly, some weight should be attached to Wittgenstein's letters to Russell soon after the completion of *TLP*.[11] But since they were evidently composed with much impatience, they too will need to be handled with caution. Thirdly, the writings in *Notebooks 1914–16* should not be relied upon directly. They should rather be used as background material, giving an indication of the issues with which Wittgenstein was wrestling in the period leading up to the composition of *TLP*. For since they date from between two and six years previously, there is evidently much scope for further development and shifts of direction.

Most importantly, Wittgenstein's later reported or written comments on *TLP* (either in the conversations with Waismann or his lectures at Cambridge,[12] or in *Philosophical Remarks, PI* and elsewhere), together with those remarks which are generally taken to refer to *TLP* (many of the early passages in *PI*, on names, Simples and analysis fall into this category), should be given no independent weight in the interpretation of his early thought. This is a severe, but defensible, restriction. For notice that eleven years elapsed between the completion of *TLP* in 1918 and the first of the recorded remarks in 1929, during which time Wittgenstein not only did very little philosophy, but found thinking about his own work extremely slow and painful.[13] Notice also that the writing of *TLP* seems to have been highly intuitive, with much apparently going unsaid, even in Wittgenstein's own thoughts.[14] He may therefore, in later years, have had difficulty in thinking his way back into the full complexity of his earlier text – especially given the restless and forward-looking nature of his intellect. In any case, if we wish to assess the conflict between Wittgenstein's early and later philosophies, then we had better not assume at the outset that he both understood and had the measure of his earlier way of thinking. So I shall abide by this restriction in what follows, controversial though it no doubt is.[15]

(C) Notes on style

Anyone can see that *TLP* is a work of extraordinary beauty; yet what makes it attractive is partially responsible for its obscurity. Firstly, because it is written in the style of pithy aphorism, without properly developed explanations of its own doctrines. And secondly, because it is mostly presented in the form of oracular statements, without supporting argument. (Wittgenstein is said to have replied to Russell's admonition that he should give more arguments, by remarking that they spoiled the beauty of his conclusions, like dirtying a flower with muddy hands.[16]) Such a mode of writing serves no one well. In attempting to ride two horses at once (truth and beauty), it risks falling between them. In philosophy it is clarity and explicitness that matter above all. For only what is plainly stated can be reliably assessed for truth, either by oneself or others. To adapt a remark from *TLP* itself: what is to be said at all should be said clearly.[17] In my own writing, therefore, I try to be as open and straightforward as possible.

In order to leave the main text of this book as uncluttered as possible, my disagreements with other commentators are mostly confined to notes. But references to *TLP* are given by section-number within the text itself, so as to keep the numbers of notes from spiralling out of all control.

Throughout this work I opt to use the colloquial plural pronouns 'they' and 'their' in impersonal contexts, in place of the pernicious masculine singular required by strict grammar.

(D) Acknowledgements

My main debts are to Roger White, who was my first teacher of *TLP*, and from whom I derive many of the interpretations which follow; and to Michael Dummett, whose work on semantic realism forms the background to much of this book. I am also grateful to the following for their helpful comments on earlier drafts: David Bell, Laurence Goldstein, Jane Heal, Hidé Ishiguro, Susan Levi, Christopher McKnight and Tim Williamson. Thanks also go to Gregory Currie for his comments on versions of Chapters 2–4, and to Crispin Wright, both for his criticisms of an early version of Chapter 15, and for his advice and encouragement over many years.

Some of the ideas presented here are based upon previous papers of mine, in particular my (1981), (1984) and (1985). Although this material has been substantially revised and corrected, I am grateful, respectively, to the editor of *Aristotelian Society Proceedings*, to the publisher of *Synthese* – Kluwer Academic Publishers – and to the editor of *Philosophia* for permission to make use of it.

I am grateful to Wittgenstein's trustees for permission to quote from posthumously published sources, as to Routledge for permission to quote from *TLP* itself.

1 Semantic background

In this opening chapter I shall explain the main aspects of my interpretation of the semantic doctrines of *TLP*. These were defended at considerable length in *TS*. Readers already familiar with that work may like to move on immediately to Chapter 2.

(A) *Sinn* and sense

In order to interpret *TLP* properly, it is crucial to understand Wittgenstein's use of the terminology of '*Sinn*', '*Bedeutung*' and '*Satz*', and to elucidate the semantic doctrines within which these terms are embedded. My view is that the word '*Sinn*' in *TLP* should be translated as 'truth-condition', instead of the more usual 'sense'. (More accurately, it should be translated as 'directed set of truth and falsity conditions', in the light of the *TLP* doctrine of the essential directedness of *Sinn* – see 3.144.[1]) For the *TLP* notion of *Sinn* is not a cognitive one, as is Frege's notion of sense. Rather than being a *mode of thinking* about the world, it is what we *think about*, the existence and non-existence of possible states of affairs.

In order to see that this is so, notice that when the notion of the *Sinn* of a picture is first introduced at 2.221, it is said to be *what* a picture represents, rather than the *way* in which it represents what it does (as we might have expected given Frege's famous metaphor of *Sinn* as the 'mode of presentation' of *Bedeutung*). Then at 3.13 we are told that a proposition – that is to say, a sentence standing in its projective relation to reality (3.12) – does not actually contain its *Sinn*, does not contain *what* is projected. This makes it clear that the *Sinn* of a sentence is something which belongs at the level of reference, rather than of Fregean sense. Indeed, 4.1211 implies that the *Sinn* of the proposition 'Fb' will contain the object b itself. So it is the referents of the component expressions of a sentence which figure in its *Sinn*, and not their senses (supposing that they have senses). We get the smoothest reading in all this if we assume that '*Sinn*' means something like 'truth-condition' throughout.

My view concerning the *TLP* use of '*Bedeutung*' is that it should be translated neither as 'reference' nor '(Russellian) meaning', but rather as 'semantic content'; though this will take some explaining. Firstly, notice that Wittgenstein is prepared to speak of the *Bedeutung* of expressions where it is perfectly clear that he does not regard those expressions as referring to anything in reality, such as the sentence '−P' and the sign '+' (5.02), the negation-sign '−' (5.451), and number words such as '1+1' and '2' (6.232). This suggests very strongly that the *Bedeutung* of an expression cannot be its referent, or anything like its referent. Yet on the other hand, at 3.203 we are told that a name *bedeutet* an object, the object being the name's *Bedeutung*. We may be puzzled how this remark is supposed to be understood if '*Bedeutung*' does *not* mean 'referent'.

In fact there is no special difficulty here. First of all, let us introduce the notion of the *semantic content* of an expression, to mean whatever must be known by one who is to understand it; or alternatively, as whatever that expression contributes to what is literally communicated by statements containing it. (I regard these formulations as equivalent.) The crucial point here is that there is nothing in the notion of semantic content as such to require that a semantic content be a possible object of reference − an item in reality. Then if we suppose that '*Bedeutung*' means 'semantic content' throughout *TLP*, it is easy to understand how the negation-sign can have *Bedeutung*, since it certainly makes a contribution to the communicated content of statements which contain it. Yet we can also understand how the *Bedeutung* of a name can be an object, if we suppose that Wittgenstein's doctrine is that in order to understand the contribution made by a proper name to a statement containing it, you are only required to know *which* thing the person in question is talking about (see Section C below).

Notice that on the reading of the *TLP* terminology of '*Sinn*' and '*Bedeutung*' presented here, it turns out that *Sinn* is a kind of *Bedeutung* − thus explaining how 5.02 can speak of sentences as having *Bedeutung*. Indeed, *Sinn* is the distinctive sort of semantic content that sentences have, in that Wittgenstein's view is that in order to understand a statement, it is only necessary to know its *Sinn* (truth-condition). Thus see 4.02–4.022, where it is implied that to understand a proposition is to know its *Sinn*, which is a matter of knowing the situation it represents − of knowing how things stand in the world if it is true (see also 4.024). And see also 4.03, which implies that what a proposition communicates is its *Sinn*. So a *Sinn* is the communicated content (*Bedeutung*) of a sentence.[2]

Although in *TLP* terminology the *Sinn* of a sentence is its truth-condition, Wittgenstein does in fact find room for a notion similar to that of Fregean sense, expressed in (the normal use of) the terminology of 'symbol' ('*Symbol*') and 'proposition' ('*Satz*').[3] But sense is not, as in Frege, detachable from the use of signs (see Section E below). Rather, a symbol is a sign together with its sense – together with the mode of thinking which it expresses, or with its mode of projection on to reality; and a proposition is a kind of symbol (at least throughout most of *TLP*).

That this is so is strongly suggested by the fact that a proposition is defined, at 3.12, as a sentence in its projective relation to the world, and that 3.11 implies that a proposition is a sentence used as a projection of a possible situation. These remarks are highly reminiscent of Frege, in a way that must surely have been intended. For the idea of the *projection* of a sentence on to the world seems to be the exact mirror-image of the Fregean metaphor of sense as the *mode of presentation* of *Bedeutung*. Moreover, 3.321 implies that a sign may express different symbols by virtue of signifying in different ways, which again suggests that the notion of a *symbol* is being tied to that of a *way of signifying* (which must be something like a Fregean sense).[4]

While Wittgenstein employs the notion of a symbol in such a way as to suggest that a symbol is a sign together with its mode of projection on to reality (that is, together with its Fregean sense), he also implies that the use of any particular symbol is never essential to what is said (see 3.344, 4.465). Indeed, this is how the idea of there being different symbols with the same *Bedeutung* gets introduced again and again throughout *TLP*, namely under the guise of a distinction between essential and inessential aspects of language. In Wittgenstein's view, the substitution of one symbol for another makes no essential difference, provided that *Sinn* and *Bedeutung* (semantic content) remain the same.

I think we can understand what is going on here, if we see Wittgenstein as endorsing one aspect of Frege's theory of sense, but rejecting another. He is accepting that thought about reality cannot be immediate (as Russell would have it),[5] but is always mediated by modes of presentation; accepting also that the reference (more generally the semantic content) of a sign is determined by the mode of thinking which it expresses. But he is denying Frege's thesis that mutual knowledge of sense is necessary for communication. In Frege's view speakers only understand one another in the use of an expression if they both associate it with the very same sense.[6] This is what Wittgenstein is denying when he denies that differences in symbol are essential. Rather, for the purpose of communication it is sufficient that speakers should know that their sentences share the same truth-conditions (*Sinn*), and more generally know that their expressions possess, in their respective idiolects, the same semantic contents (*Bedeutung*).

Wittgenstein's doctrines concerning *Sinn* and *Bedeutung* then contain a theory of communication to rival Frege's. Since he holds that it is sufficient for two sentences to say the same thing (to possess the same *Sinn*) that they be analytically equivalent (5.141),[7] two speakers may be said to understand one another in the use of a sentence provided that they know that it is, in their respective idiolects, true in the same possible worlds (as a matter of conceptual rather than metaphysical necessity).[8] And since (as we shall see in Sections C and D below) two atomic sentences possess the same *Sinn* just in case they make analytically equivalent predications of the very same individuals, two speakers may be said to understand one another in the use of such a sentence provided they know that it serves, in their respective idiolects, to say the very same things about the same individuals. But it is not as if we are supposed to be able to think about sets of possible worlds or individual objects directly. It is merely that the modes of thinking (senses, cognitive contents) involved are relegated to the province of psychology, in that mutual possession of them is not required for communication.[9]

(B) Sense and nonsense

In my view Wittgenstein's showing/saying doctrine, together with the doctrine of philosophy as nonsense, flows fairly directly from the theory of communication outlined above. The more usual way of accounting for these doctrines, however, is in terms of the impossibility of using language to represent what is essential to language or the world without presupposing exactly what is being described. This idea is certainly there in *TLP* (see 2.172), but it cannot be the whole story. For what this account fails to explain is why we should not be able to rely upon our inchoate, implicit, grasp of logical form in order to make that very same form articulate and explicit. For Wittgenstein does in any case acknowledge that the logical form of our language can be hidden from our conscious awareness (4.002).

In fact the correct way to explain Wittgenstein's views is as follows. Tautologies, contradictions and the propositions of mathematics are said to be senseless (*sinnlos*), because they fail to mark a division within the set of possible worlds. A tautology is true in all worlds, whereas a contradiction is true in none. Then since neither has a directed truth-condition (a *Sinn*), neither can succeed in saying or communicating anything. They are nevertheless well formed, consisting of legitimate combinations of signs each of which possesses semantic content. Propositions of philosophy and metaphysics, on the other hand, are said to be nonsensical (*unsinnig*), because they characteristically contain terms (such as 'necessary' or 'impossible') which can only ever figure in sentences which are necessarily true or necessarily false.[10] These terms then lack semantic content (*Bedeutung*), since they fail to make a contribution to the semantic content (*Sinn*) of sentences in which they occur. Nevertheless, Wittgenstein thinks that tautologies and contradictions (and even, in some obscure way, the nonsensical propositions of philosophy, since these can help us to see the world aright – 6.54) can *show* us something about the essential structure of language and the world.[11]

In my view these doctrines are unjustified. Wittgenstein has taken a theory of semantic content which provides an adequate account of communication for factual (broadly scientific) discourse, and attempted to extend its scope to cover discourse of all kinds, including that of mathematics and philosophy. What ought rather to be said is that the concepts of semantic content and of understanding are purpose-relative, varying in the conditions of their application according to the context in question. Roughly, to know the semantic content of an utterance of a sentence is to know *enough about the mode of thinking which it expresses for the purposes in hand*. Where the context is a factual one, the condition for understanding will be mutual knowledge of truth-conditions, just as Wittgenstein claims. But where the context is that of an *a priori* investigation of some sort, the condition for understanding will be mutual knowledge of sense (cognitive content). And for other forms of discourse the conditions for understanding will be different again.[12]

An account of the above sort enables us to provide for the significance of statements in philosophy and logic, while recognising the correctness of the *TLP* theory of communication within the crucially central area of fact-stating. Since the account can be combined with a univocal (if purpose relative) definition of semantic content, it is even consistent with Wittgenstein's project of uncovering the essence of language. It then follows that the doctrine of philosophy as nonsense may simply be excised from *TLP*, without damage to the remainder. It is for this reason that I feel myself justified in laying Wittgenstein's official attitude towards philosophy to one side in my discussions of his metaphysics.[13]

(C) Name and object

The correct interpretation of the *TLP* terminology of 'name' and 'object' will prove crucial, not only for our understanding of the *TLP* semantics of proper names and predicative expressions (see below and Section D), but also for our account of Wittgenstein's metaphysical views and programme of analysis, to be considered extensively in the present work. I maintain that this terminology should be interpreted narrowly, with *TLP* names being proper names (excluding predicates and relational expressions) and *TLP* objects being individuals, not including properties or relations (universals). There is a great deal of textual evidence in support of this reading, and no insuperable textual evidence against it – though the story is far too complex to be gone into in any detail here.[14]

It should be stressed, however, that a large part of the case for the narrow reading is not textual at all, but turns rather on considerations of Charity. For if 'name' and 'object' are interpreted widely, to cover predicates and universals respectively, then many of the *TLP* doctrines become weak and anodyne as a result.[15] In contrast, if those terms are interpreted narrowly, these same doctrines become powerful and interesting, and the Picture Theory can be understood to embody a new and correct account of the semantics of predicative expressions (see Section D below). So my view is that we should, in charity to Wittgenstein as well as in fidelity to his text, prefer the narrow interpretation.

Perhaps the most powerful textual argument supporting the narrow reading of the name/object terminology is provided by the spatial metaphors which dominate Wittgenstein's presentation of the Picture Theory. States of affairs are said to be 'combinations' or 'configurations' of objects (2.01, 2.0271–2.0272); and it is said to be the determinate relation obtaining between the names in a sentence which enables it to signify (2.14), with a sentence being compared to a *tableau vivant* (4.0311; see also 3.1431). These images become entirely inappropriate if objects include relations as well as individuals, and if names include relational expressions as well as proper names.

In order to see that this is so, notice that Wittgenstein would then be saying that in a state of affairs of the form aRb, the individuals a and b and the relation R stand in a determinate relation to one another – inviting the question '*Which* relation do they stand in, then?' and threatening a vicious regress. And in connection with sentences he would face a dilemma. Either he would be saying that in the sentence 'aRb' the names 'a', 'R' and 'b' stand in a determinate relation to one another, which precisely conflicts with what is held to be the main point of the Picture Theory by those who adopt the wide interpretation – namely that what really signifies the relation in 'aRb' is not the sign 'R' itself, but rather the *relation* obtaining between the signs 'a' and 'b' when they are written on either side of the sign 'R'.[16] Or, on the other hand, he would be saying that in 'aRb' the signs 'a', 'b' and the relation which obtains between two signs when they are written on either side of the sign 'R' stand in a determinate relation to one another. This, too, would threaten a vicious regress. So at the very least, we can say that if the wide reading of Wittgenstein's terminology is adopted, then his metaphors turn out to have been chosen most unhappily.

It might be replied that the narrow interpretation is in fact no better equipped to deal with the spatial metaphors of *TLP*. For where an atomic sentence has the subject/predicate form 'Fb', how can it be the case that there is a determinate relation between the names, if the only name present is 'b'? Equally, in a state of affairs such as Fb, where an individual possesses a monadic property, how can there be a combination of objects, if b is the only object involved? I think the correct answer to these questions is that Wittgenstein believed that there would not be any elementary propositions of subject/predicate form, or any states of affairs except relational ones.[17] (This is how I interpret the famous remark at 2.0232, that in a manner of speaking objects are colourless.) The best way of explaining why Wittgenstein should have believed this is that he already had in mind the outline of a programme of analysis which would have such a consequence. This hypothesis will be confirmed in Chapter 14, where I shall defend a model for the elementary propositions of *TLP*, which enables them to meet many of Wittgenstein's constraints, as well as leaving no room for there to be any elementary propositions of subject/predicate form.

With the terminology of 'name' and 'object' interpreted narrowly, Wittgenstein's account of the semantics of names will be as follows. The semantic content of any given proper name is (aside from its logical grammar which it will share with all other names for the same type of thing) exhausted by its bearer (3.203). In order to understand a statement involving a proper name it is sufficient (so far as the contribution of the name goes) that you know which thing the statement concerns – that you know the reference of the name. Mutual knowledge of sense is not (as Frege would have it) required. Nevertheless each name must be associated with a sense (a mode of thinking of the bearer) within the idiolect of each person who understands it; in virtue of which it has the reference which it does (3.3411, together with 3.31 and 3.321).[18]

My view is therefore that Wittgenstein agrees with Frege that names have (idiolectic) senses which determine their reference, but disagrees with him about the contribution of names to the semantic content (*Sinn*) of sentences in which they occur. Here the *TLP* account is purely referential. This combination of views seems to me to be actually correct, enabling us to retain a notion of sense for use in psychological explanation, while employing a purely referential semantics in our account of linguistic communication.[19]

While the above interpretations were in my view sufficiently established in *TS*, there remained two lacunae in the discussion, which will be taken up in the chapters which follow.[20] The first was that Wittgenstein combines the above account of the semantics of names with a commitment to analyse names for contingent physical objects into descriptions of the manner in which those objects are constructed out of their parts (3.24). Here he runs together conceptual with metaphysical necessity. For while it is plausible that at least some types of physical object are necessarily made up of their actual parts,[21] on no account will this be so as a matter of conceptual necessity (the sort of necessity for which it is appropriate to look in an *a priori* analysis). So the question arises why Wittgenstein might have felt himself pressured into accepting such a doctrine. We shall return to the issue in Chapters 7 and 12 below.

The other lacuna in the *TS* discussion concerned Wittgenstein's commitment to the transparency of simple names (the names which constitute the end-point of analysis). For at 4.243 he implies that one cannot understand two such names without knowing whether their reference is the same or different, which seems to conflict with the idea that names (even simple names) have idiolectic senses. My suggestion is that he may here have had in mind the outline of a programme of analysis, within which simple names would be introduced by means of general rules, in such a way that one would be capable of working out *a priori* whether or not two names must have the same reference.[22] We shall return to this suggestion in Chapter 14 below.

(D) The Picture Theory

Part, at least, of what is involved in Wittgenstein's Picture Theory is the doctrine that sentences represent isomorphically – for example, that a relation between two individuals will be symbolised by a relation between two proper names (see 3.1432). But we can distinguish between stronger and weaker versions of the doctrine of isomorphism. In its strong version, the idea would be that not only the names but also the significant relations between them will stand in a relation of reference to the world. In its weaker version, on the other hand, the idea would only be that relational facts will be symbolised by relational sentences, there being no requirement that the significant relation in such a sentence will, like the names involved, have reference. So from the fact that *TLP* certainly endorses a doctrine of isomorphic representation, it does not follow that it is also committed to predicative expressions having reference.

It is clearly the case that Wittgenstein accepted the strong isomorphism thesis in his earliest writings – see *NB* 99, 111. Yet I believe we can trace his increasing worries concerning this version of Picture Theory through his ensuing notebooks, culminating with a rejection of reference for predicative expressions, and a version of Picture Theory which is committed only to the weak version of the isomorphism doctrine. Very roughly, the worry took the form a dilemma, depending upon whether the significant relation in a sentence was supposed to refer to a relation *token* or to a relation *type* (a universal). The dilemma may be developed as follows.

Suppose first, that the significant relation in 'aRb' refers to a relation token which obtains between the objects a and b in particular. Then it will be impossible to explain how such a sentence can both have semantic content and be false. For if 'aRb' is false, then there *is* no appropriate relation obtaining between the objects a and b to be referred to. Suppose second, that the significant relation in 'aRb' refers to the universal Rness. Then since this universal can exist in the absence of a and b, there must be something which in fact relates it to those objects in the particular case in hand, in virtue of which it is true that they are related to one another by that relation. But this is precisely the doctrine of the copula (that the state of affairs aRb contains not only the objects a, b and the relation R, but a copula relating together the other three) which it was one of Wittgenstein's earliest concerns to reject (see *NB* 120–1). I believe that he came to feel that the only way out of this dilemma was to deny reference to predicative expressions altogether.[23]

I interpret the mature version of Wittgenstein's Picture Theory in *TLP* as embodying just such a non-referential semantics for predicative expressions, as follows. The fact that the elementary propositions which constitute the end-point of analysis consist only of proper names in immediate combination (note that I here presuppose the narrow reading of *TLP* names) would be supposed to reveal to us something of the essence of our ordinary propositions. For just as there would be two distinct aspects to the understanding of an elementary proposition (there would be knowledge of the reference of the names involved, as well as knowledge of the rules for comparing a given arrangement of names with the world, so as to test it for truth), so too our ordinary propositions involve two quite different aspects: names referring to items in the world, and predicative expressions which bring with them rules for mapping objects on to truth-values.

I thus see Wittgenstein as being committed to a non-referential semantics for predicative expressions. A one-place predicate, for example, serves not to refer to some item in the world (a property), but rather to express a rule for classifying objects in virtue of the property-tokens which they possess.[24] Thus consider the sentence 'Mary has freckles.' The role of the predicate here is not, as is that of the name, to refer to some item in the world, but rather to express a rule for determining, of any given object, whether or not it has freckles. This rule will apply to Mary, if it does, in virtue of her possessing a token of the property of being freckled (in virtue of the fact that she enters into a token state of affairs of the type *being freckled*). But this is not to say that the predicate then refers to that property-token; for if it did, then there would be a problem in explaining how such a sentence could be both significant and false, as we saw earlier. Yet all the same, there can be a number of predicates with different senses (which express cognitively distinct rules of classification) which nevertheless have the same *Bedeutung* (semantic content). For in Wittgenstein's view, all predicates expressing rules which are analytically equivalent to one another may be said to make the same contribution to the *Sinn* (truth-conditions) of sentences in which they occur.[25]

These views are both substantive and interesting. Indeed, my own assessment is that they are actually correct, with respect to at least most predicative expressions of natural language (some uses of natural kind terms excepted). They may certainly be preferred to a number of referential alternatives – for example, that predicative expressions serve to refer to extensions, or to 'incomplete' but extensional entities (Frege's view); that they refer to transcendent (Platonic) universals; or finally that they refer to universals of an immanent (Aristotelian) sort.[26] Then since this interpretation of the Picture Theory is only possible given a narrow reading of the terminology of 'name' and 'object', we have here yet another argument – from Charity – for adopting that reading.

In contrast, if the wide reading of the name/object terminology is adopted, then the Picture Theory will contain nothing of any deep philosophical significance. For the isomorphism thesis (in either its strong or weak versions) would then constitute the whole content of the theory. Yet this thesis represents, at best, a deep contingent fact about many natural languages, rather than anything belonging to the essence of language as such. For example, it is easy to imagine a language which would represent *contra*morphically, in which individuals would be signified by properties of the predicative expressions.[27] Moreover, if it were a strong version of the isomorphism thesis which were endorsed, as defenders of the wide reading generally assume, then we should still be caught on the horns of the dilemma outlined above. So all in all, the best interpretation of the Picture Theory provides strong support for the narrow reading of the name/object terminology.

(E) Thought and language

Finally, it is worth explaining how I interpret the *TLP* account of thought and its relation to language, since this will play some role in the investigations which follow. I maintain that for Wittgenstein both private thinking and public language-using are activities on a par with one another, each consisting of structured arrangements of sign-tokens which are projected on to the world by virtue of the thinker/speaker's grasp of the conventions which govern their use. Certainly the *TLP* account of how a public sentence comes to possess its semantic properties is not a psychologistic one – the view is not that it is through association with private mental processes that public words get their life. But then nor, on the other hand, need Wittgenstein be committed to the quasi-behaviourist thesis that conscious thought is only possible for a being who possesses a public language. On the contrary, as I say, his view is that thinking and speaking are essentially similar (and no doubt closely contingently connected) but logically independent activities.[28]

The textual evidence for a psychologistic interpretation of *TLP* is in fact very thin on the ground.[29] Firstly, there are 3.11 and 3.5, which say respectively (in the Pears and McGuinness translation) that the method of projection of a propositional sign is *to think of* the *Sinn* of the proposition, and that a thought (*Gedanke*) is a propositional sign applied and *thought out* (my italics). But each of these is in fact *mis*translated, the literal renderings given by Ogden being greatly preferable. When properly understood, 3.11 equates the concepts *projected propositional sign* and *thought (Gedanke) of a truth-condition* as being necessarily co-extensive with one another. This then does not begin to support the psychologistic interpretation. Rather, it suggests a quasi-Fregean use of the term 'thought', to cover all significant uses of signs, whether public or private. As for 3.5, this should be understood as saying that an *applied* propositional sign may be equated with one *expressive of a thought*. Neither does this support a psychologistic reading.

The only other textual evidence generally cited in support of a psychologistic interpretation of *TLP* is Wittgenstein's 1919 letter to Russell (*NB* 129–30). But this evidence could, if we wished, easily be discounted, since the letter was evidently written with much impatience – though in fact, when properly interpreted, it actually supports my own account. For how could the psychical constituents making up an act of private thinking have the *same* sort of relation to reality as words (which is what Wittgenstein says), if the latter are supposed to be related to reality *via* the former (which is psychologism)?

In all other respects the terminology of *TLP* supports the view that thinking and language-using are being regarded as equivalent in status. For example, at 3 the concept of a thought is equated with the concept of a logical picture of facts, suggesting that the term '*Gedanke*' is being used generically to cover all picturing of facts, whether external (spoken or written sentences, pictures, maps, etc.) or internal (thinking, imagining, etc.). Again, 4 says that thoughts are propositions with *Sinn*, again suggesting that they are to include all forms of significant representation of the world, and not just private acts of thinking. Moreover, there are a number of passages in *TLP* which imply that what confers significance on our signs is not some sort of private mental process, but rather the rules and conventions determining their use – see, for example, 3.315, 3.342, 4.002 and 4.0141; see also the discussion of the Picture Theory in Section D above.

One further aspect of the *TLP* theory of thought which should be mentioned here is this. In tying the notion of sense (cognitive content) essentially to the significant use of public or private signs (reflected in the *TLP* terminology of 'symbol', 'proposition' and 'thought' outlined above), Wittgenstein should be seen as rejecting Frege's heavily Platonic theory of thinking, according to which this activity consists in thinkers coming to 'grasp' necessarily existing abstract *Gedanken* (thoughts, assertable senses). Since I hold that this view of Frege's is not only inadequately supported by the available arguments, but makes a complete mystery of the whole business, the *TLP* account of the matter is greatly to be preferred.[30]

This is not to say, however, that Wittgenstein has no use for the notion of thoughts and propositions as abstract (but mind-dependent) entities. For propositions may be said to have an existence which is prior to, and independent of, their ever being entertained by a thinker, in virtue of the conventions which determine the significance of combinations of their component terms. (There are many propositions of English which no one has ever entertained, or ever will.) But this is not existence in all possible worlds, or even genuinely mind-independent existence. Rather, a proposition has a mode of existence which supervenes on the rules embodied in the systems of signs employed by historical thinkers.[31]

Summary

The main points to take into the discussion which follows are these:

(a)   that '*Sinn*' in *TLP* terminology means 'truth-condition', and that '*Bedeutung*' means 'semantic content';

(b)   that *TLP* nevertheless finds a place for a notion of sense (cognitive content), expressed in the normal use of the term 'symbol';

(c)   that the *TLP* terminology of 'name' and 'object' should be interpreted narrowly, to cover only proper names and individuals respectively;

(d)   that *TLP* endorses a non-referential semantics for predicates, being committed only to the existence (besides individual objects) of property and relation tokens;

(e)   that on the *TLP* view thinking and speaking are on a par, each consisting of structured arrangements of sign-tokens.

2　The Context Principle

While the non-referential semantics for predicates implicit in the Picture Theory does not strictly entail that there are no property-types, I believe that Wittgenstein accepted such a consequence, for the reason that metaphysical and ontological issues are secondary to semantical and logical ones. In this chapter we start our exploration of this approach to philosophy, beginning with the *TLP* endorsement of the Context Principle, that words only have *Bedeutung* in the context of a proposition.

(A) The Context Principle in Frege

Wittgenstein's employment of the Context Principle, at 3.3 and 3.314, echoes Frege almost word for word, in what must have been a conscious acknowledgement (see *The Foundations of Arithmetic* 71 and 73). It is therefore reasonable to assume, at least as a working hypothesis, that Wittgenstein understood the principle and its significance in essentially the same manner as Frege. So this is the obvious place to begin: what did Frege understand by the principle, and what did he take its philosophical significance to be?

The immediate point of Frege's deployment of the Context Principle in *FA* is to defend his view that numbers are objects, together with the corresponding view that numerals are genuine proper names. It is introduced in response to the objection that numerals cannot really be names, since we can form no idea – no image – which can adequately capture their meaning. For if we ask, outside of any propositional context, what the meaning of the numeral '4' is, then it is almost inevitable that we should attempt to conjure up some mental image or other; perhaps of four dots arranged in a square. But this is entirely inappropriate to capture the sense of the word. For whatever else may be the case, it is clear that the numerals are not names of arrangements of dots. The natural conclusion to draw, then, would be that numerals are not really names at all.

The mistake in all this, Frege believes, is made at the outset: asking for the meaning of (types of)[1] words outside of their role in propositions. What we ought rather to ask is whether we can give adequate explanations of the meanings of sentences in which numerals occur, in a way which is consistent with their being assigned the role of proper names. And this Frege thinks he can do.

It is clear, then, that one aspect of Frege's employment of the Context Principle must lie in his according a fundamental role to sentences within language. For the points above only make sense on the supposition that sentences are somehow radically different in purpose and function from proper names, since it needs to be maintained that a sign's being a proper name is just a matter of its contributing to the truth-conditions of sentences in which it occurs in a certain characteristic way. This is an important insight, expressible in the claim that a sentence is the smallest bit of language with which one can actually say anything.[2] Then since the whole purpose of individual words lies in the contribution which they make to the meanings of sentences in which they occur, it is this which should be investigated if we want to know what sort of meaning they possess.

However, there must be more to Frege's employment of the Context Principle than this. For one fairly natural account of the way in which a proper name contributes to the content of a sentence would be to say that its role is simply to stand for an individual object, the rest of the sentence then saying something which purports to be true of that object. And it would be wholly consistent with this to insist that all genuine proper names must be introduced, ultimately (that is, when the chain of explicit definitions runs out), by means of ostensive definitions. So Frege would still be left with a problem: his opponent would be objecting that numbers cannot really be objects since there can be no such thing as pointing out, or being presented with, a number. Indeed, this is surely the most sympathetic way of interpreting the objection from our inability to form adequate images of numbers. For an appropriate image would be a representation of the sort of thing which could be presented in an ostensive definition.

It is not entirely fanciful to see the Context Principle as the precursor of the later Wittgenstein's remarks on ostensive definition in *PI*.[3] Frege's reply to the above objection would be to challenge the idea that ostensive definition plays a foundational role in the explanation of the terms of a language. Since 'a word has meaning only in the context of a sentence', there must be a great deal more to fixing the meaning of a term than the bare assignment of a referent. On the contrary, its 'logical grammar' must also be fixed – it must be determined how it will fit together with other expressions to form a significant sentence, what basic principles of inference will govern the result, and so on. It is just not intelligible that all of this could be conveyed in a simple ostensive definition, or by any sort of pre-linguistic presentation of a referent. On the contrary, understanding an ostensive definition must presuppose considerable linguistic competence, since you will need to know at least what sort of thing is being pointed out to you, and the criterion of identity for things of that kind.

For example, consider what is necessary for someone to understand the ostensive definition 'This is Mary.' Firstly, of course, they must take 'Mary' to be a proper name rather than, for instance, a predicate describing a kind of appearance (the Mary *Gestalt*) or a colour of hair. Secondly, they must take 'Mary' as the name of a person, rather than of a particular item of clothing or of a point of the compass. Thirdly, they must grasp which person in particular is Mary. So they must know the criteria of individuation-at-a-time and of identity-over-time for persons. (If this is Mary, then her twin sister cannot also be Mary – persons are not sets of similarly appearanced humans; and if this is Mary in London, then I cannot meet Mary in New York tomorrow unless she travels.) So an ostensive definition can only work as an explanation (as opposed to conferring understanding by a miracle) if a considerable background of conceptual equipment is already possessed by the person to whom the definition is directed. They must already have taken on board the distinction between proper names and predicates, together with the sortal concept to which the object being ostended belongs (in this case, the concept of a person). Thus it follows that ostensive definitions cannot be the fundamental form of linguistic explanation.

It would seem that linguistic explanation must begin with some sort of training in the use of whole sentences. For the chain of explicit (verbal) definitions must come to an end somewhere, yet it cannot come to an end in ostensive definitions if these themselves presuppose linguistic competence. Moreover, it is certainly plausible, as Frege demonstrates, that one can adequately explain the truth-conditions of sentences in which numerals occur functioning as proper names. So if the primacy of ostensive definition is dethroned by the Context Principle, as I am suggesting, then nothing apparently stands in the way of taking grammar at face value, and recognising numbers to be objects. Indeed if, as I shall argue in the next chapter, we cannot settle what basic kinds of objects there are in the world by any sort of pre-linguistic looking and seeing, then what other alternative is there but to take language as our guide?

It is not just over the existence of the numbers, but in metaphysics generally, that Frege adopts this sort of approach. For example, he takes it as established that the entities which constitute the referents of predicative expressions must be in some way 'incomplete' because of his belief that such expressions themselves, and their senses, are essentially incomplete.[4] So what emerges is that the Context Principle can be seen to underlie a great deal of Frege's approach to philosophy. Given the primacy of the sentence, and the impossibility of conferring meaning on individual terms by any sort of bare presentation of a referent – indeed, since there can be no such thing as non-linguistic access to metaphysical truths – he thinks the only way of coming to discern the essential nature of reality is through the study of language.[5]

(B) The principle in *TLP*

Our question now is how much of the above survives into *TLP*. Does Wittgenstein, too, base questions of ontology and metaphysics upon considerations to do with language? And if so, is this approach founded upon an appreciation of the fundamental position of whole sentences within language, and on the impossibility of conferring meaning on words by a pre-linguistic presentation of their referents?

One initial difficulty concerning the interpretation of 3.3 and 3.314 is raised by the thesis defended in Chapter 1, that '*Bedeutung*' in *TLP* means 'semantic content', which in turn means 'contribution to truth-conditions (*Sinn*)'. For to say that it is only in the context of a proposition that a name makes any contribution to truth-conditions is so truistic that one wonders why Wittgenstein should give it such prominence. Can this really be all that he is saying? Now, one sort of answer would be to point out that we have been already told, at 3.203, that the *Bedeutung* of a name is an object. So 3.3 also tells us that a name only refers to an object within the context of a proposition. But a better reply is to draw attention to the central position accorded to whole sentences by the very notion of *Bedeutung*. Since *Bedeutung* (semantic content) is contribution to *Sinn* (truth-conditions), and since 3.3 tells us that it is only propositions which have *Sinn*, we have here an acknowledgement of the central role of the sentence within language, just as in Frege.

So what ought to be fairly uncontroversial is that the Context Principle, in Wittgenstein as in Frege's *FA*, serves to emphasise that it is only with a proposition that one can (non-parasitically) say anything. In fact it reaffirms the central position of the sentence against Frege's later – retrograde – doctrine that sentences are complex names of the True and the False,[6] as well as justifying the immediate corollary, that the meaning of a word is (is identical with) the contribution which it makes to the meanings of sentences in which it can occur. (See 3.3–3.314, 4.431, 5.02).

The other corollary of the principle – the denial of any fundamental role for ostensive definition, and consequent acceptance of the idea that the introduction of language must somehow involve training in the use of whole sentences – is also endorsed in *TLP*. At 3.263 (immediately prior to the statement of the Context Principle at 3.3) Wittgenstein writes:

The Bedeutungen of primitive signs can be explained by means of elucidations. Elucidations are propositions which contain the primitive signs. So they can only be understood if the Bedeutungen of those signs are already known.[7]

It is clear from the previous context (a discussion of names, 3.2ff.) that the 'primitive signs' spoken of here are the simple names which form the terminus of analysis. And it is being claimed that such names will have to be explained through propositions containing them, which can only be understood if those names themselves are already understood – that is, which presuppose, for their understanding, that one has already grasped what the explanation is trying to get across.

I take the above to be an explicit rejection of the primacy of ostensive definition. Since 'a name only has meaning in the context of a sentence', understanding a name will mean knowing how it fits together with other expressions to form a sentence, and the contribution which it makes to the truth-conditions of the sentences which result; and it is simply not intelligible that such knowledge might be conveyed through any kind of bare presentation of a referent. So we have no alternative, in explaining the meaning of primitive names, but to make use of propositions containing them, in the hope that the trainee will gradually 'cotton on'. In effect, what Wittgenstein is saying is that you can only teach someone to speak by talking to them.[8] And note that it does not matter to this interpretation if the 'elucidations' which Wittgenstein has in mind are themselves ostensive definitions, as some have claimed.[9] For by emphasising that to understand such a definition requires prior knowledge of (at least) the logical grammar of the name being defined, he would still be rejecting the view that ostensive definitions form the basis of language. On the contrary, the point would be essentially that made at *PI* 30–2: that an ostensive definition can only explain the meaning of a word when its overall use in the language is already clear.[10]

Thus far it would appear that Wittgenstein's understanding of the Context Principle is closely parallel to Frege's. But our main question must be whether Wittgenstein, too, draws out of these considerations a belief in the priority of logic over metaphysics. Certainly at one time he had believed this. For in the 1913 'Notes on Logic' he explicitly states that philosophy consists of logic and metaphysics, with logic forming the basis (*NB* 93). Of course this is not in itself very strong evidence of his *TLP* view. But consider 3.031, where he writes:

It used to be said that God could create anything except what would be contrary to the laws of logic. – The truth is that we could not *say* what an 'illogical' world would look like. [Italics in original.]

There is no way of making sense of the contrast being drawn here if (as some have done) you take Wittgenstein's view to be that a speaker will 'read off' their knowledge of what is permissible in language from their knowledge of what is possible in the world.[11] For what ought, in that case, to have been said is on the contrary that we cannot say what an illogical world would look like because God cannot create anything contrary to the laws of logic – that is, because the essence of the world is as it is. Whereas Wittgenstein is clearly wanting to claim some sort of priority for the logic of language over what is possible in the world.

Perhaps Wittgenstein's clearest commitment to the priority of logic comes at 3.317 (soon after the statement of the Context Principle at 3.3 and 3.314). In the course of discussing the idea that every expression can be regarded as a propositional variable, where the values of the variable are all of the propositions in which that expression can figure, he writes:

And the *only* thing essential to the stipulation [of the values of a propositional variable] is *that it is merely a description of the symbols and states nothing about what is signified*. [Italics in original. See also 3.33, whose import is very similar.]

Recall from Chapter 1 that a symbol is a sign together with its sense (together with its mode of determining a *Bedeutung*). So it is being claimed that in stipulating, for instance, that 'the book' is a permissible argument of the variable in 'x is red' whereas '7' is not, we should concern ourselves only with the sorts of sense which those expressions have, and not with their referents. It is being explicitly (and most emphatically) ruled out that we might attempt to justify the allowability of certain substitutions by appealing to essential features of the world – by saying, for example, 'Any

physical object can have a colour.' We must, on the contrary, confine ourselves to recognising, on the basis of our knowledge of sense, what is
possible or essential at the level of language.

(C) Philosophical method in *TLP*

If Wittgenstein thinks that logic is prior to metaphysics, as the above
passages suggest, then we should expect this to have implications for his
conception of philosophical method: we should expect him to take the
view that the way to do metaphysics and ontology is by reflecting on the
nature of thought and language. And this is just what we find. Of course
we never explicitly find him asserting quite this, for metaphysical and
ontological truths belong to the realm of the unsayable, on the official *TLP*
account of what it is to say something. But he certainly seems to think that
metaphysical truths can be shown, and that what shows them will be considerations to do with language. Thus 3.3421 tells us that the possibility of
alternative modes of signifying can disclose something about the essence of
the world – an idea which is then put to work at 5.53–5.5352, where an
alternative to our way of expressing identity is used to show that identity
is not really a relation.[12] Moreover, 6.12 tells us that the fact that certain
propositions are tautologies can be used to show the essential features of
the world.

As we shall see in the next chapter, the textual evidence is not wholly
unambiguous in support of our interpretation. But what has emerged
already is that there is at least a strong case to be made that Wittgenstein,
like Frege, took logic and semantics to be prior to metaphysics and
ontology; and that he too believed that the correct method in philosophy
would proceed *via* reflection on thought and language. However, this is
not to say that the two of them are wholly in agreement. On the contrary,
there is at least one crucial difference. For Frege is ready to allow himself
to be guided by surface-grammatical features of language, most notably
over the status of numbers, as we shall see shortly. Whereas Wittgenstein
always insists that we should look to what is essential in the kind of talk in
question.

For Frege, the fact that numerals function in sentences in all respects like
proper names, coupled with the fact that many of the sentences in which
they figure are true, is taken to show that numbers are genuinely existing
objects. Thus we make predications of numbers ('7 is prime'), we refer to
them by means of definite descriptions ('The successor of 6 is prime'), we
quantify over them ('Some number is prime'), we take '7 is prime' to imply

'Some number is prime'; and most importantly, we make statements of identity with respect to them ('7 is 4 plus 3'). So numerals purport to be referring expressions. In which case, how could it be true that 7 is prime unless the number 7 really exists as a genuine object of reference? (Compare: how could it be true that Mary has freckles, unless Mary really exists?) Frege feels that the only alternative to recognising numbers as objects would be to take the drastic course of rejecting all number statements as false.[13]

For Wittgenstein, however, all this is insufficient. As we shall see in more detail in the next section, he thinks that it is not enough to show that numerals do as a matter of fact function as proper names; we also need to show that they *must* do so. Or better: we need to show that there is no other way of saying what we currently use numerals to say. We need to show that there is no way of expressing numerical truths except by employing signs whose function is apparently to refer to them as objects. So for Wittgenstein, the thesis of the priority of logic and its resulting philosophical method are intimately connected with the idea of analysis. A form of expression can only reveal something about the essence of reality if it, in its turn, is essential: if there is no way of analysing what is said by it differently, or if we cannot construct quite a different form of notation to perform the same task.

(D) Numbers

If he is to make good his claim that numbers are objects, Frege recognises that he must provide a criterion of identity for them.[14] His main task is then to lay down truth-conditions for statements of the form 'The number of Fs = the number of Gs' – let us write this as 'NxFx = NxGx'. He shows how this can be done in terms of a notion of one-to-one correspondence between the instances of the concepts F and G, where this notion can be explicated without presupposing a prior grasp of number-words.[15] So we have the definition: NxFx = NxGx if and only if Fx 1–1 correlates Gx. But of course it is not enough merely to fix the truth-conditions of statements of numerical identity. He must also lay down truth-conditions for statements of the form 'There are n Fs', which play a central role in our use of the number-words. These statements for him take the form of an identity: 'n = NxFx'. This requires him, in turn, to give explicit definitions of the individual numerals. He could, had he wished, have given the following sequence of definitions: $0 = Nx(x \neq x), 1 = Nx(x = 0), 2 = Nx((x = 0) \lor (x = 1))$, and so on.[16] (His actual definitions were – disastrously, in view of Russell's Paradox — given in terms of sets of sets.) In which case the truth-condition of 'The Earth has one moon' would come out as '$Nx(x = 0) = Nx(x$ is a moon of the Earth)', which in turn would say that the concept $x = 0$ is 1–1 correlated with the concept x *is a moon of the Earth*.

For Wittgenstein, on the other hand, the very possibility of Frege's analysis shows that numbers are not really objects, since it shows how we could have a language which does not employ any expressions seeming to refer to them, but which would say all of the same things in terms of relations between concepts. I take it that this is the point of his statement at 6.021 that a number is an exponent of an operation, and of the definitions given at 6.02. The idea is that the only thing essential to a system of numbering is an iterable rule which will produce a sequence of signs in a unique order, each member of the sequence being distinct from every other. Then the statement 'The Earth has one moon' can be regarded as saying: 'The concept x *is a moon of the Earth* is 1–1 correlated with the concept x *is a move necessary to reach the sign "1" in the series of numerals*.' And something like this is, after all, what goes on when we count: for every instance of the concept under which we are counting we produce a distinct numeral, following the order of the numerals and taking care not to produce more than one numeral for any given instance; the number of things being given by the last numeral that gets produced.[17]

More needs to be said before we can pronounce Wittgenstein the victor in this debate. For after all, it is common to both parties that the surface form of a statement can be misleading. So what is to prevent Frege replying that reference to numbers is covertly taking place even in a notation like that sketched above, where we only appear to have talk of 1–1 correlations between concepts? Indeed, his position must be something like this anyway, since he regards his definitions as providing, not an eliminative reduction of number-words, but rather an epistemic route into reference to numbers.[18]

The decisive consideration on Wittgenstein's behalf is provided by the Principle of Semantic Relevance, which I think we can see as being implicit in the reasoning behind a number of *TLP* doctrines.[19] This holds that if reference is to be attributed to an expression, then the evidence which speakers would take to bear on the truth of sentences containing it (particularly, where available, anything they would count as a canonical mode of verification) should display sensitivity to the existence and nature of the referent. The idea is that a semantic theory should reflect the main features of the use of an expression — in verifying, falsifying and offering evidence. Since truth is to depend upon reference, evidence of truth should, as it were, 'point towards' the referent – especially where the evidence is of the most direct sort, where we may think of the truth of the sentence being *manifest* to us.[20]

It follows from the above principle that the most direct method for establishing the truth of a sentence containing an expression which has both sense and reference will involve a two-step process: first locate the referent, relying upon your knowledge of the sense; then determine whether or not the referent fits together with the semantic content of the remainder of the sentence in such a way as to yield a truth. Then if numerals were really proper names of numbers, we should expect their mode of contribution to a canonical verification of sentences in which they occur to involve just such a two-step process. We would first of all identify, in accordance with our grasp of the sense of the numeral, its referent (a particular number), and then see how that thing fits together with the semantic content of the other component expressions in the sentence to determine a truth-value. In particular, a canonical verification of a statement of the form 'There are n Fs' would be that which is appropriate to a statement of identity, since on a referential view of numerals this really says 'n = the number of Fs'. But in fact there is nothing in our practice of using number-words to warrant this sort of interpretation. On the contrary, the most direct way of verifying 'There are n Fs' reflects Wittgenstein's view of the matter exactly: we correlate, by counting, the concept F one to one with the sequence of moves necessary to reach the sign 'n' in the series of numerals.

Summary

Wittgenstein's employment of the Context Principle is essentially similar to Frege's. Both of them intend it to emphasise the central position of the sentence within language, to undermine the supposedly central position of ostensive definition, and to establish the priority of logic and semantics over metaphysics. But Wittgenstein goes beyond Frege in claiming that it is only essential (use-reflecting) features of language which are metaphysically significant.

3   The primacy of logic

Our task in this chapter is to substantiate further the reading of *TLP* presented in Chapter 2: responding to a contrary argument, and deploying Charity in its support. We shall also consider what it is that fundamentally makes metaphysics possible, in Wittgenstein's view.

(A) Epistemological versus metaphysical priority

The one aspect of *TLP* which is apparently in tension with a belief in the priority of logic over metaphysics is the recurring image of 'the great mirror' (5.511, 6.13). For it is logic which is said to mirror the world rather than vice versa. This suggests that the essence of reality is being given some sort of priority over the essence of language, since a mirror merely reflects what is there in the world, its image being wholly dependent upon what is placed in front of it. It suggests that what is possible in language and thought (logic) is supposed to be in some sense dependent upon what is possible in the world (metaphysics).

But in what sense dependent? Given the weight of evidence presented in the last chapter, Wittgenstein surely cannot suppose the dependence to be an epistemological one. He cannot be meaning that we come to know of what is possible in language – which combinations of expressions make sense, which result in a tautology and so on – in virtue of knowing what is possible in reality. He cannot mean that we are supposed to 'read off' the logical grammar of our language from some sort of prior acquaintance with the essential features of the world. So if, as I shall argue, this is the only available form of dependence, then our most reasonable course will be to deny that the metaphor of the mirror need be seen as carrying any such implication. For of course *any* metaphor will have accidental features, going lame at some point. And it may be that the priority of object over mirror-image is an accidental feature of this one (as is the fact that the relationship should involve the transmission of light). The significant feature of the metaphor might simply be that there exists a correspondence – a matching – between object and image.[1]

So is there, perhaps, a distinction to be drawn between epistemological and metaphysical priority? Could Wittgenstein be seen as claiming that although we can only have knowledge of essential features of the world by studying what is essential in language, nevertheless what is essential in language is so because of the essential nature of reality? But then what sort of 'because' could this be? It could hardly be causal. The idea of a causal explanation of something which is necessarily the case (at least on any objectivist construal of necessity) is surely incoherent. Moreover, the idea that the essential features of reality might have causal consequences would be puzzling in its own right. For we certainly cannot express the sort of dependency involved in terms of counterfactuals. We cannot say 'The essence of thought would not have been as it is had the essence of the world been different', since this would require us to make sense of the idea that there is a possible world in which the essence – the necessary features – of reality are different.[2]

But then the 'because' can hardly be a logical one either. For in admitting the epistemological priority of logic over metaphysics, we should already be granting that what is essential in language can have implications for the essence of reality. So the most that could be claimed is that there are implications in the reverse direction as well, with the essential features of reality implying something about the essence of language. But this would leave us with no more right to say that the essence of language is dependent upon what is essential in the world than to say the contrary.

There is, of course, a sense in which the essence of the world might be said to be temporally, or ontologically, prior to essences in language. For example, we should insist that long before there were ever any human beings or any language, it was true that no physical object could be in two places at once. And we should insist that even if there had never been any human beings, it would still have been true that no surface could be red and green all over. But nothing of any great significance turns on this. For since we have had to *use* our language in describing such past and counterfactual states of affairs, it may be that these essential truths are merely projections, in some sense, of essential structural features of our language.[3] Certainly such examples do not show that language is the way it is because the essence of the world is as it is.

Since we have failed to mark out any sense in which metaphysics is explanatorily prior to logic, given an epistemological priority in the reverse direction, I propose to adopt the interpretation of the 'great mirror' metaphor sketched above. Its point is not to draw attention to any form of priority, but simply to insist that there is a correspondence between the essential features of language and the world. This does not mean, however, that the image is wholly bland and uncontroversial. On the contrary, its point is to insist upon a realist attitude to metaphysics, claiming that there really are essential features of an independently existing reality which correspond to the essential features of language.[4] As such, it can be seen to have decisive advantages over an analogue of the Kantian doctrine of Transcendental Idealism.[5]

Given that we accept, with Wittgenstein and Frege, the epistemological priority of logic over metaphysics, it would be natural to ask whether we should adopt a realist or an idealist attitude to the latter. Should we say that the essences revealed to us through our study of language really belong to the essential nature of an independently existing reality? Or should we say that, since any apprehension of reality is language-mediated, the essential structure of language merely imposes an essential structure upon reality *in so far as it can be apprehended in thought by us*? That is, should we distinguish between the essence of reality 'as it is in itself' and reality 'as it exists as an object of apprehension by us', confining the knowledge which can be made available by our study of language and thought to the latter?

The metaphor of 'the great mirror' should be seen as rejecting any such distinction, hence endorsing a realist attitude. In order to discern the reasoning behind that rejection, it is only necessary to reflect upon the significance of Wittgenstein's remarks about the task of philosophy being to signify what cannot be thought by working outwards through what is thinkable (Preface, 4.113–4.115), and about the impossibility of stationing ourselves outside logic (3.02–3.0321, 4.12). For if it is supposed to be possible to ask whether the world really does have the essential structure which seems to be imposed upon it by the essential structure of language, then *in what language* is this question to be framed? Thus suppose reflection to have shown us the self-contradictoriness of the sentence 'The surface is simultaneously red all over and green all over', but that we are moved to ask 'Nevertheless, is it really the case (in the world as it is in itself) that no surface can be red and green all over?' Either the words 'red' and 'green' mean here what they usually do, or they do not. If they do, then our question answers itself (in the affirmative). If they do not, then we are talking about something else. It is impossible (on an objectivist construal of semantic relations anyway) even so much as to raise the question whether reality might be other than the logic of our language suggests.

(B) Charity again

As we saw in the last chapter, there is considerable evidence that Wittgenstein believed in the priority of logic over metaphysics. And we have just been arguing that the apparent textual evidence to the contrary – the image of 'the great mirror' – can not only be explained away, but can be seen positively as an endorsement of a realist attitude to metaphysics. We shall return once more to the question of metaphysical realism in Chapter 8. But for the moment let us consider whether our interpretation is also supported by Charity. Is it true that there can be no such thing as non-linguistic access to the essential nature of reality, and that the only way of coming to discern that nature would be by seeing what is essential in language?

Let us suppose, then, that there is such a thing as metaphysics; holding that there are various essential features of an independently existing world. Could we have access to these features which is not linguistically mediated? The idea is barely intelligible. The point here is not that there can be no such thing as access to (cognitive contact with) a reality which is unconceptualised, or which is not describable in language by the one who has that access. For of course a dog can see – 'enter into cognitive contact with' – physical objects.[6] But can a dog discern that no object can be in two places at once? Or that every physical object must occupy some position in space? It is just not intelligible that a non-linguistically competent creature (by which I mean 'a creature which employs no significant system of signs, whether public or private') might come to discern these essential features of physical objects. Nor is there anything which it could do to manifest its grasp of the corresponding principles. On the contrary, it is, and must be, *via* a grasp of a symbolic system that one is able to discern the essences in reality, if such a thing is possible at all.

It might be objected that it does not follow from the fact that language-users alone can be aware of the essences of things that the only way to discover such essences must be through reflection upon the structure and workings of language. For it is equally true that only a language-user can effect discoveries in sub-atomic physics; but no one thinks that the mode of discovery in such an area is in any sense linguistic. Yet if the mode of discovery of essences is not itself linguistic, then we must be supposed to have some other form of access to them. There must be something in addition to language-use, which for the metaphysician plays a role analogous to that of experiment and observation in physics. We are thus led to the hypothesis of an essence-sensitive faculty, which for some reason can only be possessed by a linguistically competent creature.

There will be familiar objections to the idea of such a faculty. For one thing, what reason could we possibly have for believing that we possess it, or for believing that it does not systematically deceive us if we do?[7] More importantly, how are we to make sense of the idea of causal influence being exercised by states which exist necessarily? For is not the idea of A causing B at least connected to the idea that if A had not existed, B would not have? But if A is something which is necessarily the case, then the antecedent of the counterfactual will be impossible.[8] Yet if the connection with our supposed faculty of metaphysical insight is not a causal one, then of what sort is it? What ensures that the states of the one (our metaphysical beliefs) accurately map the states of the other (the essence of the world)?

What finally gives the lie to the idea of an essence-sensitive faculty, however, is that someone could presumably lack such a faculty, or be guided wrongly by it, while still retaining a complete grasp of their native tongue. For that faculty was only supposed to presuppose linguistic competence, not be guaranteed by it; grasp of a language was not supposed to be sufficient in itself to confer knowledge of essences. But if someone were to say that they believe it to be possible for a number to have a colour, or for a physical object to be in two places at once, would we really be prepared to allow them an understanding of the terms which they use (supposing we took them to be serious)?[9] On the contrary, do we not take failure to recognise essence (in simple cases like this at least) as implying an imperfect grasp of some part of the language? But then by contraposition, if someone does have an adequate understanding of a language, they must already be in a position to recognise essences. If an understanding of a language is sufficient, by itself, to put us in position to discern the essences of things, then this can only be because it is through reflection upon the character of our understanding that such knowledge is to be attained.

It is worth noting that the approach to philosophy which I have been defending on Wittgenstein's behalf, which would accord logic and semantics pride of place over metaphysics, is consistent with the modern doctrine of Real Essence. For if it is true that water is necessarily H_2O, for example, then such a thing would have to be discovered in the following way. By reflecting upon the manner in which we understand the term 'water', and considering our linguistic intuitions in the face of various imaginary examples, we are led to conclude that we should not count any description of a substance as a description of water – where that substance is described as existing in circumstances other than those which obtain in the actual world – which ascribed to it an internal constitution different from that which water has in the actual world. We then discover empirically that the actual internal constitution of water is H_2O. So no substance described in another possible world would count as water which did not consist of H_2O. But on this account it still remains the case that the essential nature of the world is only revealed to us *via* reflection upon language (together with an empirical discovery).[10] It would not be as if the essential nature of water were open to direct inspection, so to speak.

(C) What makes metaphysics possible?

As we have seen, there is much to be said in support of Wittgenstein's views. If there are necessary truths about the nature of reality, then the only way for us to know them would be by reflecting on the forms and structures of language. Moreover, such truths would have to relate to the nature of the world itself, and not just to the world in so far as it is an object of apprehension in thought by us. Nevertheless, the doctrine is an extremely strange one. We seem to be required to believe in a sort of pre-established harmony between the essential structures of language and the world, which is little short of miraculous. Now, the one unexamined assumption in our exposition so far is that metaphysics is even so much as possible. We have left unchallenged that there is a class of necessary truths about the world. So let us ask what it is about Wittgenstein's philosophy which makes this assumption seem plausible. Why should he believe that there are essences in reality corresponding to the essential structures in language?

Besides throwing light upon *TLP* itself, an answer to this question will be of importance in understanding the relationship between Wittgenstein's early and late philosophies. For one major shift which takes place in his views concerns the possibility of metaphysics. Of course metaphysics had been stigmatised as nonsense in *TLP*; yet there remained a clear sense in which it was supposed to be possible. For although there were said to be no essential truths about the world (or indeed about language) which could be reported in a significant proposition, we were still supposed to be capable of showing what belongs to the essence of the world by displaying what is essential in language. In *PI*, however, all this is swept away, there being no longer even this way in which genuine metaphysics is held to be possible. What remains to philosophers is merely to gain a clear view of the workings of their language (*PI* 122–8). So by raising the question of what underlies the *TLP* belief in the possibility of metaphysics we may hope to identify the basis for this change of view.

Before we go any further, however, there are important distinctions to be drawn between three different kinds of supposed metaphysical truth. Firstly, there are truths which might be reached by transcendental argument, based upon the fact that language exists, or has whatever features it has. The major premisses of such arguments take the form 'If language (or such-and-such a feature of language) exists, then the world must be thus and so.' Although such premisses are necessary (if true), the conclusions will be contingent because of the contingency of 'Language exists.'[11] (As we shall see in Chapter 12, the *TLP* argument to the existence of Simples is of this transcendental sort.) Now, the existence of this kind of metaphysical truth is relatively unproblematic, since it must remain possible on any conception of philosophy which leaves room for argument and for tracing (or even inventing) conceptual connections. Moreover, far from being rejected by the later Wittgenstein, it seems likely that many of his arguments (for example those against the privacy of sensations) take precisely this sort of form.[12]

Secondly, there are truths which might be reached from the discovery of alternative notations to those which currently exist in our language, such as non-referential ways of handling the numbers. As I showed in Chapter 2, such arguments must make essential use of the Principle of Semantic Relevance, which seems at least closely related to the later Wittgenstein's insistence that we should pay attention to the sort of *use* which our words have. Moreover, instead of being stated in overtly metaphysical mode ('Properties and numbers do not exist'), the conclusions of such arguments are most naturally stated with respect to language ('Predicates and numerals are not used to refer'). So there is no reason to think that the later Wittgenstein need have rejected this sort of metaphysics either.

But then thirdly, there are truths which are supposed to be discernible from specific (but necessary) structures within language, such as the mutual incompatibility of the predicates 'red' and 'green', and the non-sensicality of '7 is blue'. Metaphysical truths in this category are supposedly discoverable from the internal relations between the various expressions in a given natural language. It is this kind of metaphysics which is most naturally described in the image of 'the great mirror', and whose existence seems both inexplicable and puzzling. And it is this which is definitely rejected by the later Wittgenstein. So it is here that we need to focus our attention: just what is it, on the *TLP* view, which makes this sort of metaphysics seem possible?

I believe the answer lies in the *TLP* commitment to a kind of determinacy and objectivity in concepts and conceptual relations. For if the impossibility of describing an object as both red and green all over, for example, derives from the fact that the senses of the words 'red' and 'green' really do − objectively − conflict with one another, then the use of the material (metaphysical) mode of speech becomes inevitable. For the words 'red' and 'green' are used ('referentially') in the sentences 'The surface is red all over' and 'The surface is green all over', whose conjunction yields an objective contradiction.[13] In which case the denial and generalisation of that contradiction in 'No object can be red and green all over' must be about the colours as well. And then, of course, the question whether an object might really − 'in itself' − be red and green all over immediately answers itself in the negative.

(D) Logical objectivism

In fact the underlying commitment in question is to what I shall henceforward call 'logical objectivism'.[14] The idea is that all internal relationships between symbols, and between symbols and reality, must depend only upon the nature of those symbols themselves, having been rendered wholly determinate − in an objective, mind-independent way − as soon as the senses of the signs in question were fixed. Internal relations are thus held to exist independently of being ratified by us; indeed, independently even of the possibility of our ratifying them. Their existence requires neither that we be able nor that we be disposed to recognise them: they are objective.

Logical objectivism should be sharply distinguished from the Fregean doctrine of necessarily existing thoughts (*Gedanken*).[15] To say that relationships between senses exist mind-independently is not at all the same as saying, with Frege, that senses themselves have mind-independent existence. On the contrary, those relations may be supposed to have sprung into existence when appropriate senses were first introduced. It should also be distinguished from any form of ontological realism.[16] The claim is certainly not that there exist 'logical objects' independently of the human mind (a claim rejected by Wittgenstein at 4.441 and 5.4). It is rather that logical relations *obtain* objectively.

It is logical objectivism to which Wittgenstein gives expression at 3.342 when he writes:

Although there is something arbitrary in our notations, this much is not arbitrary
– that *when* we have determined one thing arbitrarily, something else is necessarily
the case. (This derives from the *essence* of notation.) [Italics in original.]

The idea is that when we have fixed the meanings of our signs – say by
giving definitions – then all the internal relationships between signs have
already been determined in a way which is independent of anything
empirical. Logical objectivism is also expressed at 4.03, where Wittgenstein speaks of propositions being *essentially* connected with situations
(italics in original). What he has in mind is that a proposition must reach
out to its truth-condition in a wholly objective manner – the fact that a
proposition is true on a given condition having been determined *a priori* by
its sense, independently of any capacity or inclination of ours to take it as
verified on that condition.[17] On the contrary, we take it to be true in that
circumstance (if we do) *because of* our knowledge of its sense. Finally, it is
logical objectivism which is at issue at 6.113, where it is said to be the mark
of a logical proposition that it can be recognised to be true from the symbol
alone: such truths are to reflect relations between senses, and *only*
relations between senses (see also 5.132).

In the next chapter we shall consider how strong a case can be constructed in support of logical objectivism. And in the chapters which
follow we shall explore the extent to which it is involved in Wittgenstein's
programme of analysis and resulting metaphysical claims. Our conclusion
will be that it is ultimately responsible for many of the distinctive theses
(and not a few of the sins) of *TLP*. Then in Chapter 15 we shall argue that
it is logical objectivism which is the direct target of attack in the later
Wittgenstein's remarks on rule-following. So it will turn out to be not only
the main pivot on which the early philosophy turns, but also the crucial
locus of conflict between Wittgenstein's earlier and later selves.

In order to see clearly the role which logical objectivism is playing in the
TLP conception of metaphysics, consider what would result from its
denial. In that case a necessary truth could no longer be viewed as expressing, so to speak, a *hard* conceptual fact. Certainly it could not be seen as
expressing an objective, mind-independent, connection between the senses
of the expressions involved. Quite what it would then express is less easy
to see – perhaps a linguistic convention or rule, or perhaps our deter-
mination not to accept as admissible certain forms of description. But anyway there would be something misleading about casting such necessary
'truths' in the material (metaphysical) mode at all. If 'No object can be red
and green all over' serves really to express a rule, for example, then it

would be less misleading to say 'You must not describe an object as being red and green all over.' And that does not even appear to be stating something about the essential nature of reality.

From the standpoint of logical objectivism the sentence 'Nothing can be red and green all over' is most naturally regarded as a statement about the colours themselves, as we saw earlier. But if logical objectivism is rejected, then it will have to be viewed very differently. Its acceptability could no longer be thought of as forced upon us by the nature of our understanding of the concepts involved. There would, on the contrary, be nothing intrinsically wrong with the conjunction 'The surface is red all over and green all over', since there would be no objective conflict between the concepts *red* and *green*. So if that conjunction is excluded from the domain of possible truth, this can only be in virtue of something external to it; for example that there is a rule to that effect, which either forms an explicit part of the training in the use of colour-words, or is naturally endorsed by all those who have undergone such training. In any case there would be every reason to deny that it should properly be regarded as expressing something about the nature of the colours themselves.

Would this mean that there would then be room, after all, for a genuine metaphysical question whether an object can be red and green all over? For if the predicates 'red' and 'green' do not objectively exclude one another, then such a question does not immediately answer itself in the negative, at any rate. But what could the question mean? If it means 'Is it allowable to describe an object as being red and green all over?', then the answer is (presumably) 'No'. And if it means 'Could there be a coherent use of colour-words without a colour-exclusion rule?', then the answer is (perhaps) 'Yes'. But none of this establishes anything metaphysical. Of course what one would want is to drop the talk about 'rules' and 'allowable descriptions', and to ask about the essential natures of the colours themselves. But from an anti-logical-objectivist point of view it is unlikely that the sense of such a question can be intelligibly explained.

Summary

We have shown how the claim of Chapter 2, that Wittgenstein takes questions of logic and semantics to be prior to those of metaphysics and ontology, can be made consistent with the image of 'the great mirror'; and we have argued for it on grounds of Charity. We have also seen how his position (thus interpreted) is founded ultimately on his logical objectivism.

4 Logical objectivism

We shall consider a number of arguments supporting logical objectivism, all of which probably influenced Wittgenstein to one degree or another. Some of them can be stated quite explicitly, but turn out to fail. Those which remain are more intuitive, though seemingly very plausible. It will be left as an open question whether or not they succeed.

(A) Describing in advance

At *PR* 20–6, written soon after his return to philosophy in 1929, Wittgenstein is to be found arguing for what is apparently logical objectivism, attempting to reduce its opposite to absurdity. In fact the immediate targets of attack are the causal theories of meaning developed by Russell and Ogden and Richards.[1] But as Wittgenstein himself says, the details of these theories are inessential: what he really wants to undermine is the idea that the relation between thought and reality (or between expectation and expected event) might depend upon 'some third thing' (*PR* 21). Then since the defining characteristic of logical objectivism is that internal relations should depend upon sense alone, independently of anything contingent, it seems clear that he is wanting to undermine any kind of denial of logical objectivism.

One recurring theme in these passages is that language must be able to set up internal relations to the world in advance of experience, since otherwise the whole function of language would collapse (*PR* 20, 22, 26). At the very least this argument seems to echo the *NB* and *TLP* insistence on what I shall call 'the requirement of determinacy-in-advance', which we shall see in Chapter 5 is a form of logical objectivism. So it may be that in these passages Wittgenstein is exploring once again arguments which had underlain an aspect of his earlier views. At any rate the hypothesis is not an unreasonable one.

The best way I know of fleshing-out the argument is as follows: the functions of language are to serve as a vehicle for communication and to provide the means for us to formulate our own thoughts; but if the relationship between our symbols and reality were contingent (dependent upon some 'third thing'), then we could not know in advance of experience what those symbols represented, and communication and thought would become impossible; so the relationship between our symbols and reality cannot be dependent upon any third thing (that is, logical objectivism is true).

It is easy to see what Wittgenstein might have in mind. For suppose that the relationship between a proposition and its truth-condition were dependent upon some third thing, such as the way in which a speaker (or perhaps most speakers) of the language were inclined to react in using that proposition in the light of the linguistic training which they have received. Then how could anyone tell you anything in advance of your seeing the facts for yourself? If they say to you 'My car is green', must you not wait to discover how they (or most people) react in the use of the term 'green' before you can know what they mean? In fact must you not wait to see the precise shade of colour of their car for yourself (by which time, of course, their information can be of no use to you)? How, indeed, could you even think of anything in advance? If you make the prediction 'Her new car will be green', how can you know in advance what shade of colour you are expecting? Must you not wait upon events, observing how you are inclined to respond in the use of the term 'green' before you can know which shades of colour your thought concerns? In which case – if you do not know what you are thinking of – you might just as well be incapable of thinking at all.

Although superficially plausible, this argument turns out merely to beg the question, taking for granted that in order to know what someone is talking of, or what your own thoughts concern, symbols would have to be related intrinsically (that is, in the manner of logical objectivism) to their objects. But in order to see this we need to outline briefly the most plausible form of anti-logical-objectivist position, which holds that a speaker's understanding of a symbol is to be equated with a practical capacity or set of such capacities (contrasting with the logical objectivist view that a speaker's capacity to use a sign is to be *explained in terms of* their understanding, which may perhaps outreach any capacity they may have). On this account the connection between symbol and world is not intrinsic, but is mediated by the speaker's disposition to employ that symbol in judgements. These dispositions will also include a normative element, the speaker being disposed to correct their mistakes and to accept correction from others, perhaps also being inclined to accept the judgement of the majority of their speech-community as binding in cases where their own dispositions are out of line. (If most other speakers of English describe as 'red' an object which I am disposed to call 'pink', then I shall give way.)

Now, consider how such a view might be placed to reply to the argument from describing in advance. Take the case of communication first: in denying logical objectivism we should be saying that to know in advance what someone is talking of is a matter of your possessing, yourself, various dispositions for the use of the signs in question, against a background assumption that you have both been given the same sort of linguistic training. So when someone says to you 'My car is green', you can know in advance what they mean because you yourself have dispositions for the use of 'green' – you could immediately point to a whole range of samples to which you would be inclined to apply the word – and because of reasonable assumptions about shared linguistic capacities. In fact you would not have to wait to see how your informant reacts, even though the connection between their symbols and the world is effected by their dispositions, because it would be reasonable for you to assume that you yourself share the same dispositions.

Consider, then, the case of symbols employed in thought: here we can say that knowing in advance what your thought concerns is simply a matter of being disposed to make use of its constituent signs in such a way that they would apply to the object in question. Wittgenstein seems to assume that if logical objectivism were false then we should be forced to wait to discover the connection between symbol and world, the phrase 'waiting to discover' suggesting that we should be incapable of rational action until the connection in question emerged. But of course if we suppose that the connection is constituted by the manner in which I am inclined to act, then it need not be like this at all. If the connection between my symbol 'green' and a certain range of shades of colour is constituted by my dispositions for the use of that symbol itself, then I do not have to wait to observe my own usage before I can act. (This would be like saying that I have to act before I can act!) Having entertained the thought 'Her new car will be green', I can immediately begin to act – for example selecting a tin of paint to match the colour which I am expecting – thus *exercising* the disposition in question.

(B) Frege's Regress

The other main argument which Wittgenstein employs at *PR* 20–6 is a regress, attempting to reduce the denial of logical objectivism to absurdity.

(See especially *PR* 22, 26.) It immediately puts one in mind of Frege's famous regress argument against correspondence theories of truth.[2] Indeed, it is possible that Frege's argument had been known to the Wittgenstein of *TLP*, perhaps influencing the development of the Picture Theory. For the regress certainly appears at its strongest when deployed against theories of truth (theories of the relation between symbols and reality) which see the connection in terms of some 'third thing'.[3] And one way of expressing at least part of the point of the mature Picture Theory is that it is to bring out how the relationship between a proposition and its truth-condition is intrinsic, any new arrangement of elements in a picture showing you what configuration of things in the world would make it true *without more ado*.

Frege first published his regress argument in the essay 'Thoughts', which appeared in 1918 – too late to influence the author of *TLP*. But in fact he had used it as early as 1897, in an unpublished paper entitled 'Logic', primarily against the imagist theory of meaning.[4] Now, we know that Wittgenstein visited Frege early in 1914, and that they corresponded for some time afterwards.[5] So it seems likely that Wittgenstein made the discovery of his Picture Theory in the Autumn of that year, he would have communicated it to Frege. It seems equally likely that Frege would have responded with the argument he had deployed some years earlier against a rather different version of correspondence theory. (Unfortunately we can only speculate, since their letters were destroyed in the bombing of the Second World War.) This would then explain why the 1918 version of the argument is not just directed against the imagist theory, but also against the idea that truth might consist in a correspondence between *pictures* and reality. But in any case, whatever the historical facts, it is worth considering whether anyone who rejects logical objectivism must be committed to a theory of truth which will generate a vicious regress.

The argument can best be developed as follows. Suppose we held that the relationship between our symbols and reality were not intrinsic, but rather resided in some third thing – for example the way in which most speakers of the language would respond to their training in their use of those symbols. Then the truth of a proposition 'P' would depend, not just upon its sense and the state of the world, but also upon the way in which most speakers of the language would respond in their use of 'P' when faced with that aspect of the world. So in order to establish the truth of 'P', should we not first have to discover how most speakers would react? For example, if 'P' is the proposition that Mary has a red car, then in order to establish its truth it seems we should have to discover whether most speakers of English would concur in describing the car as 'red'. But now we have another proposition to establish ('Most speakers of English . . . '), whose truth-condition, in turn, will depend upon the way in which most speakers would respond. So in order to establish the truth of this other proposition we must first enquire how most speakers of English would respond in the use of *it*: would most people agree that most speakers of English would concur in describing Mary's car as 'red'? And so on – the regress is vicious, since no truth can ever be established.

In fact the argument fails. It only appears to succeed by conflating the idea of a criterion, or test, of truth with substantive philosophical theories of what truth consists in. Sure enough, if the reactions of most speakers of English were being proposed as a criterion of truth – as the basis of our explicit normative practice in establishing truths – then the attempt to discover any truth would generate a regress. For in order to apply the criterion we should have to discover a truth which is distinct from our target truth; but then applying the criterion to this in turn would require us to establish a truth which is distinct from that, and so on. Frege's Regress therefore rules out any possibility of a general criterion of truth. But there is no reason to suppose that the denial of logical objectivism must commit us to any such thing. We could accept that the only norms in operation are those which result from the explanations and training which speakers are given in the use of the signs of their language. And yet we can, consistently with this, bring in the reactions of most speakers as part of a substantive philosophical thesis about the nature of the relation between symbols and reality.

As we saw above, the most plausible version of the anti-logical-objectivist position would hold that the result of the explanations and training purporting to fix the content of the symbols of our language would be to set up a complex of dispositions in us: dispositions to use those signs in assertions, dispositions to justify and accept correction of that usage in various characteristic ways, dispositions to hold one's use responsive to that of the majority of other people in cases of conflict, and so on. To say this is not at all to say that in order to establish a truth we would first have to discover what most speakers of the language would be disposed to say. Rather, a speaker will employ the signs in a proposition in the way they have been trained to do, thus exercising (as opposed to describing or investigating) the dispositions which they have in common with other speakers. For we may suppose that it belongs amongst their meaning-conferring dispositions, as a legitimate part of their practice, that they are only inclined to consult the dispositions of others in cases of conflict. So no regress is generated. Yet a philosopher reflecting on this practice, and wishing to give the most general account of what the truth of a sentence will consist in within such a community, may correctly say that it will be true in whatever circumstances most members of the community would regard as verifying it.

It might be said that either a vicious regress or a vicious circle must be generated, at least in the case of an attempt to establish the theory itself, which is our alternative to logical objectivism.[6] For suppose I were trying to establish that for a proposition to be true is for there to exist circumstances which most speakers of the language would (if suitably placed, etc.) regard as conclusively warranting its assertion. Can I simply take what steps seem to me appropriate in the light of my training in the use of the terms involved? However, this would apparently presuppose both that there is such a thing as agreement in reactions to training, and that I react with the majority. Yet this would be part of the very thesis whose truth I was trying to establish. But then if I set out to consider explicitly whether there is agreement in reactions, without relying upon my own linguistic dispositions, I should be launched on a regress.

The correct reply to this argument, however, is that merely exercising my linguistic dispositions in attempting to establish a theory of the relationship between language and reality is no more taking for granted what I am trying to establish than is a physicist who walks across a room in the course of investigating the laws of gravity. I should be employing my terms in the way that I have been trained to do, thus exercising the very dispositions which as a matter of fact confer meaning on them. And as we said, it may be a legitimate part of the practice that I can in general rely upon my own dispositions, only appealing to others in cases of conflict. So it is the practice itself which embodies an assumption that there is general agreement in reactions, which is not the same thing as saying that such an assumption enters into my investigation as a premiss. In which case there would be nothing untoward or question-begging about my procedure.

I can see no prospect of deriving a *reductio* from the denial of logical objectivism, by attempting to show that it would result either in a vicious regress or a vicious circle. So whether or not the Wittgenstein of *TLP* was actually influenced by Frege's Regress, we are still without any real support for logical objectivism.

(C) Objective necessity

When we reflect upon simple patterns of argument, or simple necessary truths, they tend to strike us as being wholly objective. We tend to think of the validity of valid arguments, and the necessity of analytic truths, as obtaining in a manner which is independent of us and our capacities, purely in virtue of the concepts – the senses of the signs – involved. For if logical objectivism were false, and thus if the relations between the concepts determining the analyticity of an analytic truth depended upon some contingent fact about us or the world, then what would become of the *necessity*?

The point here needs stating with some care. For if the question 'What would become of the necessity?' means 'What would become of truth in all possible worlds?', then the argument hinted at in the question would be unconvincing, for reasons similar to those which in fact undermine Frege's argument for the necessary existence of thoughts.[7] In effect it would mean that the argument in support of logical objectivism would be this:

(1)   If the internal relations in a tautology depended upon something contingent – such as people's reactions to their linguistic training – then it would fail to be true in all possible worlds (in particular, it would fail to be true in worlds where people's reactions differed).

(2)   But a tautology is a necessary truth: it is true in all possible worlds.

(C)   So the internal relations in a tautology must depend only upon the senses of the terms involved. That is to say: logical objectivism is true.

The correct response to this argument is to distinguish between truth *in* a world and truth *about* a world. And it must be the latter notion which is involved in the idea of conceptual necessity, else we shall be committed to the necessary existence of concepts (and perhaps also signs).[8] Then it need not in any way compromise the idea that a tautology is a truth *about* all possible worlds, if it were true that relationships between concepts depended upon contingent facts about human reactions. For these concepts get *used* by us, now, in a world where our reactions are as they are. They can constrain our talk about all possible worlds, despite the fact that in some of these worlds our reactions would have been different.

Thus to take up our example from the last chapter: if the mutual exclusiveness of the predicates 'red' and 'green' consists in the fact that speakers of English refuse to countenance their conjunction, we can still say (exercising this very disposition) that it would have been impossible for a surface to be red and green all over, even had all speakers been favourably disposed towards such a description. For we may take such an imagined disposition as showing that they must either mean something different by the words 'red' and 'green' or be mad.

On the other hand, the question 'What would become of the necessity?' may mean 'What would become of the objectivity – the mind-independence – of necessity?' Although many would maintain the mind-dependent existence of senses themselves,[9] there remains a strong inclination to believe that conceptually necessary truths must be wholly objective. Think, for example, of some arbitrarily long formula of the predicate calculus: are we not inclined to insist that it either is – determinately – a necessary truth or it is not? And this despite the fact that we may be incapable – certainly in practice, perhaps even in principle – of discovering its status. In which case, the way in which the senses of our signs interact to determine whether a sentence is necessary or contingent must surely be independent of any capacity of ours. For the relations which constitute a sentence as a necessary truth are being thought to obtain in cases which outreach our capacities.

This argument appears extremely powerful, although the main premiss – the objectivity of necessary truth – has been left merely intuitive, without the backing of any further argument. However, the intuitions involved are almost unavoidable for anyone who is actually engaged in doing logic (or, for that matter, anyone who is doing mathematics, if it is appropriate to think of the truths of mathematics as being conceptual, or sense-based). Someone attempting to construct a proof will naturally tend to think of the result as being there, already determinate, waiting to be discovered. They tend to think of themselves as tracing out connections between concepts which already exist, determined in a manner which in no way depends upon them or their capacities.

This way of thinking may itself be a product of something more general, namely the idea that the senses of new sentences are determined by the senses of their component parts in a mind-independent way. When we come across a new sentence we tend to think of its sense as already fixed, independently of our capacities and dispositions. Certainly we do not feel as if we have any *choice* in how to understand it. We think of the senses of the component words of the language as combining to determine the sense of any new sentence (thereby determining the status, as such, of tautologies and contradictions); determining even the sense of sentences which it would far outstrip our mental powers to comprehend.

Thus one strong argument in support of logical objectivism is founded on our intuitive belief in the objectivity of necessity – which may itself be founded on our intuitions concerning the objectivity of relations between senses generally. Quite what the source of these intuitions may be, and whether what is of value in them could be consistent with the denial of logical objectivism, are questions which we must leave to one side until the penultimate chapter.

(D) Objective truth

We tend to think of truth as being objective, at least within a fairly wide domain such as truths about physical objects and their states, the mental states of other people, and past and future times. We believe that within one of these domains, whether or not a proposition is true is wholly independent of facts about the person who entertains it. Rather the truth-value of such a proposition depends only on the way things are (or were, or will be) in the real world, as well as, of course, upon its content (sense). We think of these domains as consisting in judger-independent ranges of states of affairs: the facts being as they are no matter what we believe, and no matter whether or not we are capable of coming to know them. And we think of ourselves as having attached senses to our signs such that they and the states of affairs in the world can settle between them the truth-values of our propositions in advance of investigation by us. Indeed, we think of those senses and the states of the world as being able to settle truth-values even in cases which outstrip our capacities, such as propositions about the remote past, or generalisations about all future times.

It appears that the above conception of the objectivity of truth must commit us to logical objectivism, requiring us to picture the senses of our signs as reaching out to reality in a manner which does not in any way depend upon us and our capacities. For suppose that logical objectivism were false. That is, suppose that the relationship between propositions and their truth-conditions were dependent upon some fact, or facts, about those who use those propositions. In that case, how could truth be objective? For what does it mean to say that a truth is *sub*jective, except that its truth is a function, not just of states of the world and the content of the proposition, but also of states of the judging subject? Moreover, if logical objectivism were false, then how could there be truths about states of the world which transcended our capacities for discovery? For if the very manner in which a proposition gets projected on to reality depends upon our capacities and dispositions, then propositions could apparently reach no further than our capacities do.

If asked to justify our belief in the objectivity of truth there is perhaps not a great deal that we can do, any more than we can justify our belief in the objectivity of necessity. But we can at least point out that our reliance upon classical logic might be unwarranted if truth were not objective. (Although whether this is really the direction of support or whether, on the contrary, it is our belief in the objectivity of truth which supports our reliance upon classical logic is perhaps not obvious.) For in relying upon the law of Excluded Middle (the unrestricted validity of 'P ∨ −P') we appear to be taking for granted the principle of Bivalence ('every proposition is determinately either true or false'). And this seems to presuppose in turn that the truth-values of propositions depend only on their sense and the state of the world (thus committing us to the objectivity of truth and to logical objectivism). At any rate, if we think that logical laws have to be validated by general semantical considerations, then it is hard to see how Excluded Middle could be retained if our belief in the objectivity of truth were given up.[10]

Summary

We have considered a number of arguments in support of logical objectivism. Three of these − from the possibility of describing 'in advance', from a vicious regress, and from necessity as truth in all possible worlds − have turned out to be less than convincing. But we are left with two arguments − from the objectivity of conceptually necessary truth, and from the objectivity of contingent truth − which although intuitive appear extremely powerful.

5 *Determinate* Sinn

Our discussion of *TLP* has so far been conducted with its associated programme of analysis largely bracketed off. In the present chapter we begin to put this right, with an investigation of the *TLP* requirement that *Sinn* be determinate.

(A) Preliminaries

As is well known, *TLP* contains a programme for the analysis of ordinary language. In outline, Wittgenstein thinks that any adequate analysis would have to satisfy the following constraints. Firstly, all propositions of ordinary language are to be logically equivalent to truth-functional compounds of a base-class of elementary propositions (5, 5.3). Secondly, these elementary propositions are to consist only of names in immediate conjunction with one another (2.03–2.032, 2.13–2.131, 3.2–3.21, 4.22–4.221). Thirdly, elementary propositions are to be logical pictures of states of affairs (2.1–2.1515, 3.2–3.21). Fourthly, the elementary propositions are to be logically independent of one another (2.061–2.062, 4.211, 5.134, 5.152). Finally, each of the names in an elementary proposition is to stand for a simple necessarily existing object – what I have been calling 'a Simple' for short (2.02–2.023, 2.026–2.0271, 3.202–3.261).[1]

Some of these ideas have already been discussed. Thus the second and third constraints were briefly dealt with in our discussion of the Picture Theory in Chapter 1. The others will receive discussion later. Here we shall consider what promises to be the corner-stone of the whole programme of analysis, underlying the first and last of the above constraints in particular. For at 3.23, in the context of a sequence of remarks on the idea of analysis, we are told that the requirement that simple signs be possible is the requirement that *Sinn* be determinate. Now the 'simple signs' of *TLP* are the names which would figure in the elementary propositions of a fully analysed language, referring to the simple objects which constitute the substance of the world (2.02–2.0272, 3.2–3.26). So it looks as though the requirement of determinacy is going to be pivotal, not only for our understanding of the *TLP* idea of analysis, but also for our appreciation of the basis of Wittgenstein's metaphysics.

(B) Determinacy in *TLP*

Since we are not told explicitly how the requirement of determinacy of *Sinn* is to be understood, we are forced to cast around for indirect evidence. The word 'determinacy' ('*Bestimmtheit*') is the noun formed from the verb 'to determine' ('*bestimmen*'), and related to the adjective 'determinate' ('*bestimmt*'). Each of these occurs at various points in *TLP*. So we might expect either or both of these semantic connections to be of some help to us in interpreting the import of 3.23.

The *TLP* use of '*bestimmen*' does seem to be accurately translated by the English verbs 'to determine' or 'to fix'. For Wittgenstein speaks of the use of a sign determining its logical form (3.327), of a proposition determining a place in logical space (3.4, 3.42), and of determining the truth-conditions of a sentence by determining under what circumstances it should be called true (4.063). If we take this as our guide, then we shall interpret the requirement of determinacy as the requirement that the *Sinn* of any proposition should have been determined (fixed). But this would leave us with a requirement of doubtful significance. For if we remember that the *Sinn* of a sentence is its truth-condition, this would tell us only that we must fix the truth-conditions of our sentences, which seems entirely truistic. We should also be left no further forward in elucidating the argument for Simples, since 3.23 would merely tell us that their existence is presupposed to our having fixed truth-conditions for our sentences, it being left obscure just why this might be supposed to be so.

The *TLP* use of the adjective '*bestimmt*', on the other hand, seems rather closer to the English use of 'certain' or 'particular' in such constructions as 'a certain relation' or 'a particular relation'. This would be a natural reading of 2.031, for instance, where we are told that the objects in a state of affairs stand in a determinate (that is, particular) relation to one another. For this is not very likely to mean that the objects stand to one another in a relation which has been fixed (that is, caused), or that the relation between the objects is fixed (that is, changeless). (See 2.032, 2.14, 2.15, 3.14.) And it is actually forced on us as an interpretation of 4.466, where we are told that determinate logical combinations of *Bedeutungen* correspond to determinate logical combinations of signs; this is immediately glossed with the remark that it is only to uncombined signs that absolutely any combination of *Bedeutungen* (that is, none in particular) corresponds. Then read in this light the requirement of determinacy of *Sinn* would be the requirement that every sentence should be assigned some particular truth-condition. But again ít would be left wholly unclear why this should be a requirement worth insisting on, as opposed to just the merest platitude; or why the existence of Simples might be thought to follow from it.

So if we were to concentrate upon the connection between '*Bestimmt-heit*' and Wittgenstein's use of the corresponding verb, then we might think of translating (somewhat barbarously) the requirement of the *Bestimmtheit des Sinnes* as 'the requirement of the *fixedness* of truth-conditions'. But concentrating on the connection with the corresponding adjective, we might think of translating it as 'the requirement of the *particularity* of truth-conditions'. There may be something of value in either, or both, suggestions. (Indeed I shall argue as much later.) But it is, to say the least, hardly very perspicuous what the requirement of determinacy would amount to, on either reading.

We might try pushing the connection with the *TLP* use of the adjective '*bestimmt*' – or one of its uses – rather harder. Perhaps we should interpret 2.031 as saying, not merely that in a state of affairs objects stand in some particular relation to one another, but also that they stand to one another in a 'quite particular' relation – that is, a relation which is sharply marked off from any other in which they might stand. For note that Wittgenstein is about to introduce, at 2.061, his doctrine that states of affairs are logically independent of one another. This doctrine would be indefensible if the relations in which objects stand to one another in a state of affairs were to admit of degrees, in such a way that the particular relation in which they do in fact stand is just one of a number of mutually exclusive relations in which they might have stood. Think, for instance, of spatial relations. If the objects in a state of affairs stand in spatial relations to one another, then from the fact that they stand in some particular spatial relation it would follow, *a priori*, that they do not stand to one another in any of the infinitely many other spatial relations.

We might therefore think of taking Wittgenstein's talk of a 'determinate relation' at 2.031 to mean a relation which does not admit of degrees,[2] in consequence taking the requirement of the *Bestimmtheit des Sinnes* to be the requirement that the truth-conditions of sentences should be sharply demarcated. It would claim that a sentence should be associated with a truth-condition which is 'quite particular', in the sense of being sharply marked off from any other possible truth-condition.

Such an interpretation would at least have the advantage of attributing to Wittgenstein a substantive and interesting thesis. Moreover, it would enable us to make some sort of sense of the *TLP* insistence on the existence of simple objects. The idea would be that the truth-condition of a sentence could never be perfectly sharp unless reality were *discrete*. Think, for example, of the colour-spectrum: if this is infinitely divisible, then at whatever level of description you choose to define the boundary between two colours, that boundary will still be vague relative to the further analysis which is still possible. For to define a sharp boundary between yellow and green, say, we should have to lay down which is the last shade of yellow, and which is the first shade of green. But if the spectrum is infinitely divisible there will still be infinitely many distinct shades between these two, about which our explanation would remain silent. Only if there exist atoms of colour, so to speak, will it be possible to draw a sharp boundary. We could then pick on an atom to be the last shade of yellow, and the very next atom would be the first shade of green, there being no atoms in between.[3]

It would obviously be ill-advised, however, to accept this interpretation on the basis of these few textual hints alone. Moreover, Charity militates against it in two ways. Firstly, the resulting argument for the existence of Simples would be extremely weak, as we shall see in Chapter 8. Secondly, Wittgenstein would be committed to the absurd thesis that none of the propositions of ordinary language really do have vague truth-conditions, as we shall see shortly.

Failing, as we have done, to extract an interpretation of the requirement of determinacy of *Sinn* from the text of *TLP* itself, we may turn to *NB* for guidance.[4] For the latter contains a lengthy sequence of passages (roughly 60–70) which discuss the programme of analysis and the demand for Simples, as well as a number of (apparently different) demands on *Sinn*. It not only contains the phrase 'requirement of determinacy of *Sinn*' (*NB* 63), but also speaks of the requirement that *Sinn* be *complete* (*NB* 61, 67), and the requirement that *Sinn* be *clear* and *sharp* (*NB* 67, 68). Although he does not say so in so many words, I think it reasonable to assume that Wittgenstein saw these as being different aspects of (or at least as being entailed by) the requirement of determinacy.

(C) The principle of sharpness

Not only is the Wittgenstein of *NB* concerned about the vagueness of ordinary language and ordinary concepts, but he seems to have thought that analysis would remove this vagueness, or rather reveal it to be illusory.

Thus at *NB* 67, having raised the question whether the sentence 'The book is lying on the table' has a complete clear *Sinn*,[5] and having insisted that since we certainly mean *something* by the sentence, as much as we *certainly* mean must surely be clear, he then notes that there may occur cases in which one would be unable to say whether or not the book should properly be called 'lying on the table'. Then at the top of 68 he suggests that this phenomenon may result merely from a certain looseness in expressing what we mean. It may be that in context – with the book lying on the table in front of me – I use the phrase 'lying on' in such a way as to refer to that particular relation in which the book and the table now stand to one another, although I should in other circumstances use that very same phrase to refer to other relations.[6]

The suggestion is, in effect, that vagueness be assimilated to ambiguity. This would enable one to insist that 'what I *mean* must always be sharp' (*NB* 68). By *NB* 70 this idea seems to have been positively adopted. There, having insisted that the vagueness of ordinary sentences can be justified, Wittgenstein says that one always knows what – in context – one means by a vague sentence. Although I may not know, in general, what I should be prepared to call 'lying on', in present circumstances I know that I mean *that* relation (pointing to the book lying on the table).

Of course this doctrine is indefensible. It perhaps has some slight plausibility in a case where I am actually confronted by the state of affairs being described. (I imagine Wittgenstein sitting with his book on the table in front of him, saying over and over again 'I mean *that*.') But it becomes absurd as soon as one thinks of descriptions of states of affairs which are not immediately, and have not recently been, before me.[7] Suppose, for example, that I assert 'I had fair hair when I was born.' Is there a sharp line here between what I mean and what I do not? Am I prepared to say precisely what shades I should be inclined to call 'fair'? Am I prepared to draw a sharp line between being born with hair and being born without? (Is being born with just sixteen hairs a case of being born 'with hair'?)

Moreover, the proposal would involve drawing a distinction in almost every case between what *I* mean and what *the sentence* means, which would make it hard to see how communication could be possible. For if what I mean by 'The watch is lying on the table' is *this* particular relation between watch and table, then how can anyone else know what I mean? Of course they cannot, at least until they themselves can see the position of the watch, by which time my information can be of no rational use to them. Nor can we get around this difficulty by saying that communication does not require knowledge of a speaker's actual meaning, but only that one should get sufficiently close to it. For this would still leave us with vagueness in the hearer's understanding of the statement. (How close is 'sufficiently close'?) And if there is a problem about vagueness, it will surely be equally a problem for hearer's understanding as for speaker's meaning.

We must insist against the Wittgenstein of *NB* that many of the propositions of ordinary language, and many of the thoughts of an ordinary thinker, are genuinely vague.[8] In which case, there can be no question of removing that vagueness by analysis. For if the vague proposition comes out under analysis into a proposition which has a perfectly sharp truth-condition, then it has not been analysed but replaced by another – different – proposition. It might conceivably be replied that although the propositions of ordinary language are genuinely vague, this vagueness is not an essential part of their sense, but is merely the product of a kind of laziness on our part. So although analysis, in providing us with a sharply defined proposition, would yield a proposition which is in certain respects different from the original, the two propositions may be regarded as essentially the same proposition. Analysis, on this view, would merely tidy up the neglected corners of the language, leaving us with a structure which is, in all essentials, the same.

This response is unacceptable for at least two reasons. In the first place, there will always be a number of distinct but equally acceptable ways of sharpening a previously vague concept. So the resulting sentences will have different – and essentially different – truth-conditions, since there will actually be circumstances in which they differ in truth-value. And the transitivity of identity prevents us from saying that there can be two sentences, whose senses differ essentially from one another, which each have essentially the very same sense as a third (vague) sentence. In the second place, it can be shown that the vagueness of many of our concepts does not result merely from laziness, but on the contrary is essential for those concepts to fulfil our purposes.[9] With colour concepts, for example, we need terms whose applicability will be memorable. So it is crucial that they should not be defined any more sharply than our memories will allow. Similarly, with concepts such as *heap* and *pile* we require terms whose applicability can be taken in at a glance. So once again it is essential that they should not be defined any more sharply than a glance will allow.

In the next chapter we shall raise the question whether a concern to eradicate vagueness survives into *TLP* (remember, we have been offered no evidence of it as yet); and if so, whether there is anything which can be said in Wittgenstein's defence. How could he have been tempted into such a blind alley? Are there any powerful arguments for thinking that vagueness is strictly speaking impossible? But for the moment we must, in charity to Wittgenstein, see whether we cannot find a textual basis for some rather different interpretation of the requirement of determinacy of *Sinn*.[10]

(D) Determinacy in advance

During the discussion of determinacy in *NB*, Wittgenstein demands not only that *Sinn* should be sharp, but also that it must be complete (*NB* 61). This is then glossed by saying that every proposition must be a picture of reality in such a way that what is not yet said in it simply cannot belong to its *Sinn*, which in turn is echoed at *NB* 64, where Wittgenstein writes:

We might demand determinacy in this way too: if a proposition is to have Sinn then the syntactical employment of each of its parts must be settled in advance. – It is, e.g., not possible *only subsequently to come upon* the fact that a proposition follows from it. But, e.g., what propositions follow from a proposition must be completely settled before that proposition can have Sinn! [Italics in original.]

Now, this passage is by no means easy to interpret. But there is evidence to suggest that it may be of crucial importance. For in *PTLP* it gets included, with only minor alterations, almost immediately after the remark that the demand for simple signs is the demand that *Sinn* be determinate (*PTLP* 3.20101–3.20103). So it may be here in this passage, despite its awkwardness of expression, that we shall find the clue to what the Wittgenstein of *TLP* really has in mind in requiring that *Sinn* be determinate.

There are two immediate difficulties in interpreting the above passage. The first is to understand what is meant by the 'syntactical employment' of the parts of a proposition. For this phrase is, on the face of it, almost wholly opaque. The second difficulty is to see why Wittgenstein should insist that in order to determine the truth-condition of a proposition it must already have been completely settled what propositions follow logically from it. For since 'P ∨ Q' follows logically from 'P, no matter what 'Q' may be, the effect of this would be to lay it down that no proposition may be said to have a truth-condition until the truth-conditions of all other sentences have been determined.

Such a position would be extremely puzzling in its own right, as well as being quite out of line with Wittgenstein's general approach. For it would mean that there could be no question of a step-by-step construction of language, in which we fix the truth-conditions of a range of atomic propositions first, and then go on to fix on that basis the truth-conditions of molecular and general propositions. On the contrary, we should somehow have to fix the truth-conditions of all propositions simultaneously. It is doubtful if such a view is even coherent, let alone whether Wittgenstein ever held it. For how could the truth-condition of 'P ∨ Q' be fixed unless the truth-conditions of 'P' and 'Q' have *already* been fixed? Moreover, in *TLP*, at least, Wittgenstein palpably intorduces the senses of the propositional connectives and quantifiers in such a way that the trurh-conditions of all elementary propositions must be taken for granted. (See 4.4, 4.51, 5, 6.)

Both of the above difficulties may easily be cleared up if we take the quoted passage in its context in *NB*. It occurs as part of a discussion of the possibility that reality, and the truth-conditions of propositions, may turn out to be infinitely complex. And just a little higher up the page Wittgenstein had written as follows:

> But suppose that a simple name denotes an infinitely complex object? For example, perhaps we assert of a patch in our visual field that it is to the right of a line, and we assume that every patch in our visual field is infinitely complex. Then if we say that a point in that patch is to the right of the line, this proposition follows from the previous one, and if there are infinitely many points in the patch *then infinitely many propositions of different content follow* LOGICALLY *from that first one*. And this of itself shows that the proposition itself was as a matter of fact infinitely complex. That is, not the propositional sign by itself, but it together with its syntactical application. [Italics in original.]

Here we have a pointer to what was meant, in the passage quoted earlier, by the 'syntactical employment' of the parts of a proposition. What Wittgenstein has in mind is the way in which the use of a sentence-part contributes to determining the logical relations between the sentences in which it occurs and others. Note, moreover, that whenever he talks of 'syntax' in *TLP* (usually 'logical syntax', at 3.327 'logico-syntactical employment'), he seems to have in mind the sense, or kind of sense, possessed by a sign – where possession of a sense may be equated with the way in which that sign is conventionally used. So when he says that the syntactical employment of each of the parts of a proposition must be settled in advance, he is saying that it must be completely determinate, from the senses of the component parts of a proposition, just what exactly its logical consequences are to be.

Our second puzzle may also be cleared up if we assume that when Wittgenstein talks, in the passage previously quoted, of the propositions which follow logically from a given proposition, he is still thinking of an example like that above, where the entailed propositions themselves belong within the truth-condition of the given proposition. In effect he is thinking specifically about propositions whose truth-conditions are conjunctive in form – in the way that the truth-condition of 'The patch is to the right of the line' might be said to take the form 'This point is to the right of the line, and this point is to the right of the line, and so on.' So when he expresses the requirement of determinacy by saying that the propositions which follow from a given proposition must be completely settled before that proposition can have *Sinn*, he has in mind only those propositions which themselves belong within the truth-condition of the given proposition, rather than literally all which are its consequences.[11]

It appears that Wittgenstein's requirement is really this: that the truth-condition of a proposition must be completely settled in advance before that proposition can have a truth-condition. (Hence the exclamation-mark in the first of the above quotations from *NB* 64!) The substance of this remark then lies in its insistence that the truth-condition of a proposition must have been settled all at once and in advance of its being used to say anything; and in its denial of the converse possibility that one might have occasion to discover, *a posteriori*, that a certain state of affairs is such as to render a given proposition true. I thus see the passage as belonging alongside 4.064, where Wittgenstein stresses that every proposition must *already* have a *Sinn*: since its *Sinn* is just what is affirmed, it cannot be given *Sinn* by affirmation.

The requirement of determinacy which has emerged here may be expressed thus: the truth-condition of a proposition must have been completely fixed in advance, in all its (possibly infinite) particularity, depending only on the sense of that proposition. (So here we have a connection with the suggestion made earlier in this chapter, that what is involved might be a requirement of the 'fixedness' and/or the 'particularity' of truth-conditions.) Now, this is just an instance of the more general doctrine of logical objectivism, which holds that logical relations generally (including the relation between a proposition and its truth-condition) must be determined in a wholly objective manner by sense alone. The claim is that the relationship between language and the world must be objective, determined *a priori* by the senses of the component expressions in a way that is independent of anything empirical; and in particular, independently of any human belief, capacity or disposition.

We have finally found a requirement to stand alongside the requirement of sharpness, which I propose to call 'the requirement of determinacy-in-advance';[12] this is one aspect of Wittgenstein's logical objectivism. Then since, as we saw in Chapter 4, the latter is a doctrine which can be powerfully supported by argument, we have already gone some way towards complying with the principle of Charity. It will be the task of later chapters to investigate the role of this requirement within the structure of argument of *TLP*.

Summary

We have discovered two very different strands to the *NB* discussion of determinacy of *Sinn*: on the one hand there is the requirement that *Sinn* should be sharp, and on the other that *Sinn* should be fully determined in advance of anything empirical. Since the first of these requirements appears to have been a blind alley, whereas the second can be powerfully defended, we have some reason to equate the *TLP* version of that requirement with the latter.

6 Vagueness

Our task in this chapter is to see what could have tempted Wittgenstein into trying to eradicate the vagueness of ordinary language by analysis. Why should he have wished to show it to be illusory? Part of the point of the investigation will be to see whether there is any reason for thinking that the requirement of sharpness of *Sinn* survives from *NB* into *TLP* itself.

(A) Fuzziness versus indefiniteness

One suggestion is that Wittgenstein's concerns may have resulted partly from confusion over the different senses of 'vague' (also reflected in the corresponding German '*Vagheit*'). For on the one hand the term can be used to characterise concepts with fuzzy boundaries (such as *green*) or sentences with blurred truth-conditions (such as 'Joan is still young'). But on the other hand it can describe sentences whose truth-conditions are merely unspecific or indefinite. Thus a sentence such as 'Joan married someone sometime last year' could correctly be described as 'vague' relative to a more specific sentence such as 'Joan married John on 16 June last year.' And this despite the fact that it may have been defined as sharply as you like what is to constitute a marriage, and what it is for a marriage to take place in one year rather than the next. Nor is it merely the presence of the existential quantifier which renders sentences vague in this second sense either. For 'The watch is lying on the table' is similarly unspecific in relation to sentences describing the particular position of the watch, such as 'It is lying at a point eight centimetres from the right edge of the table and four from the front.'

Now, as we shall see in Chapter 7, the unspecificness of most ordinary propositions was something which Wittgenstein could be, and was, legitimately concerned about. (In fact it raises a threat to the requirement of determinacy-in-advance.) It is also something which can be rendered genuinely innocuous by means of analysis. So it may be that his worries (in *NB*) over the fuzziness of ordinary language were merely a spill-over, so to speak, from his legitimate concern at the indefiniteness of many ordinary statements. We would then be free to suppose the requirement of sharpness to have been dropped by the time of writing *TLP*, since it receives no explicit mention in that work.

(B) The principles of logic

A second explanation may be that Wittgenstein inherited his worries concerning the fuzziness of ordinary language from Frege, who believed that in a properly constructed language no fuzziness could occur at all. Thus at *The Basic Laws of Arithmetic* section 56 Frege writes:

The law of excluded middle is really just another form of the requirement that a concept should have a sharp boundary. Any object A that you choose to take either falls under the concept φ or does not fall under it; *tertium non datur*.

Clearly Frege thinks that the existence of fuzzy concepts would conflict with a fundamental principle of logic. However, it is not entirely clear which, since he does not distinguish between the Principle of Excluded Third ('No proposition can be neither true nor false') and the Principle of Bivalence ('Every proposition must be determinately either true or false'). The reference to Excluded Middle suggests that it is Bivalence which he has in mind; but the phrase *'tertium non datur'* suggests Excluded Third. Of course, since Bivalence entails Excluded Third (on any conception of entailment),[1] he may have believed that fuzzy propositions would fail to satisfy Bivalence *because* they conflict with Excluded Third. Or he may have believed that there would be a conflict with Bivalence in its own right. Both possibilities will be investigated later.

If Wittgenstein, too, believed fuzziness to be in conflict with logic, then from here on their paths would have diverged considerably. Frege takes the view that since the propositions of ordinary language are in fact fuzzy, ordinary language is thereby revealed to be radically defective. The only remedy is reconstruction, replacing natural language with a language suitable for use in strict science (by which he means 'suitable for use in any systematic enquiry after truth'), in which no fuzziness would occur.[2] Wittgenstein, on the other hand, believes that the propositions of ordinary language are in perfect logical order as they stand (5.5563). For him there is no question of anything being radically wrong with sentences which we use, and use successfully, every day. He would then be committed to showing the fuzziness of ordinary language to be merely apparent.

This divergence in response would reflect different perspectives on the nature of logic itself. Frege seems to have regarded the principles of logic as prescriptions, telling us how a language should be constructed and used if it is to be fit to serve in the systematic pursuit of truth. On this view, if ordinary language fails to live up to these prescriptions, then that only shows it is not entirely suitable for use in strict science. Wittgenstein, on the other hand, views logic as the structure – the 'inner scaffolding' (4.023) – of all language and thought, regarding it as necessarily governing all representation, no matter whether as part of a systematic enquiry or of a casual conversation. On this view, an illogical language would be one which was incapable of expressing thoughts at all (5.4731).

Wittgenstein's position appears to be the stronger (though we shall return to the matter in Chapter 11 below). For does not Excluded Third say, for example, '*No proposition* can be neither true nor false'? In which case, if a sentence like 'The table is green' really does have a fuzzy truth-condition, and as a result conflicts with Excluded Third, then this could only show that it does not express a proposition. Yet how can this be, since that sentence may, after all, be determinately true? For how can a sentence express a truth unless it expresses a proposition? Frege might try to respond by restricting the scope of Excluded Third to the form 'No proposition suitable for use in strict science can be neither true nor false.' But this would be to let go of the unrestricted generality and subject-independence which are supposed to be the distinctive mark of a principle of logic.

There may perhaps be rather more subtle ways in which ordinary language could be shown to be incoherent. For example, it could conceivably turn out that there is no consistent description which can be given of our normative practice in the use of our language, rather as there would be no coherent description to be given of the norms governing a game whose rules contain a contradiction, even though the players themselves may manage to play the game quite successfully through failing to notice it.[3] But what surely stands firm is that if we believe, as both Wittgenstein and Frege did, that the principles of logic express objective constraints, then those principles must be supposed to govern all of our propositions; and whatever else may be the case, 'The table is green' does express a proposition. It would thus have been no mere thoughtlessness on Wittgenstein's part which set him off down the blind-alley of trying to show the fuzziness of ordinary language to be merely apparent, if we suppose that he had good reason to believe, with Frege, that such fuzziness would bring ordinary language into conflict with logic.

Would a proposition's possessing a fuzzy sense entail that it fails to satisfy Excluded Third? It is certainly tempting to think so. For then we should apparently have to acknowledge the existence of a third possibility alongside the possibilities of truth and falsity for that proposition – namely 'indeterminate' – which would be the fuzzy area between the cases where it would be determinately true and the cases where it would be determinately false. But in fact this would be a mistake. We cannot take indeterminate to be a third possibility alongside truth and falsity, since it would not really be mutually exclusive of either of them. For if a state of affairs falls within the fuzzy area between the clear truth and the clear falsity of a vague proposition, this does not mean that the proposition is not true, or that it is not false. It only means that we cannot say either that it is true or that it is not true, or either that it is false or that it is not false.

Consider the example of the statement 'The table is green.' What are we to say if the actual colour of the table is indeterminate between green and yellow? Would it be correct to say 'It is not true that the table is green'? Obviously not, any more than it would be correct to say 'It is true that the table is green.' Neither would it be correct to say 'It is not false that the table is green', unless this means that it is not clearly false. But there is nothing in the principle of Excluded Third to suggest that 'false' should be equated with 'clearly false', or 'true' with 'clearly true'. (In fact what we should say, of course, is that the table is greenish-yellow. This suggests a strategy for dealing with vagueness using a notion of degrees of truth, which will be discussed below.)

The fact of the matter is that the statement 'It is true that the table is green' has a sense no more and no less fuzzy than the statement 'The table is green' itself. And this is just what we might have expected had we realised that the notion of truth is governed by the Same Sense Principle, the sentence 'It is true that P' always having the very same sense as the sentence 'P' itself. (This follows from the criterion of sense-identity as cognitive content, together with the fact that it is surely impossible for anyone to enquire whether P without enquiring whether it is true that P, and vice versa; and so on for all propositional attitudes – believing, doubting, etc.)[4] For this principle implies that the predicate 'true' will always take on exactly the fuzziness of the proposition which it governs. So you could say that the reason why indeterminate cannot be a third truth-value – and so the reason why fuzziness fails to conflict with Excluded Third – is that the fuzzy borderline itself becomes absorbed into the vague area between this particular application of the concepts of truth and falsity themselves. Thus 'indeterminate' does not name a third possibility because the vagueness in this use of the terms 'true' and 'false' itself covers that possibility.

If fuzziness does not conflict with Excluded Third, then is there any reason to think that it conflicts with the stronger principle of Bivalence? Here the appearance of conflict is, if anything, even greater. For it may be difficult to see how every proposition can be determinately either true or false, if there exist circumstances in which fuzzy-sensed propositions are neither clearly the one nor the other.

It is not open to us to reply that 'The table is green' might in fact be clearly true (or clearly false), although we mere mortals are incapable of establishing it. (Compare the way in which someone might say that 'A city will never be built on this spot' might really be determinately true, although we could never live long enough to know it.[5]) For we might easily be in the best imaginable position for judging the truth-value of 'The table is green' (that is, standing in front of the table in white light, etc.). Our inability to establish its truth-value results not from any obstacle being placed in our path – on the contrary, everything is, so to speak, laid out before us for our inspection – but rather from the kind of sense which we associate with it. So if we really were to insist that its sense is such as to determine a clear truth-value in cases where we cannot do so, then we should be forced to draw the conclusion that none of us in fact knows its sense, which would be absurd.

Nevertheless, it is a mistake to think that Bivalence either has to be, or should be, construed in such a way as to rule out the possibility of fuzziness. Suppose we distinguish between two different senses of 'determinate', in one of which it means 'clear' and in the other of which it means 'objective'. Then we could understand Bivalence to say that all propositions are objectively either true or false. In which case, so long as fuzziness does not conflict with Excluded Third, there would be no conflict with Bivalence either. We could insist that 'The table is green' is either objectively true or objectively false – insisting that its truth-value is in no way dependent upon us and our capacities – while allowing, as before, the fuzzy borderline to become absorbed into the application of the terms 'true' and 'false'. For when we say that 'The table is green' need not have a determinate truth-value, all we mean is that it need not be *clearly* true or *clearly* false. But this in no way compromises the thesis of objectivity.[6]

As we shall see in Chapter 11, Bivalence not only can but should be understood in this way. For what it contains, over and above what is involved in Excluded Third, is nothing other than a commitment to a certain conception of the objectivity of truth (indeed, the very same conception as was involved in the final argument for logical objectivism presented in Chapter 4). Anyone espousing this principle must be thinking of the truth-value of a proposition as being entirely independent of anything which we may believe about the matter; independent, indeed, of whether or not we are capable – either in practice or in principle – of establishing it. They must then apparently picture the sense of the proposition as 'reaching out' to the world in a mind-independent way, so as to fix, in conjunction with the facts, a determinate (that is, objective, not necessarily clear) truth-value.

I conclude then, that there is no reason to think that the existence of fuzzy-sensed propositions raises any threat to the principles of logic. Frege and (perhaps) Wittgenstein were sent chasing a will-o'-the-wisp, the one in believing himself required by logic to undertake a reconstructive programme to eradicate vagueness, the other in believing (if he did) that logic required him to show it to be illusory.

(C) The programme of analysis

The third, and perhaps the most important, reason why Wittgenstein might have felt himself compelled to deny the fuzziness of ordinary language is that there is no way of finding a place for fuzzy truth-conditions within the constraints imposed by his programme of analysis. As we shall see in Chapter 7, he felt himself obliged on other grounds to adopt such a programme, and to regard it, not as a kind of Fregean reconstruction, but as uncovering what is already implicit in ordinary discourse. Then if a fully analysed language would necessarily have to be fuzziness-free, he would have had no option but to treat the apparent fuzziness of ordinary statements as being somehow illusory.

The *TLP* doctrine is that all propositions may be analysed into truth-functions of elementary propositions, which are the most detailed possible descriptions of states of affairs (3.2–3.261, 4.2–4.2211, 5). Now, if we were correct in arguing above that 'indeterminate' cannot be regarded as the name of a third truth-value, then there can be no question of introducing the vagueness of ordinary propositions by means of a truth-function of elementary propositions which are not themselves vague. But then on the other hand, any proposition which is vague cannot be elementary. For suppose that a proposition P is true under just one circumstance s, is indeterminate under just one circumstance t, and is false on any other condition. Then consider the possible propositions Q (which is true on condition s, false on any other) and R (which is true on condition t, false on any other). Clearly if any of P, Q and R is elementary then it must be Q and R rather than P, since they are more detailed and specific. In short: any proposition which is vague could be subjected to further analysis, and so cannot be elementary.

Even if 'indeterminate' could be regarded as a third truth-value we would not be able to introduce fuzziness by means of a truth-function of sharply defined elementary propositions. For the borderlines between 'true', 'indeterminate' and 'false' would themselves be vague. Thus suppose we tried to capture the vagueness of 'The table is green' by means of an analysis having the following sort of form: the sentence is true if and only if the table has any of the shades u or v or w, it is indeterminate if and only if the table has either of the shades x or y, and it is false otherwise. This would still leave us with a sharp boundary between the cases in which the proposition is true and those in which it is indeterminate, since the propositions ascribing particular shades are, by hypothesis, themselves sharply defined. So the analysis must fail to capture the sort of fuzziness which the proposition actually has, since for us there is no sharp line between the circumstances in which it is correct to say 'It is clearly true' and those in which we should say 'It is no longer clearly true.' Moreover, the lack of a sharp boundary here must be regarded as an essential feature of the proposition, for reasons similar to those advanced in Chapter 5: namely that we want the conditions for the use of colour predicates to be memorable.

Perhaps the most promising strategy for introducing fuzziness into an analysis employing only sharply defined elementary propositions would be to use a function which maps the elementary propositions on to *degrees* of truth. (But note that this would mean Wittgenstein having to give up his idea that analysis may be conducted using ordinary truth-functions.) We could then represent the truth-condition of a sentence like 'The table is green' by means of a *graph* (see Figure 1), in such a way that there will be a range of shades where we say 'Certainly green', a range where we say 'Green with a touch of yellow', and so on. But one immediate difficulty with this idea is that the lines in the graph would need to have thickness, and indeed blurred edges. For there is no precise shade at which we begin to say 'Green with a touch of yellow', or at which we say 'Just as much yellow as green'. So we would need, not just a function mapping shades of colour on to degrees of truth, but a *vaguely defined* function. In which case we would still be left with the same problem of how to introduce vagueness by means of notions which are not themselves vague.

Another difficulty for the proposal is as follows. Either the shades described by the elementary propositions can be discriminated from their nearest neighbours or they cannot. Yet either way we shall run into trouble with the familiar fact of the non-transitivity of discriminability. Thus consider three distinct objects A, B and C, such that object A is indiscriminable in shade from B, and B indiscriminable from C, and yet A can be discriminated from C. If atoms of colour are to be always discriminable, then A and B (being indiscriminable from one another) will possess the very same shade; and so the propositions 'A is green' and 'B is green' will have to be assigned the very same degree of truth, as will the propositions 'B is green' and 'C is green.' But then since A and C possess distinct shades, it will be possible for 'A is green' and 'C is green' to be assigned distinct degrees of truth, and we will have a contradiction. If, on the other hand, distinct atoms can be indiscriminable from one another, then A and B may possess distinct shades, and the propositions 'A is green' and 'B is green' may be assigned distinct degrees of truth, despite the fact that their colours are indistinguishable. But this would be absurd. If a sense were fixed for 'green' such that its correct application may vary in cases where we are incapable of seeing a difference, then that would only show that we do not know any such sense.

It might be replied that A and B can be indistinguishable from one another while yet coherently giving distinct degrees of truth to substitution-instances of 'x is green', by virtue of the fact that A is, whereas B is not, distinguishable from C. We merely have to allow that degrees of truth may depend, not just upon the immediate look of a shade of colour, but upon its relationship with other shades. This is indeed a formally adequate response to the second horn of our dilemma. But it means that the analysis must here lose touch with our ordinary concept of colour. For suppose that I am faced with two objects – a lemon and a lime – which are

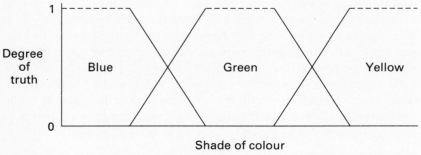

Figure 1

an indistinguishable shade of yellowish-green. If you now show me a grapefruit which is indistinguishable from the lime but slightly more green than the lemon, would it be correct for me to say that the lime had been more green than the lemon after all? Surely not. For if you had given me the order 'Bring me something which is no more and no less green than this lime', then I would not have failed you had I come back with the lemon. Similarly if you had previously asserted 'The lemon is exactly as green as the lime', you would not have said something false. Once again the point is that for the purposes for which we require colour-concepts, we want exact sameness of colour to be something which can be established by a single visual comparison.[7]

I conclude that there can be no question of the fuzziness of ordinary propositions being retained under analysis, at least if we attempt to present the truth-conditions of ordinary-language sentences by means of some sort of truth-function (or degree-of-truth-function) on sentences whose truth-conditions are as specific as possible. So here we have a deep incoherence in the philosophy of *TLP*, in that the programme of analysis which Wittgenstein adopts commits him to removing the fuzziness of ordinary-language propositions, and yet he thinks of it as genuinely a programme of analysis and not of reconstruction. The only way out for him would be to declare that the fuzziness of ordinary language is illusory. Yet as we saw in the last chapter, this itself is unacceptable.

(D) Logical objectivism again

Arguably the real source of Wittgenstein's difficulties concerning the fuzziness of ordinary statements is not his programme of analysis as such, but rather his logical objectivism (and not just because it is this which lies behind the programme of analysis, as we shall see in Chapter 7). For a logical objectivist will have to picture our understanding of an expression as consisting in a grasp of a rule, this rule then determining in a mind-independent way what is to count as correct application. At any rate the one thing that a logical objectivist cannot accept is that understanding might simply be constituted by a practical capacity. For this would then make the relation between the expression and its correct application – dependent as it would be on the mode of operation of that capacity – into a contingent one. But now if the sense of a term like 'green' consists of rules, one rule which would certainly have to be included would be this:

$\forall x \forall y$ (if x is green, and y is indistinguishable in colour from x, then y must also be green).

For as we noted above, a rule which allowed distinct judgements about indistinguishable shades is not one that we use, or want to use. But then successive applications of this rule across a long series of shades, each member of which is indistinguishable from its neighbours, will give the absurd conclusion that a red post-box is also green.

The above is a version of that form of paradox known as 'Sorites', parallel versions of which can be developed in connection with all fuzzy concepts. It has been convincingly argued by Wright in his (1975) that the only adequate solution to these paradoxes is to give up the idea that all uses of terms are governed by rules (hence giving up logical objectivism also). Rather we should think of our understanding of words like 'red' as being constituted by a simple recognitional capacity, thus allowing for the fact that on being presented in sequence with such a series of shades of colour, there will come a point (perhaps different on different occasions) where a speaker will dig their heels in and refuse to go any further. If this is correct, then it turns out that Wittgenstein's logical objectivism alone leads directly to an absurdity: either we say that all colours are in reality the same colour (everything is red and blue and green, etc.), or we insist that our colour-terms are really (and despite appearances to the contrary) sharply defined.

Summary

Although some of Wittgenstein's possible motives for insisting on the requirement of sharpness of *Sinn* may have been weak, some at least are very deeply grounded in his philosophy as a whole. Both his programme of analysis and his logical objectivism commit him to denying that there are actually any fuzzy senses.

7   The programme of analysis

Our task in this chapter is to elucidate the point of the *TLP* programme of analysis for ordinary language, especially the commitment to represent the truth-conditions of our propositions in as detailed a form as possible.

(A) The notion of analysis

There are two distinct strands to our (and Wittgenstein's) notion of analysis, which together lay down the constraints which any adequate analysis should meet. The first is that *analysans* and *analysandum* should say the very same thing – that they should share the same semantic content. The second is that the correctness of an analysis should be recognisable *a priori*, there being at least a conceptually necessary equivalence between the two expressions.

When taken together with the theory of semantic content outlined in Chapter 1, the first of these strands entails that a correct analysis of a sentence is one which succeeds in capturing its truth-condition. That is, it must say the very same things about the very same individuals, where the criterion for 'saying the same' is analytic equivalence. Any analysis meeting this constraint will thus say the same as the analysed proposition, but may do so in a different way (it may possess a different cognitive content).

However, the second of the above strands in our notion of analysis, when taken together with the account of the semantic content of ordinary proper names outlined briefly in Chapter 1, entails that such names cannot be subjected to analysis. For their contents are objects in the real world, whose individual natures cannot be known *a priori*. This then leads immediately to a criticism of the *TLP* programme of analysis. For as we also noted in Chapter 1, Wittgenstein's view is that ordinary names as well as ordinary predicates and relational expressions will disappear under analysis – see 3.24. (Moreover, we noted that the precise form which he thinks an analysis of a name will take – namely a description of the manner in which the object is constructed out of its parts – results from a confusion between metaphysical and conceptual necessity.) This criticism is important, and part of our task in the present chapter will be to see how Wittgenstein could have been tempted into adopting such a position. But I shall mostly set it to one side in the discussion which follows, concentrating on the programme of analysis as it applies to predicative expressions.

(B) Perspicuous representation

The idea that a correct analysis may provide us with different ways of expressing the things we say in ordinary discourse leads immediately to one of its main purposes, on the *TLP* conception. This is that since the modes of thought and speech embodied in ordinary language may be in some respects radically misleading, the provision of alternative ways of saying the same things, through analysis, will help us to see matters aright (3.323–3.325). For as Wittgenstein claims, ordinary language disguises the true form of our thoughts in ways which can easily lead to the most fundamental philosophical confusions (4.002–4.0031). One of our aims in providing an analysis of a given proposition should therefore be to find some way of expressing what is said by it which will be philosophically perspicuous ('*klar*' – see 4.115–4.116).

Wittgenstein thus shares with both Russell and Frege the aim of constructing a language whose syntax would reflect all important semantic and logical distinctions on its surface (a *Begriffsschrift* – 3.325).[1] Like them he sees the business of analysis as the production of a language which will be logically perfect. But note that, in contrast with Frege at least, this is not because he thinks there is actually anything wrong with ordinary language. On the contrary, it fulfils its function perfectly (5.5563). It is only when we come to do philosophy that its structure leads us astray (4.002).

Although Wittgenstein agrees with Russell and Frege about one of the main aims of analysis, he also goes beyond them in a number of respects. Some of these have already emerged in the course of our previous discussions. Thus we noted in Chapter 1 how an analysis of ordinary language in terms of a notation containing no predicates or relational expressions (the Picture Theory) would be supposed to reflect the fundamental distinction between referring and classifying. And in Chapter 2 we saw how Wittgenstein tries to provide a notation for dealing with the numbers in a non-referential way, showing that they are not genuine objects. Moreover, at 5.53–5.534 he provides a notation which is intended to enable him to do without a distinct sign of identity, taking this to show that identity is not really a relation.[2] Finally, I believe Wittgenstein thought that a successful analysis should reflect logical form on its surface in a much more specific way than either Frege or Russell ever contemplated; for example, believing that in a philosophically perspicuous notation a nonsensical sentence such as 'Seven is heavier than five' should be ill formed in precisely the sort of way that '∃xa' is.[3]

When coupled with the thesis of the priority of logic over metaphysics, the idea of a perspicuous representation thus comes to hold a central place in the methodology of *TLP*. More than anything else, it is the construction of such notations which is to enable the philosopher to show the essential features of thought and reality, while dispelling philosophical confusions. By presenting clearly whatever can be thought, analysis will show what is mere nonsense. And by providing alternative ways of expressing those thoughts, it will help us to be clear about the fundamental semantic distinctions at work in our language, and to discern, in consequence, the basic metaphysical structure of the world. This aspect of Wittgenstein's conception of the role of analysis is thus best seen as a development of the Frege/Russell idea of a conceptual notation, coupled with his own version of the thesis that logic and semantics are prior to metaphysics and ontology.

(C) Complete analysis

Nothing in the above discussion of perspicuous representation has yet done anything to explain why Wittgenstein should think that it must be possible to provide a *complete* analysis of the propositions of ordinary language (3.2–3.201, 3.25), unless this only means that the result of analysis should be complete perspicuity. But plainly he means more than this. Analysis, in *TLP*, is not just a matter of providing propositions logically equivalent to, but more perspicuous than, the originals; it also entails seeking ever more detailed representations of their truth-conditions. For as we noted at the outset of Chapter 5, analysis is to represent all propositions as truth-functions of a base-class of elementary propositions which cannot themselves be analysed further (3.26, 4.221, 5). Now, why should this be a goal worth pursuing? What would be the point of seeking a completely detailed representation of the truth-conditions of our ordinary-language propositions?

Part of the answer no doubt lies in the *TLP* commitment to Simples, if

Wittgenstein's reasons for believing in them should turn out to be independent of the programme of analysis itself. For if the very existence of language requires that there be a class of simple necessarily existing individuals to serve as possible objects of reference, then analysis must presumably be able to bring out how our ordinary discourse is, on some deeper level, related to such things. We shall return to the issue in Chapters 9, 10 and 12.

For the remainder of our answer we may once again consult *NB* 60–70. For discussion of the idea of complete analysis is there interwoven with discussion of the requirement of determinacy of *Sinn*. This suggests that, in one way or another, the search for ever more detailed representations of truth-conditions is to enable us to comply with this requirement. But as we discovered in our previous discussion of determinacy, there is not one requirement here but two. So the immediate question before us is whether analysis is to help us to meet the requirement of sharpness of *Sinn*, or rather the requirement of determinacy-in-advance.

We saw in Chapter 6 that it is impossible to introduce the fuzziness of ordinary statements by means of a truth-function of elementary propositions. So if we simply turn this around, it of course follows that analysis of ordinary language by means of such truth-functions would be precisely the way to show that it does – despite appearances to the contrary – conform to the requirement of sharpness of *Sinn*. Successful completion of such a programme of analysis would reveal fuzziness to be illusory. But we also saw that Wittgenstein lacks any independent reason for insisting on the requirement of sharpness. More precisely, we saw that some of the reasons which might have influenced him – namely confusion between two senses of 'vague', or a belief that fuzziness conflicts with the principles of logic – were poor ones. And we saw that the other reason which may have influenced him was none other than his commitment to his programme of analysis itself. As for the final possible reason – that Sorites paradoxes must remain insoluble for anyone with a commitment to logical objectivism – there is nothing to suggest that Wittgenstein was actually influenced by it. So in the interests of both Charity and historical plausibility, we would do well to seek evidence that his programme for the complete analysis of ordinary language was somehow motivated by the requirement of determinacy-in-advance.

Our first clue is to be found at *NB* 61, in the midst of a discussion of the idea of complete analysis. Wittgenstein remarks that every proposition must have a *complete Sinn* (italics in original), and that whatever is not yet said in a proposition cannot belong to its *Sinn*. This suggests very strongly that it is the requirement of determinacy-in-advance which is at issue. But then in the next sentence he says that it must be explicable HOW THIS proposition has THIS *Sinn* (capitals in original). So it appears to be the business of analysis to provide an explanation of how a given proposition – a sentence with a particular Fregean sense – comes to have the truth-condition which it does. And it appears that the demand for such an explanation is somehow forced on us by the requirement of determinacy-in-advance (which is one aspect of logical objectivism). But what is it that needs explaining? And what is the connection with logical objectivism?

A second clue is to be found at *NB* 70, again in the midst of a discussion of analysis, where Wittgenstein remarks that he wants to justify the vagueness of ordinary propositions. Now, since (as we saw in Chapter 6) the notion of vagueness is ambiguous, this remark too is ambiguous. Does Wittgenstein mean that he wants (through analysis) to justify the unspecificness of ordinary propositions? Or does he mean that he wants to justify their fuzziness? In fact there is sufficient textual evidence for us to answer 'Both'. For just a little further down the page he is clearly discussing fuzziness, since he raises the possibility that there may be relative positions of watch and table such that it would be uncertain whether the one could be said to be lying on the other.[4] But at the bottom of the previous page, separated only by some remarks about the extraordinary complexity of the conventions governing ordinary language, he had remarked that the proposition 'The watch is lying on the table' obviously contains a lot of indeterminacy ('*Unbestimmtheit*'), declaring it to be apparent to the uncaptive mind that the *Sinn* of that proposition is more complex than the proposition itself.

Now, he could hardly have thought it obvious that the proposition 'The watch is lying on the table' is really extremely fuzzy, since his strategy for dealing with fuzziness is to try to show it to be merely apparent, as we have seen. And indeed, in the paragraph immediately following the remark about justifying vagueness, he speaks of the demand that propositions should be given in more *detail* still (my italics). So when he speaks about the indeterminacy of the proposition here, he must surely have in mind its unspecificness or generality.[5] This is confirmed by the previous page (*NB* 69), where he says that there will be an indeterminacy in any proposition containing a name of a complex object, and that this derives from the *generality* of such a proposition (my italics). So it would be the business of analysis, we may suppose, to justify this unspecificness by expressing the truth-condition in complete detail.[6]

Wittgenstein seems to take it to be a fact with which we have to reckon that the states of affairs which render our propositions true or false are always, themselves, entirely particular and specific. There can be no indefiniteness in the world itself. (*NB* 62: 'The world has a fixed structure.') Yet we might naturally wonder where the truth of such a claim is supposed to come from. For who is to say that the world does not contain (perhaps at a sub-atomic level) states or events which are irreducibly indeterminate in some respect? Indeed, do not most physicists now believe that there is an indeterminacy in the position and/or velocity of sub-atomic particles, thus implying that their position is to some degree unspecific? It might be replied that such questions are anachronistic, since the various indeterminacy theses in physics had not been published at the time when Wittgenstein was writing. He may simply (and reasonably) have been taking for granted what was believed by the physicists of his day (Einstein included). But in any case it seems likely that his argument only really requires a weaker claim: that the states of affairs which make our ordinary propositions true are a great deal *more* specific than the propositions which describe them.

Wittgenstein's demand is thus to explain how an ordinary (unspecific) proposition can be made true by a quite specific (or at least more specific) state of affairs. And this is to be accomplished by analysing the unspecific proposition into one which is just as detailed as the states of affairs which might render it true. So the demand to explain how a proposition comes to have the truth-condition which it does, which we gleaned from *NB* 61, is the demand to show by analysis how an ordinary unspecific proposition can nevertheless be made true by a specific state of affairs. But still we need to ask why such an analysis is needed. Quite what is it here that calls out for explanation?

The answer lies in the requirement of determinacy-in-advance itself. For the relationship between the specific state of affairs and the unspecific proposition is an internal one. (If that state of affairs exists – if the watch is lying in *this* particular position on the table – then the proposition in question *must* be true.) So it must somehow be completely determinate, from the sense of the unspecific proposition alone, that it would be made true by this particular state of affairs. And if this is so, then in Wittgenstein's view it must be possible to *display* the content of the proposition in such a way that it will be *manifest* that it is so.

The idea behind the programme of analysis is then that the content of the unspecific ordinary-language proposition should be displayed as a truth-function of elementary propositions, each of which could be made true by one and only one specific state of affairs. It would then be manifest that the relationship between proposition and state of affairs is an internal one, since the truth of the proposition would follow logically (truth-functionally) from the truth of elementary propositions stating the existence of states of affairs. To take a crude model, the idea is that if we were to analyse 'The watch is lying on the table' into a truth-function of propositions describing particular positions of the watch on the table, then it would be made clear how that unspecific proposition can be made true by (can 'reach right up to'[7]) a specific state of affairs.

In this exposition of Wittgenstein's ideas I have thus far focussed on the predicative element in sentences, reflecting on the variety of different positions of the watch which could correctly be described as 'on the table'. But a similar point would appear to hold equally in connection with ordinary names. For consider the variety of changes in the watch itself which would be consistent with the truth of 'That watch is on the table.' Its hands may be reading any number of different times; it may be broken or recently repaired; it may be scratched, dented or have lost its strap; and so on. In each one of this wide variety of circumstances the sentence in question would still have to be true (provided the watch were positioned somewhere on the table). So determinacy-in-advance will require that the sense of the sentence should somehow contain a representation of each of them. In which case it must be possible for analysis to display the content of the proposition in such a way that it will be manifest that the connection between it and the variety of states of affairs is dependent upon sense alone. In particular, it must be possible to analyse this use of the term 'That watch', in order to explain the variety of different ways in which the watch may enter into a state of affairs. And although this does not actually entail that the term may be replaced by a description of the various ways in which the watch may be made up of its parts, consistent with its existence, it is perhaps hard to see what other form the analysis might take.[8]

(D) The rejection of intuition

What has emerged from all this textual detective-work is that Wittgenstein's programme for the complete analysis of ordinary language is based upon his logical objectivism. Since the truth-conditions of our propositions must be determined in advance of anything empirical in all their particularity (the requirement of determinacy-in-advance), it must be possible to demonstrate that this is so – to show that language reaches right up to the world – by means of a completely detailed representation of the truth-conditions of the unspecific proposition.

But why should it be either necessary or possible to provide such a complete analysis? Why should we not simply say that anyone who understands the unspecific proposition will have the capacity to see – by intuition – that such-and-such a particular state of affairs must render it true? What would be wrong with saying that the connection with a particular state of affairs will be self-evident to one who has grasped the sense of the unspecific proposition?

Clearly Wittgenstein would reject any attempt to introduce intuition or self-evidence into the explanation of the internal connection between propositions and reality, in precisely the way that he rejects any attempt to find a place for intuition in logic. (See 5.4731, 6.1271, 6.233.) His reasons are not entirely easy to interpret, and we shall return to them in Chapter 13. But I believe we may see him as setting a dilemma. Either the appeal to intuition imports quite inappropriate psychological considerations into the account (the thinker's feelings of intuition being what *determines* that the unspecific proposition is made true by some given state of affairs), thus conflicting with the requirement of determinacy-in-advance; or it simply repeats the assertion that there really is an internal relation between the proposition and the state of affairs, without taking us one whit closer towards showing that this is so.

Considering the second horn of the dilemma first, we might wonder why it *has* to be possible to show that the relation between unspecific propositions and specific states of affairs is internal. Perhaps the relation is one which admits of no explanation, so that if we were asked what the proposition 'The watch is on the table' says, one could only reply: It says that the watch is on the table. But in response to this we need only reiterate that the proposition is, after all, made true by quite specific positions of the watch on the table. So if the requirement of determinacy-in-advance is complied with, the proposition must somehow determine – *a priori* – the truth-condition in all its particularity. And since the truth-condition is, so to speak, that much more specific than the proposition itself, it must at least be possible to set it out in all its particularity. This task is not only possible, but is required of us if we wish to show determinacy-in-advance to obtain. And it is hard to see how this could be done except by analysing the unspecific proposition into a truth-function of elementary ('particularised') ones. So it is not that there is anything really wrong with the answer 'It says that the watch is on the table' in itself. It is simply that this answer is compatible with either the truth or falsity of determinacy-in-advance (logical objectivism). If we are to show that the unspecificity of ordinary language raises no threat to logical objectivism, then we have no option but to embark on a programme of analysis.

To the first horn of the dilemma – the charge that any appeal to intuition which is doing genuine explanatory work will conflict with the requirement of determinacy-in-advance – we might object that even analysis itself will have to appeal to intuition at some point. For we should have to rely upon speakers' intuitive judgements in the use of the ordinary-language proposition in setting up the analysis in the first place. ('Would this be a case of the watch being on the table? And would this? And this?') And be our account of the truth-functional connectives as precise and explicit as you like, we shall still have to rely in the end upon our intuitive sense of what the rules and definitions require of us in particular cases. In short: if appeals to intuition are unavoidable in any case, then there can be no objection to the introduction of such an appeal into the defence of determinacy-in-advance; thus removing the need for a programme of analysis.

This reply overlooks a crucial distinction between a form of account which actually brings an appeal to intuition into the truth-condition of the proposition itself, and one which merely relies – externally – upon intuition to justify itself, or in seeing what is required of us in particular cases. The former really does threaten to undermine logical objectivism, whereas the latter merely reflects the fact that there must always be some latitude left to intuition, for the logical objectivist, by any rule or definition no matter how explicit. For while the sense of the rule may determine unlimitedly many applications, all that one can be given (or that one can give oneself) in explanation are some other symbols which themselves have to be understood, or various gestures and examples which themselves have to be interpreted. Understanding, for the logical objectivist, must always be to some extent a matter of 'cottoning on' to the intended sense. (Compare 3.263.)

The distinction I have in mind might also be expressed in terms of the difference between appealing to intuition in answer to a question of the form 'What does "P" mean, or say?', and in answer to one of the form 'How do you know that "P" means that?' In the first case, an appeal to intuition is either incoherent or conflicts with determinacy-in-advance. It will conflict with determinacy-in-advance, and with logical objectivism generally, if feelings of intuition are introduced as the link between propositions and reality. For this would be to suppose that it is speakers' feelings of intuition which determine that a sentence with a given sense has a given truth-condition, which is precisely to say that the relationship depends upon 'some third thing'. Incoherence will result, on the other hand, if intuition figures in the account of the sense of the proposition itself. For suppose that in answer to the question 'What does "The watch is lying on the table" say?', one replied that it says things stand in such a way that anyone who understands it (and is suitably placed) will see by intuition that it must be true. This would be viciously circular, since we should have referred to the proposition itself within what was supposed to be an account of its content.

The second sort of case, on the other hand, is entirely innocent. If the question asked is 'How do you know that the proposition is true in these circumstances?', or if it is 'How do you know that it is equivalent to such-and-such a truth-function of elementary propositions?', then an appeal to intuition can be perfectly legitimate – indeed at some point unavoidable.

(D) Complexity in thought

Are we, on Wittgenstein's account, to think of the complexity of the fully analysed proposition as being somehow already implicitly there – perhaps 'added in thought' – in the ordinary-language proposition?[9] If so, then the idea would be extremely counter-intuitive. Are we really prepared to believe that my understanding of an ordinary proposition somehow involves a huge – perhaps infinitary – truth-function of elementary ones, or that I somehow run over all these propositions in thought (extremely fast!) when I think the ordinary proposition? For of course I may have not the faintest idea of what these propositions are, as Wittgenstein himself acknowledges (5.55).

At *NB* 70, when remarking on the complexity of the conventions governing our language, Wittgenstein does say that enormously much is added to each proposition in thinking it ('*dazugedacht*'). But this is dropped from the otherwise similar passage in *TLP*, 4.002. Moreover, when discussing the possibly infinite complexity of ordinary propositions earlier in *NB* (at 64), Wittgenstein had remarked that this complexity was not in the propositional sign by itself, but in it *together with its syntactical application* (italics in original). This suggests that the complexity results, not from what is added in thought, but rather from the conventions determining the use of the sign. But in any case the 'added in thought' interpretation would conflict with the thesis defended briefly in Chapter 1, that for Wittgenstein thinking and speaking are on a par, each consisting of structured arrangements of symbols. So when he speaks of the way in which the complexities of our language may be hidden from us, at 4.002, I take it he has in mind not just perceptible but also imperceptible languages.[10]

There is no reason to interpret Wittgenstein as believing that the complexity of the fully analysed proposition is already there, in some mysterious way, in the ordinary one. His view is simply this: since the two propositions will (if the analysis is accurate) be logically equivalent, and since identity of semantic content is sameness of truth-conditions, both *analysans* and *analysandum* will say the very same thing, and will be (essentially) the very same proposition. There will then be no harm in saying that the ordinary proposition is (that is, has the same truth-condition as) a truth-function of elementary propositions (see 5). And we can use the fact that the one clearly complies with the requirement of determinacy-in-advance as an explanation of how the other does.

Summary

Analysis, in *TLP*, is to fulfil two distinct functions. On the one hand it is to provide notations which are philosophically and semantically perspicuous. And on the other hand it is to demonstrate how thought reaches right up to reality: showing how unspecific propositions can be made true by specific states of affairs, consistent with logical objectivism.

8   *Sense-data and solipsism*

In this chapter we shall consider, and reject, a phenomenalist interpretation of the *TLP* programme of analysis, the main evidence for which is provided by Wittgenstein's apparent endorsement of solipsism.

(A) Preliminaries

There is a long tradition, championed especially by the Logical Positivists in the thirties but revived again recently, of taking the 'simple objects' of *TLP* to be the data of immediate experience – sense-data.[1] Now it is certainly true that Wittgenstein began to play around with phenomenalism and its associated verificationism soon after his return to philosophy in the late twenties (perhaps responding to the interests of the Vienna Circle), and that he often thereafter seems to have thought of his early work in broadly phenomenalist terms.[2] But in line with the general interpretative strategy adopted throughout this book, I propose to ignore this later evidence as being of doubtful reliability. (Given the forward-looking nature of Wittgenstein's intellect, it would be entirely natural that once stimulated to an interest in verificationism he should throw himself wholeheartedly into developing his old thoughts in this new direction, even to the extent of losing touch with their original significance.) We shall confine our attention to our primary sources: *TLP* and (cautiously) *NB*.

No doubt some have read *TLP* through the prism of Russell's 'Lectures on Logical Atomism', which he says reflects what he learned from his conversations with Wittgenstein in the period leading up to the Summer of 1914,[3] allowing themselves to be guided by the fact that the programme of analysis envisaged in the 'Lectures' is clearly phenomenalist, as had been Russell's earlier publications. But in reality the evidence provided by the 'Lectures' is negligible. Notice firstly, that even if they were an accurate record of Wittgenstein's pre-1914 thinking, there are still four full years to elapse before the completion of *TLP*, leaving much scope for development and changes of mind. Notice secondly, that Russell nowhere claims that the 'Lectures' are intended to be a record of Wittgenstein's thought. The views expressed are his own, with due acknowledgement of Wittgenstein's influence. It may then be that this influence is confined to the logical matters which take up the bulk of the 'Lectures', Russell merely slotting his own phenomenalism into this framework.

Now, of course Russell's phenomenalist programme of analysis was motivated by considerations of an epistemological nature. Indeed, the same is true of phenomenalism generally. The project of reducing all ordinary talk to descriptions of sense-data (and experience-based universals) only really makes sense as part of an attempt to show how our common-sense items of knowledge can be adequately justified on the basis of our experiences. It is then a powerful argument against a phenomenalist reading of *TLP* that Wittgenstein treats epistemological questions disparagingly, identifying the theory of knowledge with the philosophy of psychology, where psychology is said to be no more closely related to philosophy than any other natural science (4.1121). Indeed, theories of knowledge seem to play no role whatever amongst the main doctrines and arguments of *TLP*, Wittgenstein's major concerns being logic and semantics, and the nature of representation generally.[4] Since there is then a strong presumption against a phenomenalist reading of *TLP*, it will require explicit textual evidence to overcome it.

(B) Phenomenal objects

What are the simple objects of *TLP*? Is there any reason to think that they are sense-data? The evidence that they are is extremely thin on the ground, mostly being provided by Wittgenstein's apparent endorsement of solipsism (5.62), together with some related remarks. These will be discussed in the next section. Some have thought to find evidence in Wittgenstein's remark at *NB* 45, that as examples of simple objects he always thinks of points in the visual field.[5] But against this can be set many remarks which pull in a contrary direction. For example, just a few pages later he describes parts of space (note, *not* visual space) and spatial objects as 'things' (*NB* 47). And then later again he is to be found treating the material points of physics as examples of genuinely simple things (*NB* 67, 69).[6] The truth seems to be that at this early stage his ideas were extremely fluid and unformed.

One direct objection to a phenomenalist interpretation of *TLP* is pro-

vided by the doctrine that elementary propositions are logically independent of one another (1.21, 2.061–2.062, 5.134). For if they were to take
the form 'There is a red sense-datum at such-and-such a point in my visual
field', then this would of course be incompatible with a wide range of other
elementary propositions, for example 'There is a green sense-datum at that
same point in my visual field.' However, I do not wish to press this objection too hard. For as we shall see in Chapter 14, it is by no means obvious
that we cannot devise a system for describing sense-data which would
enable us to comply with the independence requirement.[7] (Rather than
employing names for sense-data it would employ names for the lines in a
system of coordinates imposed upon the various sense-fields.) In fact it will
turn out that a phenomenalist interpretation of *TLP* can be maintained
without identifying simple objects with sense-data. Nevertheless, I shall
continue to focus on such an identification for the remainder of this section. For the argument I am about to present against it can be developed in
such a way as to apply to the other form of phenomenalism also, as we
shall see in Chapter 14 when it comes to be explained.

The main objection to identifying Simples with sense-data is provided by
the doctrine that simple objects have necessary existence. How could they
be sense-data, if they are supposed to exist at all times in all possible
worlds? For it is surely certain that sense-data do not have necessary
existence. On the contrary, such things as pains and sensations of red exist
extremely fleetingly: on the most natural view, no longer than our awareness of them.

However, in reply it might be said that Wittgenstein nowhere explicitly
commits himself to the necessary existence of Simples. He says that they
make up the substance of the world (2.021), and that they exist in all
possible worlds (2.022–2.023).[8] And he says that they are unalterable and
changeless, since it is their changing configurations which are responsible
for changes in the world (2.027–2.0272). But none of this actually implies
that they exist at all times in all possible worlds. For their changelessness
is consistent with their existence having a beginning and an end in time.
And they may exist in each and every possible world merely in the sense in
which Moses exists in our world: that is, existing for a while at some time
or other within it.

The following interpretation would therefore be consistent with the
text.[9] Simples are fleeting experiences, or sense-data. However, all talk,
and all thought, is built upon references to individual sense-data, in such a
way that every conceivable world must consist of recombinations of those
very same experiences which actually exist at some time or other in the real

world. (This would be implied by the fact that elementary propositions contain references only to Simples, and that each possible world is described by a complete assignment of truth-values to the set of elementary propositions – see 2.0124, 4.22, 4.26, 5.) Since all thought is built upon references to the sense-data which actually occur, there is no possible world which does not contain those very items. We can conceive of a world in which these sense-data are differently arranged, but we cannot think of a world in which they do not exist, or in which others exist instead of, or in addition to, them.

Although this interpretation is consistent with what Wittgenstein actually says, it produces a reading which is intrinsically very implausible. For example, suppose that I have just trodden on a drawing-pin and experienced pain. Then on the above account it would be logically impossible that I should never have felt that sensation. For there is supposed to be no possible world in which that pain does not exist. It hardly needs to be said that this is counter-intuitive. For we believe very firmly that undergoing the individual experiences which we do is a contingent matter: I believe that if I had not stepped on that drawing-pin, I should not have felt that pain. Similarly, if we suppose that I suffer from exactly sixteen migraines during the course of my life, then on the above account it would be logically impossible that I should ever have had more. Again this is highly counter-intuitive.

Plausible assumptions about the conditions for sense-data identity reduce the scope for contingency still further, rendering the above account even less acceptable. It is natural to think that the time at which an experience occurs (indeed the time at which any event occurs) is essential to its identity. Then if I had stepped on the drawing-pin five minutes later, it would not have been that individual pain which I felt, but another similar one. If this assumption is granted then the above account will imply that my life must contain exactly the experiences which it does, occurring at times when they do. The only scope left for contingency would concern the relative positioning of my experiences within the various sense-fields. And even this may be limited. For it is by no means obvious that the very same sensation of red which is currently in my left visual field might have occurred in my right. Nor is it obvious that the pain in my foot might have occurred in my back. If these things are not possible, then it will not even be possible that I might now have had a pain in my back rather than my foot (that is, had I lain on the drawing-pin rather than stepped on it).

These doctrines are so intrinsically counter-intuitive that anyone wishing to attribute them to Wittgenstein had better provide at least one of the following two things: either some seemingly powerful argument for their truth, or some unambiguous textual evidence for their presence in *TLP*. The arguments will have to wait until the next chapter, where we begin to consider the various possible reasons for believing in Simples. But it will turn out that there is no real support for such draconian restrictions on contingency. The main textual evidence, on the other hand, is provided by Wittgenstein's supposed solipsism, to which we now turn.

(C) Solipsism

Wittgenstein's remark at 5.62, that what the solipsist means is quite correct, certainly seems to support a phenomenalist reading of *TLP*. For solipsism, as ordinarily understood, is the doctrine that the world consists of my mental states, only my experiences being real. Now, of course, there is nothing in the above remark by itself to show that Wittgenstein understands solipsism in the usual way. But additional evidence can be adduced. For he goes on almost immediately to say that the world and life are one (5.621), which certainly makes sense if the world is supposed to consist in my experiences. And then later he says that at death the world does not alter, but comes to an end (6.431). This can only be taken literally if the world consists of my conscious states.

In fact a phenomenalist reading of 5.621 seems explicitly to have been excluded by Wittgenstein, at least when it was originally written into his notebooks.[10] At *NB* 77 he writes:

The World and Life are one. Physiological life is of course not 'Life'. And neither is psychological life. Life is the world.

In saying that psychological life is not what he understands by 'Life', Wittgenstein is at least denying that life (and the world) might consist in the set of his experiences. But quite what he does mean is left almost wholly obscure. I shall return to it later.

As for the remark about the world coming to an end at death, there is simply no way of taking this literally except as an endorsement of solipsistic phenomenalism. But then there is no particular reason why we should take it literally, since it occurs within a sequence of remarks in which metaphor and hyperbole are rife. (For example, it occurs immediately after the claim at 6.43, that the good or bad exercise of the will causes the world to wax or wane as a whole!) We could take it as saying merely that at death the world *as represented from a particular point of view* (mine) comes to an end. This idea will be explained in the discussion which follows.

The main difficulty for a phenomenalist interpretation of the *TLP* endorsement of solipsism is the claim that it coincides (when strictly thought out) with pure realism (5.64). For realism, as normally understood, is the doctrine that there is a real world of objects and states which exists independently of our experiences. And this is just flatly inconsistent with the claim that the world consists of nothing but my experiences (solipsism). We therefore have no alternative but to seek another interpretation. In particular, Wittgenstein must be understanding either 'solipsism' or 'realism' in something other than their standard sense.

When Wittgenstein says at 5.62 that the element of truth in solipsism makes itself manifest, he immediately goes on to say:

The world is *my* world: this is manifest in the fact that the limits of *language* (of that language which alone I understand) mean the limits of *my* world. [Italics in original.]

This suggests very strongly that he understands solipsism to be encapsulated in the slogan 'The world is my world.' It is also clear that he is equating the limits of his world with the limits of what he is capable of representing in language. Indeed, throughout the 5.6s when he talks either of 'the world' or 'my world', it is clear that he has in mind a set of possible, not actual, states of affairs. What is at issue are possibilities, not actualities – see in particular 5.61.

The limits of the world are thus the set of metaphysically possible states of affairs, whereas the limits of *my* world are the set of possible representations. The claim that the two coincide is then the claim that metaphysical possibility (real world) and conceptual possibility (my world) are one and the same: it is the 'great mirror' doctrine once again. So part of the point of 5.62 is to insist upon a realist attitude to the logic/metaphysics relationship, of the sort we outlined and defended in Chapters 2 and 3.[11] This is one reason why there is truth to be found in solipsism: for in saying 'The world is my world' the solipsist in fact utters something correct, since the set of real possibilities coincides with what it is possible for me to represent in language. But it is also part of the reason why solipsism coincides with pure realism (5.64): for the realist too says something correct in stating that there is a set of real possibilities existing independently of our representations. This is what I understand Wittgenstein to mean by saying that the world and life are one (5.621): not that the actual world coincides with the set of my actual experiences (solipsism as it is standardly understood), but

that the set of possible states of affairs is correlated one to one with the set
of possible representations.

It is easy to understand why Wittgenstein should insist that the limits of
the real world and the limits of possible representation are one and the
same. For this is none other than the 'great mirror' doctrine. But why
should he introduce the self at this point? Why should he choose to express
this idea by equating the world with *my* world, identifying what is objectively possible with what it is possible for *me* to represent? I believe the
answer lies in the Kantian idea that it must be possible for the 'I think' to
accompany all my representations.[12] Wittgenstein is struck by the fact that
the world can be represented from a particular point of view: his. (See
5.631, 5.6331.) All actual facts can be represented in terms of their
temporal and spatial distance from himself, and even all possible facts can
be expressed by saying not 'This is possible', but rather 'I think this is
possible.' Indeed, I take it that this is the further truth which he thinks can
be discerned behind the statement 'The world is my world': that all
possible states of affairs can be represented from his particular point of
view, as it were positioning himself at the centre of the universe.[13] It is this
which is supposed to find a place for the self (the metaphysical subject)
within philosophy (5.641), as I shall now try to explain.

(D) The metaphysical subject

When Wittgenstein says that solipsism coincides with realism (5.64), part
of what he means is that the world which I am capable of representing is
the real world – there is nothing possible in the world which cannot
possibly be thought.[14] But he also means that there is a sense in which the
'I' – that thing from whose point of view everything else can be represented
– is not itself an item in the world (5.641). It is not something which we are
acquainted with in experience (5.631), nor can its existence be inferred
from the nature of our experience (5.6331). It is rather a 'limit' of the
world: identifiable with the inexpressible 'myness' of the point of view
which I take towards the world and my own experiences (5.64–5.641).

Wittgenstein is concerned to show that the metaphysical self (the
supposed subject of thoughts and experiences) is not really an item in the
real world (5.631). All that really exists is the bundle of representations
which the 'I think' accompanies. Hence his criticism of Russell's theory of
belief and judgement in the 5.54s. According to Russell, belief is a relation
between the believing subject and a possible state of affairs, a report of the
form 'A believes that p' stating the existence of such a relation, just as it

appears to. This then places the thinking subject very firmly within the world. Wittgenstein claims, on the contrary, that the report really has the form ' "p" says p' (5.542). It states a relation between a structured arrangement of signs (an act of thinking) and a possible state of affairs.[15] So all that really exists in the world are the thoughts of the thinking subject, not the thinking subject itself. In effect he is endorsing a version of Hume's bundle-theory of the self, at least as regards the self-in-the-world: all that exists is a particular bundle of thoughts and representations (5.5421, 5.63–5.631).

Whilst endorsing a Humean view of the empirical subject, Wittgenstein nevertheless seems to want to find room somehow for the metaphysical subject – only not as part of the world, but as its limit (5.641). How is this to be understood? We might try interpreting it as a version of the Kantian doctrine of the transcendental unity of apperception. Wittgenstein would be saying that although we cannot *know* of any unifying subject of our own experiences, we can nevertheless *think* it. Yet this would run up against the fact that he places the subject outside the world; that is: outside the realm of the thinkable (5.61, 5.641). Moreover, it ignores the fact that the truth in solipsism is somehow supposed to be *shown* by the world's being my world (5.62, 5.641), since what can be shown cannot be said (4.1212), or thought (if I am right that Wittgenstein regards thinking and speaking as activities essentially on a par).

Wittgenstein's idea is best explicated as follows. Imagine a complete objective description of the world and its contents ('objective' in the sense of being given from no particular point of view). It describes all physical objects, together with their properties and distributions. It also includes a description of all thoughts, experiences and perceptions of the world, and states which of these representations is possessed by which physical objects (human beings). Included in such a description, of course, would be mention of that body which is in fact my own, together with a description of those thoughts and experiences which are in fact mine. But they would not be described as such. Indeed, the one fact which would not be conveyed in such a description would be which of all the various experiences and perspectives is my own. One can thus imagine exclaiming, with a shock of recognition when one finally succeeds in working the matter out, 'And those experiences and thoughts must be mine!' I believe it is this 'myness' of a given perspective which Wittgenstein thinks is the truth to be found in solipsism, over and above the 'great mirror' doctrine.

Notice that this 'myness' of thoughts and perceptions is incommunicable. For the most that I could convey to anyone else by saying 'And those experiences are mine' is that they are the ones possessed by the human being who makes the assertion. But if my hearers too have been provided with the above complete description, then they will know this already. The 'myness' of a given perspective must be something over and above the relation between a particular set of thoughts and experiences and a particular human body. Yet of course it does not consist in a relation to a particular metaphysical subject either, since Wittgenstein denies that we know of the existence of any such thing; and in any case this would still leave room for the shock of recognising that I am that subject. So it is incommunicable; and because incommunicable, necessarily unique: I can form no conception of what it would be for there to exist some other 'myness' in the world. (This is not to deny that I have knowledge of other experiences and perspectives; on the contrary, this is given to me in the complete description.) And because it is incommunicable, it is also unthinkable, and hence outside (or at least at the limit) of the world. Yet for all that it does seem to be real: for there would be something which I should have failed to know if I had not realised which out of all the experiences and perspectives on the world was mine.

What emerges is that, so far from endorsing solipsism as traditionally understood ('Only my experiences are real'), Wittgenstein is making two rather different claims. Firstly, that one element of truth in the slogan 'The world is my world' is that the set of metaphysical possibilities coincides with what it is possible for me to represent. And secondly, that the only way of finding a place for the metaphysical subject of thoughts and experiences is to identify it with the ineffable 'myness' of the point of view from which these representations are formulated. Since neither of these claims either entails or is even especially closely connected with phenomenalism, we have found an interpretation of Wittgenstein's 'solipsism' which is fully consistent with a generally realist reading of TLP.

(E) Can we be charitable?

We saw in Section B above how a phenomenalist interpretation of TLP would force us into attributing to Wittgenstein some extremely counter-intuitive doctrines. We have now found our way to an interpretation of Wittgenstein's solipsism which enables us to avoid any such consequence. But we have yet to raise the question whether this, in its turn, is perhaps equally counter-intuitive. Or does Charity, as well as Textual Fidelity, also favour the reading suggested?

Of course the 'great mirror' doctrine has already been shown in Chapter 3 to be capable of powerful defence. But is anything of significance manifested by the fact that 'the world is my world' beyond this? In particular, is the 'myness' of the point of view from which I represent the world a real but incommunicable feature of it? I believe not. Although the position is by no means a foolish one (indeed, it can seem quite plausible, as I hope I have managed to bring out),[16] it is nevertheless incorrect. For the 'myness' of an experience is just the difference between knowing in the abstract that a certain experience is taking place, and being directly aware of it. It is not a further (but incommunicable) feature of that experience, but a distinctive mode of knowledge of it. Quite how this point should be expressed will depend upon one's favoured theory of self-knowledge. But one plausible account would have it that awareness of an experience is a belief caused by the presence of that experience, which is then apt to enter into the causation of the behaviour of the subject whose experience that is (where 'subject' here means 'human being').[17]

Similarly, the 'myness' of my perspective on the world is not a peculiar sort of ineffable fact, but rather consists in the way my modes of presentation of the world (my thoughts and perceptions) facilitate bodily action. Put differently, what I should lack when I have not yet worked out from the complete objective description of the world which of the described perspectives is my own is an ability to employ that knowledge in action. It is only when I know where I am, and which are the things which I am seeing, that my knowledge of the world can become practical. But this is not to say that there is some further fact which I have to learn. It is rather that I have to connect the facts which I have been told with my current perceptions in such a way as to generate action.[18]

Summary

A phenomenalist reading of *TLP* has much to be said against it. Nor does Wittgenstein's endorsement of 'solipsism' provide any real evidence for it. For part of what he means is that there is no distinction between what can be represented in my thoughts and what is possible in reality. And the rest of what he wishes to say – that the 'myness' of the point of view from which I describe the world is an unsayable aspect of it (a 'limit') – is equally consistent with realism.

9 Simples: weak arguments

In this chapter we begin our consideration of the various possible arguments for the existence of Simples, concentrating on those which seem particularly weak.

(A) Preliminaries

As is well known, the early sections of *TLP* advance a number of metaphysical theses about the nature of the objects (*Gegenständen, Dingen*) which make up the world. They are said to be simple, as opposed to complex (2.02), and all complex entities are said to consist, ultimately, of some combination of Simples (2.0201). They are the referents of the 'simple signs' (names) with which the analysis of ordinary propositions must terminate (3.2–3.25). They are unalterable and changeless (2.0271). And most importantly, they make up the substance of the world, being common to all logically possible worlds (2.021, 2.022–2.023, 2.024). The Simples of *TLP* are thus simple and changeless, and exist in all possible worlds.

Besides these explicit claims in the text, we may also add the interpretation defended briefly in Chapter 1, that Simples are individuals, not including properties and relations. We also have our argument from the last chapter that they do not merely exist in all possible worlds, but at all times within those worlds: that they exist necessarily. We shall carry these two additional claims forward into the discussions which follow, subject to reassessment if required. (Hence we shall need to ask ourselves whether the arguments we consider would be more convincing if one or other of these features of our interpretation were dropped. But given the strength of the case in their support, the answer would have to be a very powerful affirmative to force a change on us at this stage.)

Clearly the thesis of simplicity is entailed by the thesis of necessity (and indeed also by the weaker thesis of existence in all possible worlds). For 'simple' in this context means 'non-complex', which in turn means 'not consisting of parts'. And any object which does in fact consist of parts can exist only contingently, even if those parts are fused together by causal necessity. For then it will be logically possible that those parts might never have been joined together, in which case the object in question would not have existed. So any entity which is necessary, or which exists at some time in every possible world, must also be simple.

The converse entailment does not hold, however. From the fact that an object is simple it does not even follow that it exists at all times in the actual world, let alone that it exists in all worlds, or at all times in all worlds. For it is not a necessary truth that the only way for an object to begin its existence is to be created out of parts; nor is decomposition into parts the only possible way for an object to cease to exist. The ideas of creation *ex nihilo* and destruction *ad nihilum* are surely not self-contradictory.[1] One can conceive of there being an 'existence-hole' somewhere in the universe, on reaching which an object will simply disappear out of existence into nothing, and out of which new objects will sometimes spring into existence from nothing.[2] In which case the simplicity of an object certainly does not entail that it exists for all time.

Moreover, even if it were a necessary truth that a simple object would have to exist at all times in the actual world, it would not follow that it must exist in all possible worlds. Even if it were self-contradictory to claim that a simple object could ever come into existence or cease to exist, it would not follow that it is false that it might never have existed. For there might be one possible world consisting of one set of simple objects, which exist – of necessity, we may suppose – at all times within that world; and yet there might be other possible worlds which are made up of quite different sets of simple objects.

The upshot of these considerations is that no argument for the existence of Simples can be regarded as wholly satisfactory which only yields their simplicity. Whereas, on the contrary, an argument leading to the conclusion of their necessary existence, or of their existence in all possible worlds, will automatically yield their simplicity. So one constraint (a constraint of Charity) on the plausibility of attributing to Wittgenstein any given argument for the existence of Simples is that its conclusion should go beyond a claim of simplicity, the argument at least purporting to establish that Simples exist in all possible worlds.

The thesis of changelessness, on the other hand, is two-way independent of the claims both of simplicity and necessity. There could be simple entities, and necessary entities, which are subject to change. (Perhaps God might be an example of such a thing, if he were to think different thoughts at different times, but were not to consist of parts, and were to exist in all possible worlds.) And there could be changeless entities which are neither simple nor necessarily existing. (Perhaps propositions – senses of sentences – might be candidates here.)[3] So any argument for the changelessness of Simples will have to be separate from the argument for their necessary existence. In fact such an argument is provided by the claim that Simples are 'colourless', which I interpret to mean that their only properties are relational ones (2.0231–2.0232).[4] The idea is that all change is change in the relations between Simples, because Simples themselves lack any contingent non-relational properties. And as for why Wittgenstein should believe this, I suggest that he had at the back of his mind, at least, the outline of a programme of analysis which would have such a consequence. We shall return to the issue in Chapter 14, sketching just such a programme. For the moment we shall concentrate on arguments for necessity.

Although the thesis that there are such things as Simples forms the corner-stone of the metaphysics of *TLP*, explicit argumentation for it is extremely sparse in the text. At 2.0211 we are told that there must be Simples since otherwise whether a proposition had *Sinn* would depend upon the truth of another. This is by no means easy to interpret. We shall consider some suggestions in the next chapter, and another in Chapter 12. Then at 2.026 it is argued that there must be Simples since otherwise the world would not have an unalterable form. This will be considered in Section D below. Finally, 3.23 implies (when taken together with 3.2– 3.221) that there must be Simples since otherwise the requirement of determinacy of *Sinn* would be breached. One possible reading of this argument will be considered in the next section. Another will be considered in Chapter 12. In addition to these three there have been various other arguments suggested in elucidation of Wittgenstein's position which we shall need to consider, some taking their inspiration from his own later writings.

(B) The argument from sharpness of *Sinn*

This is the argument we sketched briefly in Chapter 6. There is no unequivocal evidence that Wittgenstein ever actually deployed it. What there is comes from 3.23, which equates the requirement that simple signs be possible with the requirement of determinacy of *Sinn*. But as we also saw in Chapter 6, the requirement of sharpness is only one strand in this, the other being logical objectivism (the requirement of determinacy-in-advance).[5]

The argument would proceed as follows. Suppose we were convinced that every proposition must, as a matter of logic, have sharply defined truth-conditions. Then such a thing will only be possible if reality itself is discrete. If the colour spectrum were a continuum, for example, then however precisely one tried to define the boundary between two colours, there would always remain indefinitely many shades of colour which were not determinately placed on one side of the boundary or the other. Only if there are atoms of colour – so that there exist shades x and y which are distinct, and which are such that there is no other shade z which falls between them – will it be possible to define a completely precise boundary.

This argument might conceivably be thought sufficient to establish the existence of non-complex objects. But it obviously cannot show the atoms of reality to be constituents of all possible worlds. They might be genuinely simple, thus facilitating the drawing of sharp boundaries, and yet exist only contingently. At this point it might be felt that the argument would fare better if we dropped the requirement that Simples be necessary, and returned to the phenomenalist interpretation which we discussed in the last chapter. But still it would only establish, at best, that all thought must be built on references to simple sense-data. It would not follow that these sense-data are constituents of all possible worlds.

It might be suggested that the immediate acquaintance that we have with our own sense-data is sufficient to fill the gap. For if all thought reduces, ultimately, to thoughts involving direct reference to sense-data, then how would one be able to entertain the thought that a particular existing sense-datum might not exist? How can one represent, by means of direct reference to an individual, the possible non-existence of that very thing? But in fact there is no real problem about this. One could entertain a thought of the form '$\lozenge - \exists x(x = b)$'. Nor can our certainty with respect to our own sense-data make any difference. The fact that it would be self-refuting to assert 'This sense-datum does not exist' does not imply that there is any difficulty in thinking 'This sense-datum might not have existed.' Nor does the self-verifying nature of 'This sense-datum exists' make it the case that it entails 'This sense-datum necessarily exists.'[6]

What is somewhat less obvious, but none the less true, is that the argument from sharpness is incapable even of establishing that reality must consist of non-complex individuals. For the sense of 'atomic', as it figures in the argument, relates entirely to concepts. The claim is that all those predicates and relational expressions whose conditions of application we take to involve continua in fact have conditions of application which are discrete and sharply defined. But it does not follow that the individual things to which these concepts apply must themselves be non-complex. We can easily imagine worlds in which all individual things are complex (consisting of parts which in turn consist of parts and so on) and yet in which their construction out of those parts does not admit of degrees. So it would be an all-or-nothing matter whether or not a given complex entity exists, in addition to the properties of and relations between individuals being similarly discrete.

It is clear, moreover, that the argument would fare no better if we widened our reading of 'object' to include universals. For even so the objects of *TLP* would have to include individuals as well (there could not be a world of contingent facts consisting only of universals) and we should still be left without any argument for their simplicity, let alone their necessity. Indeed, this point generalises: any argument for the existence of simple objects must purport to establish that there is a class of necessarily existing individuals, whatever it may say about universals.

(C) The argument from complexity

The simple objects of *TLP* are contrasted with complexes: it is claimed that all statements about complexes can be analysed into statements describing the relations between their simple constituents (2.021, 3.24, 3.3442). If we take this together with the later Wittgenstein's discussion of the simple/complex contrast at *PI* 39–64, then we might be tempted to read back into *TLP* the following argument:

(1)   There are complex objects in the world.
(2)   Any complex object must consist of simpler parts.
(C)   So there must exist a class of non-complex objects.[7]

Wittgenstein's main criticism of this argument in *PI* turns on the idea that there are no such notions as absolute simplicity or absolute complexity (*PI* 47–8). On the contrary, 'complex' means different things in different sorts of context, and in different language-games. This is, of course, not the sort of criticism that the Wittgenstein of *TLP* could have been expected to foresee, since it depends upon a recognition of the multiplicity of different uses of language which is distinctive of the later philosophy. So if there were nothing else wrong with the above argument it might be reasonable, in the absence of textual evidence to the contrary, to see *TLP* as endorsing it. The metaphysics of *TLP* would then derive ultimately from a certain conception of the uniformity of language.

However, there is, in fact, a great deal more wrong with the argument. To begin with, the move from the premisses to the conclusion is unsound. From the undoubted fact that there exist complex objects in the world, and the analytic truth that any complex object consists of simpler parts, it does not follow that there is any object which does not consist of simpler parts. It may be that each complex object is made up of simpler parts, which in turn themselves consist of simpler parts, and so on *ad infinitum*. To think otherwise is to commit a fallacy, involving a quantifier shift from 'Every complex object consists of some simpler parts' to 'There are some simple parts out of which all complex objects are made.'

The above error is so obvious that we surely cannot, in charity to the early Wittgenstein, suppose him to have overlooked it. Moreover, there is textual evidence to show that he was aware of the possibility of analysis *ad infinitum*. At 4.2211 he remarks that even if the world were infinitely complex, with every fact consisting of infinitely many states of affairs (*Sachverhalten*, atomic facts), and every state of affairs consisting of infinitely many objects, there would still have to be objects and states of affairs. While this is not quite the same as acknowledging that there need be no definite terminus to the hierarchy of complex objects and their simpler constituents, it does at least show an awareness that it may prove impossible ever to complete the analysis of any given proposition of · ordinary language.

In any case, even if these scruples could be overcome, the argument from complexity fails to establish what it is supposed to: the existence of Simples. For as we have already had occasion to see, from the fact that there exists a class of absolutely simple (non-complex) individuals, it does not follow that these individuals must exist in all possible worlds, let alone that they exist at all times in those worlds. So in this respect too, Charity requires that we find an alternative source for Wittgenstein's position if we can possibly do so.

(D) The argument from unalterable form

As we noted at the conclusion of Section A above, Wittgenstein argues at 2.026 that if the world has an unalterable form, then there must be simple objects. And at 2.022 he claims it to be obvious that the world does indeed have an unalterable form. So the existence of Simples is entailed, by a step of *modus ponens*.

The first thing we have to ask is what Wittgenstein means by the form of the world. At 2.0231 it is contrasted with the material properties of the world, which is presumably the set of actual truths about the world: the set of facts. So it seems reasonable to assume that the form of the world is the set of logically possible truths about the world. That is to say: the form of world w is given by the set of propositions of the kind $\Diamond A$ which are true about w. We then need to ask what it means to say that the form of the world is unalterable. In the light of the above, it presumably means that the set of possible truths about our actual world would remain the same with respect to any other possible world. That is to say: if any proposition of the kind $\Diamond A$ expresses a truth about our actual world, then $\Diamond A$ expresses a truth about all possible worlds. This is in effect the characteristic S5 axiom: $\Diamond A \rightarrow \Box \Diamond A$.[8] I propose to grant Wittgenstein its obviousness. The real question is whether the S5 axiom entails the existence of Simples, as Wittgenstein seems to claim at 2.026.

We can begin to see the connection which he may have had in mind if we notice that he speaks, not only of the form of the world, but also of the form of an object. At 2.0141 we are told that the form of an object is given by the set of possible states of affairs in which it can occur. And 2.012 tells us that the possibility of occurring in a state of affairs must be 'written into the object itself' – that is to say, be an essential attribute of it. So the set of possible situations in which an object can occur is an essential attribute of it. This too is apparently entailed by the S5 axiom. For if it is possible for an object to occur in a state of affairs (if, say, $\Diamond aRb$ is a truth about our world), then it is a truth about all possible worlds that it is possible for that object to occur in that state of affairs ($\Box \Diamond aRb$ is also true).

We also know Wittgenstein to have believed that all possibilities reduce, ultimately, to the possibility of objects occurring in states of affairs (2.0272, 4.3, 4.4, 5). Indeed, such a belief is independently plausible. It is in any case quite natural to maintain that all possibility must in the end be a matter of which atomic sentences are possibly true – that is, of which individuals could possibly possess what properties, and of which individuals could possibly stand in what relations to one another. There is then a sense in which the form of all the objects in the world gives us the form of the world itself (see 2.0231). For together with the objects we are given all possible properties of, and relations between, objects (remember their forms are essential to them), and all possibilities whatever (the form of the world) are said to reduce ultimately to these.

We are now apparently in a position to argue, by *reductio*, that the same set of objects must exist in all possible worlds. Suppose that this is not the case: suppose that there are two possible worlds, w and v, which consist of different objects. Now, the set of objects in w determines the set of propositions of the form $\Diamond A$ which are true about w ('the form of world w'). And similarly the set of objects in v determines which propositions are possibly true about v ('the form of world v'). Then since the two sets of objects are different, so must be the two sets of possible truths. But this conflicts with the S5 axiom: what is possible in one world is possible in all (the form of w = the form of v). Our initial supposition must therefore be false. On the contrary, the same set of objects must exist in all possible worlds: objects constitute the fixed form of the world.[9]

The mistake in this argument lies in the claim that if the objects in w and v differ, then so too must the possible truths about w and v. To see this, suppose that world w contains only the objects a, b and c, while world v contains only the objects f, g and h. Amongst the possible truths about a, there will be propositions relating it to b and to c. But – and this is the crucial point – there will also be possible truths relating it to f, g and h. For there will be another possible world u in which all six objects exist. (I assume that the existence of one individual thing cannot logically exclude the existence of another.) The same, of course, goes for the objects in world v: the possible truths about them will include ones relating them to the objects in world w. So the set of possible truths about w and v will be identical after all.

Take a more concrete example. I exist in this world, and amongst the possible truths about me are ones relating me differently to other things which also exist in this world. There are possible worlds in which I am friends with Margaret Thatcher, and worlds in which I am friends with Ronald Reagan. But there are other possible truths about me, relating me to objects which do not in fact exist in this world, but which exist in other possible worlds. There are possible worlds in which I am friends with Zeus, and worlds in which I go riding on Pegasus. So there is no reason why the set of possible truths about the actual world, in which I exist, should not be the very same as the set of possible truths about the world in which Zeus exists and I do not: both will include the possible truth that we are friends.

We can thus grant Wittgenstein the truth of the S5 axiom, allowing him that the world has a fixed form; and we can grant him that the form of the world reduces ultimately to the form of individuals: it is a matter of the possible properties of, and possible relations between, individual things. For it is entirely consistent with these concessions to deny that the world is made up of objects which exist in all possible worlds. Nor does it follow that the individuals which give the form of the world have necessary existence.

Although Wittgenstein does seem to have endorsed the argument for the existence of Simples which we have been discussing, it is surely reasonable to hope that he may also have had a better one. It is not unusual for a philosopher to have in mind a number of distinct arguments for the same conclusion. Nor is it unusual for them to find some of these arguments more convincing than they should, precisely because they yield a conclusion of whose truth they have already become convinced. Charity requires us to hope that something of this sort may be true in Wittgenstein's case.

(E) An argument from the semantics of names

Recall from Chapter 1 that for Wittgenstein the semantic content of a name is its bearer. So a name which lacks a bearer will lack semantic content, and sentences containing it will accordingly be without truth-conditions. How, then, am I to use a name for a contingently existing entity to describe the possibility of that thing never having existed? For this possibility is at the same time one with respect to which sentences containing that name will lack truth-conditions.

The argument here seems to be the same as that put in quotation marks by Wittgenstein at *PI 55*, apparently in exposition of his earlier self. He writes:

'What the names in language signify must be indestructible; for it must be possible to describe the states of affairs in which everything destructible is destroyed. And this description will contain words; and what corresponds to these cannot be destroyed, for otherwise the words would have no meaning.'

Yet the reply to the argument is simple and obvious. It is that one may coherently use a name which does in fact have meaning in this world to describe situations in which its bearer would fail to exist. The fact that such a situation would be one in which that name, if it were then to exist, would be without semantic content need not deprive our description now of its truth-condition. The simplest such description would take the form '$\Diamond -\exists x(x = b)$', as we saw in Section B above.

There is, however, a further possible premiss of the argument which would rule out the acceptability of this reply. This is the *TLP* thesis that all possible worlds may be described by means of assignments of truth-values to the set of elementary propositions (4.26, 5).[10] For since '$-\exists x(x = b)$' is clearly not elementary it cannot, according to this thesis, be essentially involved in the description of another possible world. Yet how else are we to describe the possibility that a contingent object b might never have existed?[11]

In fact, however, there is no difficulty in meeting the constraint introduced by the extra premiss of the argument. Using only elementary propositions we can describe a situation in which a contingent object of reference fails to exist, by negating all of them in which the name of that thing figures. Since the elementary propositions of *TLP* are to be logically independent of one another, such a description will not be self-contradictory. But since it is surely impossible for a contingent object to exist without there being anything contingently true of it, it must follow from the description that the object in question does not exist, and we shall have our desired specification of a possible world.

Of course there would remain a problem in using elementary propositions to describe, not worlds where things which do exist would not exist, but rather worlds where there would exist objects which do not exist in the actual world. For since they do not exist in this world, any names for them which we might introduce will lack semantic content, and any elementary propositions employing those names will lack truth-conditions. We might try to circumvent this problem by appealing to the distinction between the sense and semantic content of names. For example, if names for non-existent things employed descriptive senses, then although sentences containing them would lack semantic content, they would still be capable of expressing determinately true or false thoughts in the idiolect of any given speaker. But as we shall see in the next chapter, Wittgenstein has a strong argument for saying that at least not all the names in elementary propositions can have descriptive senses.

It would seem, then, that by combining together the thesis that the semantic content of a name is its bearer with the claim that all possible worlds must be describable by means of assignments of truth-values to a set of elementary propositions, we can at most derive the conclusion that the objects of actual reference which exist in our world are the only possible objects that there are. But this does not entail that they exist necessarily. It is one thing to say that all possible worlds must contain some selection from amongst the objects which exist in the actual world, and quite another to say that all or any of those objects must exist in all possible worlds. So this argument, like the others so far considered, fails to establish the desired conclusion.

Summary

We have considered four possible arguments for the existence of Simples: from the requirement of sharpness of *Sinn*, from complexity, from the S5 axiom, and from the semantics of names. Each has failed lamentably.

10   Simples: stronger arguments

In this chapter we shall develop and assess two further arguments for the existence of Simples. Each, with considerable plausibility, could be attributed to Wittgenstein.

(A) Russell's argument

As we noted briefly in Chapter 1, Wittgenstein appears to commit himself to a form of description-theory for ordinary proper names, proposing to analyse them into descriptions of the manner in which their referents are constructed out of component parts (3.24). In Chapter 7 we saw that this may have been partly motivated by his programme of analysis, which was to show how ordinary propositions reach right up to particular states of affairs. However, there is also more than a suggestion that the issue is somehow connected with his reasons for believing in Simples, since the passage in which he endorses a form of description-theory comes immediately after 3.23, which says that the requirement that simple signs be possible is the requirement of determinacy of *Sinn*. But the exact nature of the connection remains obscure.

We may reasonably expect light to be thrown on the matter by comparing Wittgenstein's position with that of Russell. As is well known, Russell not only has a theory of definite descriptions (emphatically endorsed by Wittgenstein at 4.0031) but proposes to analyse ordinary proper names by means of such descriptions, as well as believing that such analyses must terminate in names for simple objects. So it is possible that an examination of Russell's argument will help us to understand Wittgenstein's.

Russell saw a problem concerning sentences containing bearerless proper names and uninstantiated definite descriptions, and proposed to solve it by means of his celebrated theory of definite descriptions. On this account, a sentence of the form 'Fb', where 'b' is an ordinary (possibly bearerless) proper name, in reality has the form 'The G is F.' And this, in turn, is analysed as saying that there is one and only one thing which is G, and that thing is F. In symbols: $\exists x(Gx \ \& \ \forall y(Gy \to x = y) \ \& \ Fx)$. So if there is no G (if the name is bearerless) the sentence is straightforwardly false.

Now, what exactly is the problem that the theory is designed to overcome? A number of things are being assumed. Firstly, Russell is taking for granted that if a sentence 'Fb' is genuinely singular, then its truth-condition will have the following form: 'Fb' is true if the object b possesses the property F, false if the object b does not possess the property F. So if the object b did not exist, then 'Fb' would be neither true nor false. (Compare 3.24.) Indeed, stronger than this, he believed that any genuinely singular thought would involve, as one of its constituents, the object thought about itself. So if the object b did not exist, then there could be no singular thought having the form 'Fb'. Now, Russell is a Cartesian about acts of thinking: it is unintelligible to him that he might seem to be thinking a particular thought while there is, in reality, no such thought occurring. This then gives him a powerful motive for insisting that any putatively singular thought or sentence should be analysed in the manner of the theory of definite descriptions if we cannot be completely certain of the object referred to, thus revealing that it is not genuinely singular after all. For then the existence of the thought (or the meaning of the sentence) can be guaranteed in the face of the possible non-existence of the object.

But why do there have to be any genuinely singular thoughts or sentences at all? This brings us to another assumption: that the understanding of general sentences presupposes an understanding of singular ones, and that grasp of general thoughts presupposes a grasp of singular ones. In outline, the argument goes as follows. Any sentence analysed by means of the theory of definite descriptions turns out to have the truth-conditions of an existentially quantified sentence, in reality having the form '$\exists x \phi x$'. But an understanding of sentences of this form palpably depends upon a prior grasp of sentences having the form 'ϕb'. No one could know what it is for something in general to have a certain property who did not know what it would be for some particular thing to possess that property. And no one could know this who was not yet capable of understanding sentences involving singular reference to particular things. But now if these sentences, themselves, are to be analysed in terms of the theory of definite descriptions, then they too will be general in form. And then any attempt to explain the truth-conditions of general sentences will turn out to be viciously circular.[1] So if it is to remain intelligible how someone can come to understand general sentences (or to think general thoughts), then there must be a class of genuinely singular sentences which do not presuppose a prior understanding of the existential quantifier.

Putting these points together we can see that Russell is endorsing the following argument:

(1)   General thoughts presuppose singular ones.

(2)   Singular thoughts cannot themselves have general thoughts amongst the expression of their truth-conditions, on pain of vicious circularity.

(C1)   So there exists a class of genuinely singular thoughts.

(3)   Singular thoughts occur only if their objects of reference exist, since those objects are themselves part of the thought.

(4)   We have Cartesian certainty about our own thoughts.

(C2)   So there must be a class of objects of reference about whose existence we can be completely certain.

Famously, Russell drew from this argument the conclusion that the only genuine proper names are the indexicals 'this' and 'that', used to refer to the thinker's own sense-data. Our immediate task, however, is to see to what extent Wittgenstein could have endorsed such an argument; and if he could not, whether he could have employed some variation upon it.

(B) A variant of the Russellian argument

It is clear that Wittgenstein would have agreed with Russell's argument as far as the subsidiary conclusion (C1). For *TLP* explains the content of general propositions in terms of operations upon elementary ones (5.5, 5.501, 5.52). Indeed, all propositions whatever are said to be (to be equivalent to) truth-functions of elementary propositions (4.4, 5, 5.3). Clearly, then, elementary propositions cannot themselves be general in form, nor can they presuppose a prior understanding of general propositions. Indeed, at 4.411 Wittgenstein explicitly states that the understanding of general propositions depends upon a prior grasp of elementary ones.[2] The upshot is that there must be a class of genuinely singular elementary propositions, whose understanding neither involves nor presupposes a grasp of generality.

However, there can be no question of Wittgenstein accepting premiss (3), since this is in effect Russell's theory that judgement involves a direct relation between the subject and the objects thought about – so no object, no judgement. And this theory is explicitly rejected by Wittgenstein at

5.541–5.5422. His own view is that all thinking must involve some structured array of symbols, as we saw briefly in Chapter 1. And since he holds that proper names have senses (even logically proper names, as we also saw in Chapter 1), there can be no objection in principle to the idea of singular thought without an object (sense without reference). Or at least if there is such an objection, it will have to derive from quite a different quarter.[3]

Nevertheless, Wittgenstein would endorse a slightly weaker version of premiss (3), namely that a singular thought without an object would lack a truth-condition – it would have sense but no *Sinn*. For recall that his view is that the semantic content (contribution to truth-conditions) of a name is its referent. So no referent, no truth-conditions. In which case we may replace premiss (3) of Russell's argument by (3*): genuinely singular propositions only have truth-conditions if their objects of reference exist. And notice that this is already beginning to echo Wittgenstein's explicit argument for Simples at 2.0211, which we could read as saying that if the objects of reference of singular propositions existed only contingently, then whether such a proposition had *Sinn* would depend upon the truth of another, which asserts the existence of the objects referred to.

Whether or not Wittgenstein would have endorsed premiss (4) of the Russellian argument, it would certainly have been insufficient for his purposes, for it could only enable him to show that the objects of reference do certainly exist in the actual world, not that they have necessary existence. Yet precisely what he wants is to prove that there is a class of objects of reference which exist in all possible worlds. Is there then any variant of (4) which would be adequate to the task? What additional premiss would enable Wittgenstein to get from (C1) and (3*) to his conclusion? Clearly this: whether a proposition can have a given truth-condition must be independent of any contingent fact about the world. For if the objects of genuine singular reference were to exist only contingently, then it would follow, by (3*), that the possibility of a singular proposition having a truth-condition would depend upon a contingency.

Summarising, then, and conflating together the first three steps of Russell's argument into a single premiss, we have the following:

(1*)   There must be a class of genuinely singular propositions, which do not presuppose a prior grasp of generality.

(3*)   Genuinely singular propositions only have truth-conditions if their objects of reference exist.

(4*)   Whether a proposition has truth-conditions must be independent of any contingent fact about the world.

(C)   So there must be a class of objects of reference whose existence is not contingent but necessary.

This argument is valid.[4] Premisses (1*) and (3*) were almost certainly endorsed by Wittgenstein, and are in any case extremely plausible in their own right. So the questions before us are these: is there textual evidence of Wittgenstein's acceptance of (4*)? And can any convincing defence of it be given (Charity again)?

(C) Can having truth-conditions be contingent?

One point in favour of (4*) is that it enables us to make some kind of sense of 3.23, where Wittgenstein equates the requirement that there be Simples with the requirement of determinacy of *Sinn*. For recall that the best interpretation we were able to offer of the latter requirement amounted to this: the truth-conditions of a proposition must be fixed in advance in all their particularity. We took the phrase 'in advance' to be an expression of logical objectivism, the requirement insisting that the truth-conditions must be fixed by the sense of the proposition alone, independently of any such contingencies as speakers' intuitions, capacities or responses to linguistic training. But it seems only a small step from this to the claim that the possession of a truth-condition by a proposition must be independent of any contingent facts whatever, which is premiss (4*). Construed broadly, then, the requirement of determinacy is none other than premiss (4*) – which would explain why 3.23 picks it out as the fundamental ground for believing in the existence of Simples.

This interpretation would also enable us to make fairly ready sense of 2.0211, which could be paraphrased as follows:

If there were no Simples, then whether a singular proposition had truth-conditions would depend upon the contingent truth of a proposition asserting the existence of the object referred to.

Then since such a situation would supposedly involve a breach of the requirement of determinacy (premiss (4*)), and since there have to be singular propositions if there are to be any propositions at all (premiss (1*)), we could readily understand why Wittgenstein should go on to claim that if there were no Simples we could not form any representation of the world at all (2.0212). For we saw in Chapters 3 and 4 that he thinks, with some reason, that logical objectivism (and hence determinacy-in-advance) is essential to all representation.

In fact, however, the requirement of determinacy-in-advance is not the same as premiss (4*); nor is it easy to see how one could get validly from the one to the other. For what that requirement really says is that propositions must fix their truth-conditions in a manner which is independent of any contingent fact. It is the *manner* of reaching out (the mode of projection) which has to be independent of contingencies, not whatever is reached out *to*. Indeed, it seems perfectly consistent with the requirement of determinacy that a proposition might sometimes 'reach out' in the normal way, but fail to determine any truth-condition. So it is one thing to say that a proposition must determine its truth-condition in a way which is independent of any contingent fact. And it is quite another, stronger, thing to say that whether a proposition succeeds in having a truth-condition must be independent of any contingent fact. Yet it is the stronger thesis which we need if our Russellian argument to Simples is to go through.

The only argument which I know of for the stronger thesis is based upon a version of the principle of Bivalence which we know Wittgenstein to have endorsed: that a proposition must yield a determinate yes-or-no answer in the face of any possibility whatever (4.023). For notice that the effect of this is to insist that a proposition must have its truth-value fixed with respect to every possible world. And it might be felt that this is sufficient to entail premiss (4*). For if (4*) were false, because there were possible worlds in which some proposition would fail to have a truth-condition, then would it not follow that there are possible worlds with respect to which it would fail to have a determinate truth-value? For how can a proposition without a truth-condition have a truth-value?

But in fact this argument is invalid, depending upon an illegitimate conflation of truth *about* a possible world with truth *in* a possible world.[5] Bivalence only requires that every proposition for which we have fixed truth-conditions should have a determinate truth-value with respect to (that is, about) every possible world. It does not require that it be possible for someone within such a world to express a proposition with those truth-conditions. On the contrary, it is entirely consistent with Bivalence that we may have to rely upon contingent facts about our world (such as the existence of an object of reference) in determining the truth-conditions of our propositions across all possible worlds.

For example, suppose we took the proposition 'Moses is wise' to be genuinely singular. And suppose we agreed with Wittgenstein that the truth-condition of such a proposition involves the man Moses himself, in such a way that without the existence of Moses there would be no truth-condition. Now as things are – relying upon the truth-condition which the proposition does in fact have – we may truly say 'If Moses had never existed, then it would not have been true that Moses is wise.' That is: the proposition that Moses is wise gets assigned the value False with respect to a world in which there is no such person as Moses. But we may also truly say 'Inhabitants of a world in which there is no such person as Moses could not have made the false statement that Moses is wise, since no proposition with that truth-condition would have been available to them.' That is: the proposition that Moses is wise, within a world in which there is no Moses, would fail to have a truth-condition. There is no breach of the principle of Bivalence, since all actually existing propositions with truth-conditions get assigned truth-values relative to each and every possible world.

Given that the argument from Bivalence to premiss (4*) is invalid, might Wittgenstein nevertheless have endorsed it? One powerful line of reasoning against this suggestion is that a simple extension of the argument would establish the necessary existence of propositions. The extension is so simple that it would be extraordinary that Wittgenstein should have overlooked it; yet the conclusion is Frege's thesis of the necessary existence of thoughts (*Gedanken*), which he rejects.[6] The argument is this: suppose that propositions exist contingently, a proposition 'P' failing to exist in some possible world w. Since 'P' does not exist in w it would follow – by a move identical to that made in the argument for (4*) – that it cannot be either true or false with respect to w, and the principle of Bivalence would fail. So holding Bivalence firm, we could deduce by *reductio* that propositions have necessary existence. Here exactly the same distinction is being overlooked, between truth *about* a world and truth *in* a world.

There is a natural response to our rebuttal of the argument for premiss (4*). It is that if 'Moses is wise' gets assigned the value False relative to a world in which there is no such person as Moses, then the truth of that proposition, conversely, must imply that there is such a person as Moses. And this seems to conflict with the thesis that 'Moses is wise' is genuinely singular. In fact this can be turned into yet another argument for Simples, not requiring an assumption as strong as Bivalence.

(D) An argument from Excluded Third

Our quasi-Russellian assumptions are not the only way of getting validly from the thesis that there must exist a class of genuinely singular propositions to the thesis that Simples exist. The Principle of Excluded Third

('No proposition can be neither true nor false') can be deployed to the same end, as follows.

Supposing that all the objects of reference have only contingent existence, consider the singular proposition 'Fb'. Since b exists only contingently, there is a possible world w in which b does not exist. Now what is to be said about the truth-value of 'Fb' with respect to (note, not 'in') world w? Clearly it is not true with respect to world w. There can be no question of a proposition of the form 'Fb' being true in a case where there is no such object as b.[7] But then nor can the proposition be neither true nor false, in virtue of Excluded Third. So the only remaining possibility is that it is false. But if the non-existence of b entails the falsity of 'Fb', then by contraposition the truth of 'Fb' must entail that b exists. But then of course if 'Fb' entails some proposition of the form $\exists x \phi x$, it has an existential quantifier within the expression of its truth-condition, which contradicts the hypothesis of its genuine singularity.[8] So, by *reductio*, there must exist a class of objects of reference which exist in all possible worlds. That is to say: there must be Simples.

This same argument may also be approached in a slightly different way. As Wittgenstein himself notices at 5.47, the proposition 'Fb' is logically equivalent to '$\exists x(Fx \,\&\, x = b)$'. For clearly these two propositions must at least always be true together. The only possible doubt about their equivalence would be whether the falsity of '$\exists x(x = b)$' entails the falsity of 'Fb'. But since 'Fb' obviously cannot be true if nothing is b, this is forced on us if we accept Excluded Third. Now the above equivalence might seem, on the face of it, to raise a problem for the thesis that there must be a class of genuinely singular propositions, since it looks as if all propositions will be quantified. But in fact it does not, and in seeing how it does not, we shall see how it can be transformed into an argument for the existence of Simples.

If b is a Simple, then of course '$\exists x(x = b)$' will be a necessary truth.[9] In which case recognition of the entailment from 'Fb' from '$\exists x(x = b)$' will not be required for a grasp of the former's truth-condition. For since there is no possibility of '$\exists x(x = b)$' being false, there is no conceivable circumstance in which the speaker's failure to recognise the inference from 'Fb' to '$\exists x(x = b)$' could manifest itself; there are no circumstances in which they could be led to accord the wrong truth-value to 'Fb'. It will then be possible for someone who does not yet understand the existential quantifier to have a complete grasp of the truth-condition of 'Fb'. So long as they know which object is b, and so long as they know the conditions under which an object possesses the property F, they will never go wrong. If, on the other hand, b is not a Simple, then '∃x(x = b)' will be contingent. There will then be possible circumstances which would not be recognised as entailing the falsity of 'Fb' by someone who has no grasp of the existential quantifier, and this would be sufficient to show that they do not understand it properly. On the contrary, proper understanding of 'Fb' would require a prior grasp of the existential quantifier. Thus the fact that 'Fb' is equivalent to '∃x(Fx & x = b)' raises no problem for the introduction of the quantifiers if, but only if, some propositions of this form involve reference to Simples.

The argument we have been considering may be set out as follows:

(1)   There must be a class of genuinely singular propositions, which do not presuppose a prior grasp of generality.

(2)   There is no possible world, or time within a world, with respect to which a proposition is neither true nor false.

(3)   If all the objects of reference are contingent, then there are possible worlds in which those objects do not exist.

(4)   With respect to such worlds the propositions in (1) are not true.

(C1)   So, by (2), they are false with respect to such worlds.

(C2)   So, by contraposition on (C1), the propositions in (1) entail the existence of their objects of reference.

(5)   This conflicts with the hypothesis of their genuine singularity.

(C3)   So there must exist a class of non-contingent objects of reference (Simples).

This argument looks powerful. Premisses (1) and (2) seem very plausible; premisses (3) and (4) are truistic; and the argument itself is valid. The only immediate worry might appear to concern premiss (5). For after all, not every case where one proposition implies another can be taken to show that an understanding of the latter is presupposed to an understandiang of the former. For example, 'Fb' implies 'Fb ∨ Q', but no one would say that this shows the former to be molecular rather than genuinely atomic.

In fact this worry is misplaced. The difference between 'Fb' implying '∃x(x = b)' and 'Fb' implying 'Fb ∨ Q' is that the existence of b must be counted amongst the truth-conditions of 'Fb', whereas no one would say that 'Fb ∨ Q' describes a truth-condition of 'Fb'. That b exists can be stated without presupposing a prior understanding of the proposition 'Fb', and in terms of it the truth-condition of the latter may be partly specified. But obviously no one could have a grasp of the possible circumstance described by 'Fb ∨ Q' who did not already know the truth-condition of 'Fb', in which case one could not use it in specifying the latter's content.

Despite its intrinsic plausibility, there seems to be little textual warrant for attributing the argument above to Wittgenstein. Certainly it would not mesh particularly well with 3.23, since there is apparently no way in which it could be connected with either version of determinacy of *Sinn*. And although it can provide an interpretation of 2.0211, the fit is by no means exact. We should have to take this to be saying:

If there were no Simples, then whether a singular proposition was true-or-false would depend upon the contingent fact of the existence of the object referred to.

Thus if this other proposition – asserting the existence of the object – were false, then the singular proposition would be neither true nor false, since otherwise it could not be genuinely singular. But in fact 2.0211 says that if there were no Simples, and the 'other proposition' were false, then the singular proposition would *have no Sinn* (truth-condition). And to say that in certain circumstances a singular proposition would be neither true nor false is surely not the same as saying that, were those circumstances to obtain, then there would be no condition in which it would have been true and no condition in which it would have been false. So interpreted in this way, we should have to regard 2.0211 as singularly ill expressed.

Moreover, even if we could bring ourselves to accept this sloppiness of expression on Wittgenstein's part, we might find it hard to make sense of the remark which follows (2.0212), which claims that if there were no Simples then it would be impossible to represent reality at all. For it is not at all clear why the failure of Excluded Third should have such radical consequences. In fact we should have to see Wittgenstein as managing to convince himself that Excluded Third is so closely bound up with the notion of a proposition, and the notion of a symbolic representation of reality, that there could be no such thing as a system of symbols which failed to obey it.

This last thought can also be arrived at from another direction. For the existence of Simples is supposed to be a presupposition of all language and thought. In which case an argument which takes Excluded Third (or indeed Bivalence) as a premiss can only conceivably be successful if that principle, too, is a presupposition of all symbolic representation. So Wittgenstein would need to show that nothing could count as a language, or a system of representation, which allowed Excluded Third to be violated.

Now it might be replied that Wittgenstein does in fact seem to regard Excluded Third in this light. For as we noted in Chapter 6, he regards the principles of logic as providing the structure (the 'inner scaffolding') of all language and thought. This then brings us to considerations of Charity. In the next chapter we shall assess the strength of the reasoning underlying Wittgenstein's attitude. Since the principles of logic will turn out not to have the sort of inviolable status he attributes to them, the present argument to Simples will be unsound. And then we shall (out of Charity, as well as Textual Fidelity) have reason to continue our search for a better one. For Charity requires us to do the best that we can on behalf of our subject, hoping that he may, besides weak arguments, have had in mind something stronger.

Summary

We have considered two further arguments for the existence of Simples. The first (Russellian) argument can be made to fit the text quite well, but commits an obvious fallacy. The second argument is a great deal more plausible; but it fits the text less well, leaving us puzzling about why Wittgenstein should have thought a belief in Simples to be imposed upon him by the requirement of determinacy of *Sinn* (3.23).

11 *The principles of logic*

Our task in this chapter is to understand the basis of *TLP*'s commitment to two-valued logic. But we should discuss separately two principles that neither Frege nor Wittgenstein distinguishes very carefully from one another: firstly Bivalence, which says that every proposition must be determinately (objectively, mind-independently) true or false; then secondly Excluded Third, which says that no proposition can be neither true nor false.

(A) Bivalence

On any account of the matter, Bivalence must entail Excluded Third. If all propositions must be determinately true or false, then there is no room for them to be neither the one nor the other. If they must always have one or other of the two truth-values, then clearly they cannot have neither. A commitment to Excluded Third, on the other hand, does not by itself entail a commitment to Bivalence. If one thought that the truth or falsity of a proposition had to be in some way epistemologically accessible to us in order for it to possess a determinate truth-value (crudely, 'no truth except verifiable truth'), then one would hesitate to assert that every proposition must be determinately true or false; for some might fall beyond our epistemological reach. Yet one could continue to insist that no proposition can be neither true nor false, denying that anyone could ever be in a position to assert positively of a proposition that it is determinately not true as well as being determinately not false – claiming that to be able to assert of a proposition that it is not true is tantamount to the discovery that it is false.

It is clear that *TLP* is committed to Bivalence (and hence also Excluded Third). For 4.023 tells us that a proposition must restrict reality to just the two alternatives, true and false, following this up with the claim that it must describe reality completely – having a force which reaches through the whole of logical space. This suggests very strongly that the truth or falsity of a proposition is to be settled just by its sense (by the manner in which it reaches out through logical space) together with the state of reality itself, requiring no help from us, and unconstrained by whether or not we have epistemic access to that aspect of the world. Indeed, there is no suggestion in *TLP* that semantics might be in any way constrained by epistemology. On the contrary, the theory of knowledge is said to be merely the philosophy of one natural science amongst others (4.1121), whereas philosophy of language is accorded a foundational role (4.0031). Indeed, it seems that the only limits on semantics are those which result from the essential nature of representation itself (4.113–4.1213).

One can also reach *TLP*'s commitment to Bivalence by another route, premised upon Wittgenstein's dual commitments to Excluded Third and to logical objectivism. Given that it is impossible for a proposition to be neither true nor false (since there is no third truth-value, and since it is impossible for a proposition to lack a truth-value); and given that the manner in which a proposition reaches out to reality to determine its truth-value is wholly objective (being unconstrained by any limitation in our capacities); then each proposition must possess, determinately, either the truth-value True, or the truth-value False. If the sense of a proposition is able to match up against the world in a wholly objective mind-independent manner (as logical objectivism affirms), then the state of the world must either fall within the truth-condition of the proposition or not; for as Excluded Third affirms, there is no third possibility.

As we saw in Chapter 4, Wittgenstein has some reason for thinking that logical objectivism is essential to all thought and representation. He may have felt that if (*per impossibile*) it were false, then there would be no possibility of thinking or saying anything at all. So the question whether it was reasonable of him to regard the principles of logic (and in particular Bivalence) as constitutive of all language reduces to the question whether it was reasonable of him so to regard Excluded Third. Since Bivalence can be thought of as a conjunction of two distinct theses, logical objectivism and Excluded Third, and since it is not unreasonable to think that the former belongs to the very essence of representation, all attention must devolve upon the latter thesis.

(B) Excluded Third

It might seem that the existence of vague propositions would provide a good test-case for Excluded Third. But as we saw in Chapter 6, this would be a mistake. Where something falls within the fuzzy borderline of a concept we ought not to say that a proposition ascribing that concept to the thing is both not true and not false. A better test-case is provided by propositions containing uninstantiated (or multiply instantiated) definite descriptions. As is well known, Frege took the view that such propositions are neither true nor false. His reasoning was based upon an analogy with definite descriptions themselves: just as 'The father of Mary' must lack a reference if the name 'Mary' fails to refer, so too much 'The father of Mary is bald' lack reference (that is to say, be neither true nor false) if 'The father of Mary' does not refer. But in fact many others have shared Frege's view of the matter without endorsing his reasoning.[1] So Wittgenstein cannot mount an adequate defence of Excluded Third merely by virtue of rejecting Frege's doctrine that sentences, as well as names and definite descriptions, have reference (3.1–3.144).

Nor can Wittgenstein's rejection of the Fregean doctrines concerning uninstantiated definite descriptions and bearerless proper names (adopting Russell's theories in their place) provide any basis for his commitment to Excluded Third. For in the first place, even if Russell's analyses of sentences containing such expressions could be established as correct, this still would not give us the full generality of Excluded Third, which is supposed to apply to all propositions whatever. And in the second place (and more importantly), since the idea is to establish that Excluded Third is constitutive of all thought, this cannot be shown merely by analysing the forms of thought which we happen to employ. So it would not be enough to establish that sentences containing uninstantiated definite descriptions are false rather than neither true nor false. It must also be shown that there could not be a form of expression rather like our definite description, but differing from it in that sentences which contain it would lack a truth-value in cases where there is nothing, or more than one thing, satisfying it.

Any argument for Excluded Third, then, is somehow going to have to be quite general in form, even if it focusses upon sentences containing uninstantiated definite descriptions as a test-case. Moreover, we clearly need to be provided with an argument of some sort here. We cannot simply rely (or allow Wittgenstein to rely) upon an appeal to intuition, since on this issue, manifestly, intuitions can differ.

(C) Formal arguments

One argument for Excluded Third is that it is entailed by the Equivalence Principle – the principle that 'P' and 'It is true that P' are logically equivalent.[2] For if we were to allow that a proposition could be neither true nor false, then this principle would have to be given up. For in a case where 'P' was neither true nor false, 'It is true that P' would be, not neither true nor false, but false. Admittedly, this is not quite the same as saying that 'P' and 'It is true that P' can have different truth-values, since on one view of the matter to be neither true nor false is to lack a truth-value altogether, rather than to possess some third one. But at least it implies that they do not necessarily have the same truth-value, and this does seem sufficient to conflict with the Equivalence Principle.

It is clear that Wittgenstein is committed to the Equivalence Principle, and it is also clear why. For his view is that the content of a proposition is a representation of the condition under which it is true (4.022). Hence to understand a proposition is to know the condition of its truth (4.024), and fixing the content of a proposition is a matter of laying down under what condition it may be said to be true (4.063). Then since content and truth-conditions coincide, to say explicitly that a proposition is true (to assert 'It is true that P') cannot amount to anything different from the assertion of that proposition itself (to assert 'P'); which is just what the Equivalence Principle tells us. Yet this still does not amount to much of an argument. For where is it shown that fixing the content of a proposition must always be simply a matter of laying down the condition for its truth? Where is the argument that fixing the condition for the falsehood of a proposition must always be merely a matter of saying (having laid down the condition for truth) 'and false on any other condition'? For if Frege is right, and Excluded Third and the Equivalence Principle do not always hold good, then sometimes, at least, one will need to specify the conditions for falsehood separately, since there will be some situations falling in between, giving neither truth nor falsehood. No reason has been presented for saying that this cannot (or indeed does not) happen.

Another argument for Excluded Third is provided by the conception which we very naturally form of propositional negation. For on the one hand we are inclined to endorse a principle governing negation which is the analogue of the Equivalence Principle for propositional assertion: that a proposition 'P' is false if and only if '−P' is true (5.512). This connects falsehood with negation in just the same way that the Equivalence Principle connects truth with non-negated content. But then, on the other hand, we are inclined to picture negation as reversing the truth-condition of a proposition, in such a way that '−P' says something like 'Anything else, only not any of the conditions for the truth of "P"' (5.2341). These two ideas together entail Excluded Third. For suppose that a proposition could be neither true nor false. In that case '−P', in reversing the truth-condition of

'P', must be true if 'P' itself is neither true nor false. But then clearly the truth of '–P' can no longer be equivalent to the falsehood of 'P'. For '–P' can be true while 'P' is not false.

Once again the trouble with this argument is to establish the principles underlying it. How are we to show, for example, that any concept of negation would have to involve reversal of truth-conditions? And can this be shown without at some point appealing to Excluded Third? Indeed, there is at least some reason for thinking that we do not in fact employ such a concept of negation. For it might be held that the negation of 'The father of Mary is bald' is the sentence 'The father of Mary is not bald.' And it would seem that the latter, just as much as the former, must be counted as not true in a case where the name 'Mary' lacks reference. In which case negation cannot here be reversing the truth-condition of the original, or else the negated proposition would have to be true in such circumstances. Now, of course this case by itself is inconclusive, since it might be denied that the negation-sign in 'The father of Mary is not bald' really governs the whole proposition, serving rather to negate the predicate in some way.[3] But the point is that Wittgenstein cannot simply assume that negation reverses truth-conditions without begging the question against his opponent. For anyone who thinks that a proposition can be neither true nor false will be inclined to deny this, retaining merely the connection between negation and falsehood.

(D) Aiming at truth

It seems unlikely that any argument premised upon principles supposedly governing the concepts of propositional content and propositional negation can establish our commitment to Excluded Third; for these principles are themselves a crucial part of what is in question. It is even less likely that such an argument could show Excluded Third to be essential to the very notion of symbolic representation. However, Wittgenstein gestures towards quite a different sort of argument when he speaks of the danger of thinking that true and false are relations of equal status and justification between signs and what they signify (4.061, NB 95). For if it were possible for a proposition to be neither true nor false, then it would indeed have to be the case that the notions of truth and falsity stand on the same level – that they are, so to speak, coordinate with one another.

In order to see this point, consider Dummett's famous analogy between propositions and bets.[4] In connection with a bet we have three possible outcomes: it can be won, it can be lost, and it can be declared void. There is room for a middle position here because (and only because) it is possible to describe the consequences of winning and losing separately: if I win then someone has to pay me money; if I lose then I have to pay someone else money. So it is possible for there to be a case in which no money changes hands at all. Similarly then in connection with propositions: if there is to be room for a third possibility here (neither true nor false), then the significance of saying something false must be describable separately from that of saying something true. Saying something false cannot simply be a matter of saying what fails to be true, just as losing a bet is not simply a matter of failing to win it.

Wittgenstein clearly wishes to insist that the notion of truth is primary, and that truth and falsity are not in fact coordinate with one another. This is how we should read 4.022, which says that propositions show how things stand if they are *true* (my italics). It is also partly what is involved in the idea that propositions have *Sinn* (direction): a proposition directs us primarily towards the circumstances of its truth, and the circumstances of its falsity are simply those to which it does not direct us (that is, they are all other circumstances). It also seems to be part of what Wittgenstein has in mind in giving the general propositional form as: this is how things stand (4.5). The idea is that a proposition represents the world as being in a certain sort of condition (the condition of its truth), without containing a separate representation of the condition of its falsehood; rather, it is false if the condition of its truth does not obtain. But we look in vain in Wittgenstein's writing for any explicit argument for the view that truth is primary; it just seems to have struck him as intuitively obvious.

In fact what is at issue here is the significance or point of the true/false classification.[5] We need to investigate the purpose of classifying propositions into 'true' and 'false', in order to see whether there is any point in our having two separate classifications under the general heading 'not true', namely 'false' and 'neither true nor false'. What really needs to be elucidated is the kind of interest which we take in truth and falsehood: the kind of importance which they have. We must see whether or not that interest is a dual one (as it is in the case of a bet), or whether our interest in falsity is merely parasitic upon – the obverse of – our interest in truth.

Dummett in his seminal discussion of this topic suggests that the point of the true/false classification should be elucidated in terms of the significance of conventions governing the linguistic activity of assertion.[6] But this will be of no help as an exposition of Wittgenstein, who holds that assertion is merely psychological, and not a conventional matter at all (*NB* 96, 4.442). It is also unfortunate in that beliefs as well as statements can be classified as 'true' and 'false'; for since most of a person's beliefs will remain unexpressed in public assertion, it is implausible to connect the point of that classification in any very direct way with the conventions which govern statement-making. We shall do better to return afresh to Dummett's original project, taking care to consider the classification of beliefs on an equal footing with that of public assertions.

Taking our start from some remarks Dummett makes in a discussion of the concept of assertion,[7] we might suggest that the point of classifying beliefs and statements into 'true' and 'false' lies in the concept of *action*, specifically in the idea of an action's being dependent upon a belief. So perhaps the importance of the classification consists in this: that you may safely act upon a belief or statement if and only if it may be correctly classified as 'true'. Of course 'safe to act' here cannot mean that you are guaranteed to achieve the ends of your action. For you may make errors in trying to carry it out, or some event may intervene to prevent you completing it, or it may fail because of the falsity of one of your other beliefs. But it does mean this: that any failure cannot be attributable to the belief or statement in question. Moreover, if all of the beliefs on which you act are true, then the most that is needed to achieve your aims is successful execution of the action. Equally, of course, an act based upon a false belief, although 'unsafe', is not bound to fail. But any success will be purely adventitious.

From the point of view of our interest in action there is no relevant distinction to be drawn between the different ways in which a belief or statement can fail to be true. For action on a belief is safe if and only if that belief is true. If it is not true – no matter in what manner it is not true – then an action based upon it will only succeed by accident. For example, suppose that I am hungry one Sunday evening and ask you where I can get something to eat. You reply 'The restaurant in the next street is open.' Is there any relevant distinction here between the case in which there is no restaurant and the case in which there is one but it is closed? Surely not: either way, my hunger will continue unabated. (And if it does not – if I meet a hot-dog seller on the way who is only there because there is no restaurant in that street, or if there is a sign in the restaurant window directing me to another nearby which is open – then this will be an unplanned-for success.)

Of course our interest in truth and falsity is not wholly practical in orientation. Many of us also take an interest in the matter for its own sake. However, there is some reason to think that the practical is the more fundamental of our two sources of concern. For it may be possible to explain why, as practical agents, we have reason to develop an interest in truth for its own sake: because there is no telling when a true belief might not come in handy. Since we cannot predict in advance which beliefs we shall one day need to act upon, we do well to interest ourselves in trying to ensure the truth of our beliefs almost indiscriminately, without looking, in general, to possible future applications. But even if the two sources of interest were to turn out to be wholly independent, there would still be no relevant distinction between the different ways in which a belief can fail to be true. For the for-its-own-sake interest is surely an interest in *truth*: what we aim at is to build up our stock of correct representations of reality, and to avoid placing into that collection any which are not correct. A statement involving an uninstantiated definite description is just as much to be avoided, in this respect, as one which succeeds in referring but mis-attributes a property. We do not have any separate interest in collecting false representations which might leave room for a set of statements belonging to neither collection.

Since the practical and for-its-own-sake interests are the only direct sources of significance of the true/false classification, it follows that Wittgenstein is correct: there is no room for a proposition to be neither true nor false.[8] On the contrary, since both sources of interest are directed at truth, it is this notion which is primary, falsehood being characterisable as merely the absence of truth. However, this argument for Excluded Third makes essential appeal to human interests and purposes. In which case, despite its success in establishing that we do in fact operate with a notion of truth which is primary, it cannot show that Excluded Third must govern any system of representation whatever.

(E) A biographical language-game

I can see no way of validating Excluded Third except as we have done, by reference to the purposes underlying the true/false distinction. Nor can I see how one could characterise those purposes in such a way that they would not turn out to depend upon contingent human interests. This then undermines the supposed unavoidability of Excluded Third.[9] We may have shown that no proposition as used by us can be neither true nor false. But how is this to show what Wittgenstein clearly believes, that no proposition in any conceivable system of representations could be neither true nor false? Not only has this not yet been established, but we can surely conceive of at least a limited system of representation, of the sort which

Wittgenstein was later to characterise as 'a language-game', for which Excluded Third would fail.

Imagine a community of people who have a distinctive style of definite article which is only ever employed in constructions like 'The first-born of John and Mary', 'The second-born of Peter and Susan' and so on – and then only when the person involved is believed to be dead. During their life-time people are referred to by name or by means of ordinary descriptions, the special description-operator being employed for the first time on the occasion of their funeral. These descriptions then form part of a language-game of biography-telling, which we can imagine to hold a central place in the social life of the community. The game consists in the telling of facts about the dead, points being scored (either literally, or in terms of social esteem) for facts which the others did not previously know. We can imagine that much of the leisure-time of these people is taken up with researching obscure and interesting facts about their dead fellows. Perhaps they see it as a kind of honouring, a kind of remembrance. But we may suppose heavy penalties (either loss of game-points, or lowering of social esteem) attach to the making of assertions which can be shown to be false of the individual described. This is partly as an inducement to careful research, and partly as a deterrent against fabrication.

Here we have a language-game in which separate consequences attach to truth and to falsehood. Interesting truths receive rewards, whereas false-hoods attract penalties. Note also that it has no connections with action. We may suppose that the community in question never have occasion to act on their biographical beliefs, except in the making of assertions and in researching further biographical facts. Their interest in truth and false-hood, with respect to sentences involving the special descriptions, is wholly non-practical. Then it is easy to imagine that within this language-game propositions may be allowed to be neither true nor false. In particu-lar, if it is found that one of the descriptions current in the community is in fact uninstantiated (either because one of the names involved lacks a bearer, or because the named couple did not have the appropriate number of children), then the whole game of assertions and denials which has taken place with the use of that description is regarded as aborted, all rewards and penalties being rescinded. For the whole interest of the game for them lies in the discovery of truth or falsehood about historical indi-viduals. Falsehood, in this context, has to involve the misattribution of a property to an actual person. A sentence containing an uninstantiated description is not treated as false (which would entail a penalty), but rather as not properly belonging to the game: as neither true nor false.

Thus, so far from necessarily governing all language and thought, Excluded Third is in fact dependent upon contingent features of the system of representation which we happen to employ. Its validity derives from our two main sources of interest in the true/false classification – both practical and for-its-own-sake – being directed exclusively at truth. But we can imagine different sources of possible interest which would motivate other ways of drawing the true/false distinction, leaving room for the idea of a proposition being neither the one nor the other. I therefore conclude that Wittgenstein may be right, as against Frege, that Excluded Third is in fact a valid and exceptionless principle of our language. But Frege is correct at least in this, that Excluded Third would not necessarily have to govern any conceivable system of representation whatever.

Summary

We have seen how Bivalence may depend upon a conjunction of logical objectivism and Excluded Third. The former of these has some claim to be essential to the very notion of representation. But the latter principle can only be validated by reference to the kind of interest which we happen to take in the true/false classification.

12　Simples and logical objectivism

In this chapter I shall present the argument for Simples which constitutes my preferred interpretation. It both fits the text of *TLP* very well and is powerful in its own right.

(A) The argument

In Chapter 10 we saw how a valid argument for Simples could be premised upon Excluded Third. But then in Chapter 11 it emerged that this principle is incapable of bearing such weight. Now in fact a similar argument can be constructed which has no need to rely upon Excluded Third. As before, it begins by insisting that an understanding of general propositions pre-supposes an understanding of singular ones.

There must be a class of genuinely singular propositions – that is to say, a class of propositions of the form 'Fb', whose understanding does not in any way presuppose a grasp of the concept of generality. Now suppose that the object referred to by 'b' has only contingent existence, so that there is a possible world w in which b does not exist. What is to become of the truth-value of 'Fb' with respect to world w? Obviously it does not express a truth about that world. There are then only two remaining possibilities: either it is false, or it is neither true nor false. But either way we cannot, if we are logical objectivists, allow this to be settled at a later stage (that is, in world w). If the non-existence of b would render the proposition false, then this must have been determined from the start; it must somehow have been implicit in the sense of 'Fb' that it would be false on that condition. But equally if the non-existence of b would render 'Fb' neither true nor false, then this too must have been determined in advance. It could not, as it were, be a matter of accident – of contingent fact – that the proposition would be neither true nor false in such circumstances.[1] So either way the sense of 'Fb' must somehow contain within itself a representation of the possible non-existence of b, in order that it may determine that it should be false, or neither true nor false, on that condition. From this point on, the argument proceeds as before: it follows that 'Fb' is not genuinely singular, and that to be such it would have to contain a name of a Simple.

Essentially this same argument may also be presented as follows. If all the objects of reference exist contingently, then what relationship obtains between the singular proposition 'Fb' and the existentially quantified proposition '$\exists x(x = b)$'? Obviously they cannot be logically independent, since if anything is clear it is that the falsity of '$\exists x(x = b)$' would render 'Fb' not true. There can be no question of a singular proposition being true in face of the non-existence of the object referred to. So by contraposition, the truth of 'Fb' must imply the truth of '$\exists x(x = b)$'. But then given the thesis that the truth-conditions of a proposition must be determined by its sense in advance of anything empirical (the requirement of determinacy-in-advance), it follows that it must already have been contained in the sense of 'Fb' that its truth would require the truth of '$\exists x(x = b)$'. In which case grasp of the sense of any singular proposition would involve an implicit understanding of the concept of existence. But this is impossible: if it were really the case, then it would be impossible that the sense of any general proposition (or indeed of any proposition, since all singular propositions would themselves presuppose a grasp of generality) should ever be intelligibly explained. It therefore follows that some objects of reference must be non-contingent: Simples exist.

It will aid clarity to set out the argument in the form of numbered premisses, thus:

(1)   There must be a class of genuinely singular propositions, which do not presuppose a prior grasp of generality.

(2)   The truth-conditions of a proposition must be completely determined, in advance of anything empirical, by the sense of that proposition alone.

(3)   Suppose that all the objects referred to by the propositions in (1) are contingent.

(C1) Then there are possible worlds in which those things do not exist.

(4)   With respect to such worlds the propositions in (1) would fail to be true.

(C2) So, from (4), the existence of the objects referred to would be a condition for the truth of each singular proposition.

(C3) So, from (2) and (C2), the senses of those propositions must contain a representation of existence.

(5)   This conflicts with the hypothesis of genuine singularity.

(C4)   So there must exist a class of objects of reference whose existence is
not contingent.

Here at last is an extremely powerful argument for the existence of
Simples.[2] Each of the premisses can easily seem undeniable (certainly (4)
and (5) are mere truisms) and the argument itself is clearly valid. We shall
return to considerations of Charity in Section (C), asking if the argument
is really as strong as it looks. But we must first discuss whether there is any
textual basis for believing Wittgenstein to have endorsed it.

(B) The argument and the text

Let us begin by considering the evidence that Wittgenstein accepted the
main premisses of the argument. We have already noted in Chapter 10 that
there is considerable evidence for his acceptance of premiss (1), deriving
both from the foundational role given to elementary propositions within
the semantic system of *TLP*, and from his explicit statement at 4.411 that
the understanding of general propositions depends upon the understanding of singular ones. There are, however, a number of passages where he
suggests that all the logical constants including the quantifiers are already
contained in the elementary propositions. (See for example 5.47.) This
seems to pull in the opposite direction. But in fact the best interpretation
of these passages is consistent with the hierarchical approach to language
expressed in premiss (1). What he is getting at is expressed elsewhere in the
claim that the logical connectives do not 'go proxy' (4.0312, 5.4), which is
to say that they do not describe elements of reality over and above what is
mentioned in the elementary propositions. It is expressed also in the claim
that a complete assignment of truth-values to the elementary propositions
is a complete description of a possible world (4.26). And it is entirely consistent with these claims that the senses of the sentential connectives and
quantifiers should only be explicable on the basis of a prior understanding
of the elementary propositions, as premiss (1) of our argument states.

Premiss (2) of our argument is of course accepted by Wittgenstein; for it
is none other than the main strand in the requirement of determinacy of
Sinn, and is an aspect of his logical objectivism. There is no direct textual
evidence of Wittgenstein's endorsement of our other premisses. But then
they hardly make any new substantive claims, beyond the obvious one that
'Fb' cannot be true with respect to circumstances in which the object b does
not exist. They really just summarise the main moves in the derivation of
the conclusion from premisses (1) and (2).

The fact that Wittgenstein equates the requirement that simple signs be possible with the requirement of determinacy of *Sinn* (3.23) is readily intelligible if we see him as endorsing the argument above. For as we saw in Chapter 5 from our study of the relevant passages in *NB*, there is a strong case for interpreting the requirement of determinacy of *Sinn* to be the requirement that the truth-conditions of a proposition must be fixed in advance of anything empirical by the sense of the proposition alone; and this is precisely premiss (2) of our argument, which carries the main burden of the proof, as we shall see in Section C below.[3] Indeed, it is a powerful reason for attributing the argument above to Wittgenstein that it explains why he should see such a close connection between the argument to Simples and the requirement of determinacy, without our having to construe the latter requirement implausibly widely (as did the Russellian argument of Chapter 10), or implausibly weakly (as did the argument from sharpness in Chapter 9).

TLP 2.0211 can also be seen to make ready sense. Let the phrase 'whether a proposition has *Sinn*' be speaking quite generally about any proposition whatever. And let the 'other proposition' be one which describes the way in which human beings respond to their linguistic training (or whatever proposition describes how propositions determine their truth-conditions if logical objectivism is false). Then 2.0211 can be understood to say this:

If there were no Simples, then whether any proposition had truth-conditions would depend upon the truth of a further proposition describing the manner in which speakers respond to their linguistic training.[4] (Hence the requirement of determinacy-in-advance would be breached.)

This meshes exactly with the argument from logical objectivism above, if we suppose that Wittgenstein regarded the other premisses as truistic. And given the strength of the case which can be built up in support of logical objectivism, it is entirely intelligible that he should go on to say, as he does at 2.0212, that it would follow that we could not sketch any picture of the world, true or false. For there is a case for saying that logical objectivism is essential to any representation whatever, without which there could be no truth or falsity.

(C) Can the argument be avoided?

Notice, to begin with, that we cannot reject premiss (1) by denying that it is necessary to explain our concepts at all, embracing some form of innatism instead. For that premiss does not relate primarily to the teaching of concepts, but rather to the logical orderings which exist between them. The claim is that the truth-condition of a quantified proposition depends upon the truth-conditions of atomic propositions, but not vice versa. So it would be impossible to understand general propositions if one did not already understand some non-general ones; and it would be impossible to explain the quantifiers to someone who did not already understand some atomic propositions. But it is not implied that concepts do actually need to be taught.

Notice also that we cannot hope to avoid the argument by according demonstratives pride of place over proper names. It is indeed plausible that the most fundamental forms of atomic proposition, logically prior to those involving proper names, are those in which a predicate is applied to an object picked out ostensively.[5] So it is also plausible that one might be able to explain quantification to someone who did not yet understand any proper names, if they were nevertheless capable of understanding such propositions as 'This butterfly is valuable.' But none of this helps us to block the argument to Simples. For what of the possibility that the object picked out by ostension (this butterfly) had never existed? Our understanding of the ostensive proposition somehow determines what is to be said in the face of such a possibility. And it is obvious at least that the proposition would fail to be true with respect to such a possibility. So we have no option, if we are logical objectivists, but to say that the sense of the ostensive proposition must somehow contain a representation of the existence of the object, since this is a condition for its truth. In which case it too will fail to be genuinely singular. Anyone understanding it will require at least an implicit grasp of the concept of generality.

It is also worth noting here that one cannot hope to avoid the argument to Simples through the sort of quasi-Russellian hybrid which has recently become fashionable.[6] On this view, propositions like 'This butterfly is valuable' are genuinely Fregean: they represent their objects (the butterfly) in a particular way, containing a mode of thinking about (rather than direct reference to) their objects. But they are also Russellian, in that if the butterfly in question were to fail to exist, the proposition could not exist either. Those who take such a view might hope to deny that the sense of 'This butterfly is valuable' need contain a representation of the possible non-existence of the butterfly, on the grounds that were such a possibility to be realised then the proposition would not be false, or neither true nor false, but would fail to exist altogether. Yet once again this would be to ignore the distinction between the status of a proposition *within* a given possible world (in this case, non-existent), and the status of a proposition *with respect to* a given possible world (in this case, at least not true). If we were to ask, concerning the proposition-in-this-world 'This butterfly is valuable', what its truth-value would be with respect to a world in which the butterfly in question had never existed, then the unavoidable answer is: 'Not true'. In which case the argument proceeds as before: it looks as if the proposition must somehow contain a representation of the existence of its object, and thus be debarred from genuine singularity.

One way of blocking the argument would be to reject premiss (1), by giving up the assumption of semantic hierarchy (or semantic foundationalism) which it contains. We could embrace instead some version of semantic holism, arguing that atomic and general propositions each presuppose grasp of the other. On such a view the idea of a step-by-step explanation of the various forms of proposition is not only not obligatory, but actually impossible. The only way of coming to grasp the various concepts involved would be by total immersion in a linguistic practice, with light dawning gradually over the whole.

Some degree of semantic holism must be acceptable on any view. No one could understand a predicate without understanding some referring expression, and no one could understand just a single proposition without also understanding some similar, related, propositions.[7] But the above thesis goes well beyond this in claiming that the senses of whole classes of proposition are mutually interdependent. Indeed, the strongest version of semantic holism holds that language is a seamless web, no part of which can be grasped in isolation from the others.[8] Now, this strong thesis is in fact inconsistent with logical objectivism, since it leaves no room for propositions to have determinate content, or to stand in determinate logical relations with one another. But there remains the possibility of a weaker thesis, restricting itself to the claim that one cannot fully understand either atomic or general propositions without understanding the other.

The thesis of Semantic Hierarchy is an intuitively attractive one, especially for anyone who takes as their guide (as Russell and Wittgenstein no doubt did) the standard modes of introducing the various logical operators. For in logic one takes for granted an understanding of a class of atomic propositions, and explains on that basis the sentential connectives and quantifiers. But once Semantic Hierarchy is challenged, it is by no means easy to find arguments in its support. Certainly one cannot in this context appeal to the actual modes of teaching natural languages, claiming that pupils in fact grasp the idea of reference to individuals (including parents, siblings and the family dog) before acquiring the concept of generality. For the argument to Simples is designed precisely to show that such apparently singular propositions are not genuinely so. On the contrary, Wittgenstein's view must be that reference to the family dog presupposes generality after all, since the object referred to is contingent.

Consider the following argument, however. Suppose that Wittgenstein were correct that there is a class of necessarily existing individuals. This is at least epistemically possible. Then someone could surely learn to refer to such individuals, and to make atomic statements concerning them, prior to acquiring the concept of existence. Provided they were capable of identifying the appropriate individuals, and knew how to use the various predicates and rational expressions, then we would have no motive for denying them complete understanding of their atomic propositions, despite their inability to frame any sort of existence-statement. In contrast, it is obvious that no one could understand an existence-statement who was incapable of effecting singular reference. What this then shows is that the concepts of singularity and of generality are asymmetric. Since it is epistemically possible that someone should possess the notion of singular reference prior to acquiring the concept of generality but not vice versa, the concept of singular reference itself must be prior to the concept of generality; which is the thesis of Semantic Hierarchy.

If premiss (1) of the argument can be regarded as sufficiently established, and the other premisses are truistic, then the whole weight of the argument comes to fall upon premiss (2), which is the requirement of determinacy-in-advance. It is then worth considering how the argument to Simples might be blocked by its denial.

To reject logical objectivism is to allow that the relationship between a proposition and its truth-condition is not wholly independent of everything empirical.[9] It is to say that no matter how much may have been done to fix the sense of the proposition, there will always be a further (contingent) contribution required from us before the truth-condition is determined. On this view, no explanation of the sense of a sentence can alone fix its truth-condition, since that will also depend upon the way in which we respond to the explanation. And this is, of course, a contingent matter. Equally, a logical relationship between propositions will not consist in a wholly objective connection between their senses. It will rather depend upon the fact that speakers who have been given the usual linguistic training can be brought to accept that they must not believe the one proposition without also believing the other.

Looked at from this perspective, there will be no problem in fixing the truth-conditions of quantified sentences by means of propositions involving references to entities which have only contingent existence. We can begin by explaining the use of sentences having the form 'Fb'. The pupil will be able to manifest at least partial understanding, by successfully identifying the object b in a range of different circumstances, and by making successful applications of the predicate 'Fx'. But at this stage it will be indeterminate whether they have fully understood. For since they lack the conceptual equipment to represent the possibility that the object b might not have existed, we cannot test what they would say about the truth-value of 'Fb' in face of such a possibility. Now, on the basis of their understanding of the atomics we explain the quantifiers to them, and they can manifest that they understand by making the right sorts of deductive moves between general propositions and singular ones. Then, finally, we put to them the possible truth of the proposition 'Not $\exists x(x = b)$', and we may suppose that they regard themselves (without further training) as bound to say that in that case 'Fb' would fail to be true. We can then say that they had understood the proposition 'Fb' correctly all along.

None of the explanations given here would be circular, and there is no reason to think that they could not be successful. The crucial point is that by giving up logical objectivism we could allow that the singular proposition 'Fb' implies the truth of '$\exists x(x = b)$', and thus contains an existence-claim within its truth-condition, without having to think that a representation of the latter condition must somehow be presupposed in a grasp of the former. Rather, the connection between the two will consist in the fact that speakers who have had the senses of both forms of proposition explained to them regard themselves as bound to believe the latter if they believe the former.

(D) Is the argument a *reductio*?

The argument for Simples which we outlined in Section A seems to depend, ultimately, upon Wittgenstein's logical objectivism. Yet the conclusion is an extraordinary one. Not only are we asked to believe in a class of necessarily existing individuals, but we are also required to accept that they are (somehow or other) what our ordinary statements are really about, reference to them forming the foundation of all language and thought. Now, is this merely very surprising, or is it actually incoherent? That is to say, are we obliged to turn the argument to Simples into a *reductio*, using the absurdity of the conclusion to derive the falsehood of logical objectivism? Is the argument by itself sufficient to reveal a basic flaw in the system of thought of *TLP*?

If reference to Simples forms the basis of all language and thought, then how is it that none of us is aware of referring to them? How is it that we cannot even provide an example of a Simple? There are in fact two closely related problems here, each threatening *TLP* with incoherence. Firstly, how is it possible to refer to a thing without being aware that one is doing so, in such a way that one would, literally, not know what one was talking about? Secondly, how can it be a logical constraint upon the adequacy of explanations of the quantifiers that they be given on the basis of propositions involving reference to Simples, and yet no such explanations are ever given? The first sentences which a child learns will involve reference to such manifestly contingent entities as its parents and the family dog, and general propositions are seemingly explained on that basis. So are we to suppose that the child has already, without prior training, been referring to Simples it its thoughts?

The first difficulty is rather easily dealt with, since there will only be a problem here if 'Mary is talking about x' implies 'Mary knows that she is talking about x.' For only if this implication holds will the fact that we are none of us aware of referring to Simples entail that we are not in fact doing so, thus conflicting with the theory of *TLP*. But the implication fails, because the context created by the phrase 'talk about . . . ' is transparent, whereas that created by the phrase 'knows that . . . ' is opaque. Thus if Mary says, while watching a broadcast of a speech by Ronald Reagan, 'That old man looks as if he was once an actor', then it is true that she is talking about Reagan. And since Reagan was once President of the United States, it is also true that she is talking about an ex-President. But Mary need not know that she is talking about Ronald Reagan, or that he was once President. So from the fact that we none of us know that we are talking about Simples, it does not follow that we are not in fact doing so.

In order to deal with the second difficulty, we need only distinguish between the constraint that a certain mode of explanation be possible, and the constraint that it be actual. Wittgenstein would presumably say that the question how people actually acquire a grasp of their language is an empirical matter, and no business of the philosopher.[10] It may be that linguistic understanding is innate, or that it is acquired by some sort of miracle (that is to say, inexplicably). What *is* of legitimate philosophical concern is the manner in which our concepts are logically embedded in one another to form an hierarchy, with complex concepts containing simpler ones within their conditions of application. Whether any speaker ever actually acquires their grasp of complex concepts by first having the simpler ones explained to them and then having the complex ones explained to them on that basis may be an irrelevant empirical question. But it is an *a priori* constraint that it should at least be *possible* for someone to acquire their concepts in this way. For if this were not possible, it could only be because no one could understand the 'simpler' concepts who did not already understand the 'complex' ones, which would contradict the initial thesis about the manner in which they are embedded in one another.

Thus it may in fact be the case that people acquire their grasp of quantification − somewhat mysteriously − as a result of total immersion in a linguistic practice, rather than step by step on the basis of a prior grasp of singular propositions. Indeed, this is perhaps not implausible as a description of what actually happens. For one does not, in general, give children definitions, of any sort. One simply talks to them. (Compare 3.263.) All that Wittgenstein's argument requires is that it must be *possible* to acquire a grasp of the quantifiers on the basis of a prior understanding of propositions referring to Simples. And this will only be possible (given logical objectivism) if Simples do indeed exist.[11]

Note also that to say, as Wittgenstein does, that all our propositions are actually truth-functions of elementary ones involving reference to Simples is not to say anything about what is going on in our thoughts, or about the manner in which the truth-conditions of our propositions are actually determined (that is to say, their senses). As we saw in Chapter 7, it is merely to claim that all propositions are logically equivalent to some possible truth-function of elementary ones. For recall from Chapter 1 that the *TLP* view is that the criterion of identity for semantic content is logical equivalence.

Summary

There is no obvious incoherence in the *TLP* doctrine of the existence of Simples. Yet there is a powerful argument in its support, premised upon the requirement of determinacy-in-advance (more generally, logical objectivism), which also provides us with the best available interpretation of the crucial passages in the text. It is therefore not unreasonable to regard Wittgenstein as having discovered a proof of the existence of Simples, in the absence of a direct refutation of logical objectivism.[12]

13   *Independent elementary propositions*

Our task in this chapter is to see why Wittgenstein should have insisted that the elementary propositions which constitute the end-point of analysis must be logically independent of one another.

(A) Preliminaries

The independence requirement is mentioned at four different points in *TLP*. Twice it occurs in the material mode, stated in terms of the independence of the states of affairs which elementary propositions describe (1.21, 2.061). Then at 4.211 it is said to be a mark of a proposition's being elementary that there can be no elementary proposition which contradicts it. Finally, 6.3751 makes essentially the same point in the context of a discussion of colour-exclusion. However, in none of these cases does a study of the surrounding remarks throw any light on Wittgenstein's motives. Nor can we look to *NB* for any explicit guidance, since the independence requirement receives no mention there. Yet he must surely have had some powerful reason for insisting upon it, since he is prepared to do so in advance of being able to give any examples of elementary propositions. Indeed, it is far from obvious that the requirement can possibly be complied with.

There is just one other remark in *TLP* which suggests a possible interpretation. This is 5.152, which tells us that any two elementary propositions will give one another a probability of ½. When taken in the context of the theory of objective probability developed in the 5.15s, this implies that elementary propositions must be logically independent of one another.[1] Now, as Wittgenstein himself says, his theory of probability is founded on an identification of the trio 'necessary', 'possible' and 'impossible' with 'truth-functional tautology', 'truth-functional contingency' and 'truth-functional contradiction' respectively (4.464, 5.1), which itself presupposes the independence requirement if taken with full generality. So if we could construct an argument supporting such an identification it would at the same time provide an explanation of the independence requirement.

(B) Displaying necessity

Throughout the 6.1s we find Wittgenstein explaining and arguing for his thesis that the propositions of logic are tautologies. Now by 'logic' here he does not just mean 'formal logic' – logic in the narrow sense; though this is certainly part of what he has in mind.[2] Rather, by a proposition of logic he means any conceptually necessary proposition. This is in line with the use of 'logic' and 'logical' throughout the rest of *TLP*, where he generally has in mind any internal or conceptual relationship (see, for example, 2.0121, 4.015, 4.023, 4.1213, and indeed the very title of *TLP* itself). In any case, if read in this light we can see the 6.1s as providing arguments for the thesis that all necessity is truth-functional, and hence as providing reasons for the independence requirement.

Wittgenstein insists that it must be possible to recognise a proposition of logic from the symbol alone – that is to say, from our knowledge of its sense (6.113, 6.126). In part this reiterates his view that logic is epistemologically prior to metaphysics, discussed in Chapters 2 and 3 above. Since it is unintelligible that we should have to read off our knowledge of the necessity of a proposition from a prior acquaintance with the metaphysical necessities which hold in the world, it must rather derive from seeing, from our knowledge of the senses of the terms involved, that the proposition is constructed in such a way as to be true come what may. But he also wants to insist upon something more: that it must be possible to *display* the sense of the necessary proposition in such a way that its status as necessary will be manifest.[3] For 6.122 implies that it must be possible to construct notations in which we can discern that a proposition is necessary by mere inspection, as we can in the case of truth-tables.

We can begin to see what Wittgenstein has in mind here if we reflect upon another strand in the discussion in the 6.1s, namely his rejection of axiomatic approaches to logic (which now means 'logic' narrowly conceived of). He insists against Frege and Russell that there is a sense in which all the propositions of logic are on an equal footing, each one showing in and of itself that it is necessary (6.126, 6.127). Moreover, the role of proof in logic is merely psychological, enabling us to recognise necessary propositions in complicated cases (6.126). The claim is that the notion of proof of a complex proposition from simpler cases should only enter into an account of the epistemology of logic, not into an account of what logic *is*.

Wittgenstein's remark at 6.1271, expressing surprise that a thinker 'as rigorous as Frege' should appeal to degree of self-evidence as the mark of a proposition of logic, is pertinent here. For it can indeed be said that for Frege a necessary truth gets characterised as one which follows from self-evident truths by means of self-evident principles of inference.[4] But this is to introduce into the characterisation of logic just the sort of psychologism which Frege himself is so resolute in rejecting elsewhere. For how can one continue to believe in the objectivity of logic – maintaining that a proposition's status as necessary is independent of facts about the human mind – while yet holding it to be constitutive of a truth of logic that it should either strike us as obvious, or be derivable from truths which strike us as obvious by means of principles of inference which strike us as obvious?

Since Wittgenstein, like Frege, is committed to the objectivity of logic as well as the epistemological priority of logic over metaphysics, he has no option but to say that logical truths hold in virtue of relations between concepts (senses), appealing to intuition only in accounting for our knowledge of what those concepts require of us in particular cases. But then since these relationships are objective, and not in any way constituted by our intuitions, it must surely be possible to provide them with a semantic validation: setting out the relevant concepts in an analysis, in such a way that those relationships can be seen to depend only upon them. It is just such a validation that Wittgenstein is able to provide, in the case of logic narrowly conceived of, by means of his truth-table notation. This enables him to display a truth of logic in such a way that its truth manifestly depends only on the senses of the propositional connectives and their mode of combination.

Here is part of the reason, at least, why Wittgenstein should insist that the elementary propositions must be independent of one another. For if they were not, there would be a class of necessary truths which could not be exhibited as truth-functional tautologies; and yet how else could they receive their semantic validation? For example, if 'This is red' and 'This is green' were really elementary, then there would apparently be no way of explaining the necessary status of 'Not both: this is red and this is green'. But there must be something about the concepts *red* and *green* in virtue of which they exclude one another; their mutual exclusion cannot simply consist in the fact that anyone who grasps them intuitively rejects the admissibility of describing a surface as both 'red' and 'green' at once.[5] Rather, such intuitions must reflect an awareness of the inner structure of the concepts *red* and *green* themselves. Yet if 'This is red' were elementary the concept *red* would possess no inner structure. For to say that a proposition is elementary is precisely to say that the concepts involved in it admit of no further analysis.

This argument for the logical independence of elementary propositions thus turns fundamentally upon three premises: logical objectivism, the epistemological priority of logic over metaphysics, and the plausible thought that if two propositions are inconsistent with one another, then this must reflect the structures (hidden or explicit) of those propositions themselves. Of course Wittgenstein was later to attempt to explain inconsistencies between elementary propositions by means of the idea of an holistic system of concepts, all of which are involved whenever any one of its members is applied to anything (thus denying the third of the above premises – see *PR* 82–6). We shall return to this idea in Section D below. But first we shall explore a rather different way of approaching the independence requirement.

(C) Reducing necessity

Notice that on the *TLP* account a necessary truth is a truth about all possible worlds. For on the one hand, all necessary truths are characterised as truth-functional tautologies of elementary propositions (5, 5.1, 6.1). Yet on the other, to fix the sense of one elementary proposition is at the same time to fix the sense of all (5.524). Moreover, the elementary propositions can be used to describe reality completely: an assignment of truth-values to each one of them would constitute a complete description of the world (4.26). Indeed, since the objects with which these propositions deal are constituents of all possible worlds, all possible worlds may be described by means of such assignments (2.0124). Then since a tautology is a sentence which is true for all assignments of truth-values to its component elementary propositions, it will of course be true for all assignments of truth-values to the whole set of elementary propositions. So it will be a truth about all possible worlds.

Now, the important point here is this: because (and only because) the elementary propositions are logically independent of one another, Wittgenstein has to hand the materials for a reductive account of necessity. He can explain necessary truth as truth about all possible worlds (true for all assignments of truth-values to the set of elementary propositions) without taking for granted any modal notions. His account of the concept is then genuinely explanatory, in that it in no way presupposes what was to be explained: the notion of necessity. Contrast with this any attempt to explain necessity in terms of a notion of a possible world not fixed by means of a set of mutually independent elementary propositions. For example, suppose that the language contains as elementary the sentence 'This surface is red' and 'This surface is green.' Then in order to recognise that an assignment of 'True' to both of them fails to constitute a part-description of a possible world, we should have to rely on our knowledge that the concepts *red* and *green* logically exclude one another. But this would be to take for granted the very notion of necessity we were supposed to be explaining.

It might be objected that Wittgenstein's account, too, presupposes an understanding of a modal notion, since it is given in terms of assignments of truth-values to a class of propositions characterised as logically independent. But here we need to distinguish between the fact that those propositions are logically independent of one another, on the one hand, and what would be required for an understanding of them on the other. Someone could surely have a complete grasp of their senses while having neither an implicit nor an explicit grasp of the notion of necessity. In contrast, no one could understand sentences involving the words 'red' and 'green' who was not prepared to reject *a priori* the admissibility of describing an object as being red and green all over. An ability to see the mutual incompatibility of the colour-terms is a criterion for their proper understanding. We are not required to see this as such, perhaps, since we may as yet have no word for 'incompatible'; but we must at least refuse to accept the description 'is red all over and green all over'. So anyone who understands a language containing such terms will already have an implicit grasp of the notion of necessity, in a way that someone who understands the sort of elementary propositions envisaged in *TLP* would not. Thus Wittgenstein's account – and only such an account – would put one in a position to explain the concept of necessity to someone completely *ab initio*.

It may be helpful at this point to compare the *TLP* account of necessity with the form of analysis provided in contemporary modal logic, specifically in Model Theory.[6] This, too, takes as basic the idea of a set of atomic propositions in terms of which one could provide a complete description of reality; but without the requirement of logical independence. A 'model' for the language is then defined as being any sub-set of the set of all assignments of truth-values to the elementary propositions. The notion of necessity is then defined relative to a model, by saying that $\Box A$ = True for a given assignment of truth-values within a model, if and only if A = True for every assignment in the model. Note that this account neither mentions nor implicitly relies upon a prior grasp of the notion of necessity. For there is nothing to require that a model should be a set of assignments of truth-values to the atomics which is actually possible. Indeed, many models for a given language will in fact be impossible.

Someone could understand and work with the above definition of '□' who had no prior grasp of any modal notion. Given only a formal description of a language and a set of assignments of truth-values to its atomic sentences, they would be able to apply the definition. But for this very reason □ must fail to capture our notion of necessity, since the two notions will not even be co-extensive. Thus '□A' will come out as true relative to certain models where 'Necessarily A' would either be false or nonsensical. For example, '□ Mrs Thatcher is red all over and green all over' will be true relative to some models of English; yet it is hardly necessary. The best one could do would be to provide someone with an operator co-extensive with 'necessary' by giving the above definition of '□' and then presenting them with a model for English which is actually correct, which in fact describes the set of all possible worlds. But this could hardly succeed in conveying our notion of necessity. For there can be nothing in the explanation which picks out the model as special. So far as the trainee is concerned, it is simply one set of assignments of truth-values among others.

What this means is that contemporary Model Theory fails as a reductive account of necessity. This is not to say that it does nothing valuable. On the contrary, it can be seen as explicating a large part of our conception of necessity. It also has the great advantage of enabling us to use our firmly entrenched understanding of the rules governing the existential and universal quantifiers in working out the principles which govern necessity. (For example, the move from '□A' to '◇A' gets validated as the move from 'True for all assignments in the model' to 'True for some assignment in the model'.) But the *TLP* account would have all of these advantages as well as providing us with a reductive analysis.

Wittgenstein's independence requirement would then be very attractive if it could be complied with; but we have yet to show that it must be possible to comply with it. The fact that the existence of a class of logically independent elementary propositions would enable one to give an *ab initio* explanation of necessity provides us with no reason to think that there must be such a class, unless there is some reason for thinking that it must be possible to give such an explanation. So the real question which needs to be asked is what reason there is for thinking that an eliminative definition of necessity is even so much as possible.

We might wonder whether the motivation behind a reductive account is ontological. Might Wittgenstein's demand be to show that necessity is not an element of the real world, just as he wishes to show that the logical constants (*and*, *or* and the rest) do not belong to the world? Is the idea that a complete but a-modal description of reality would show that modality is not genuinely there in the world? This is not a very promising interpretation. For on no account of the matter does 'necessary' function as the name of a supposed kind of thing. It is more naturally treated as a predicate of sentences. And as we saw in Chapter 1, Wittgenstein in any case wishes to deny that predicates have reference.[7]

Nor, on the face of it, does it appear very plausible to suggest that the line of thought is this: if it were to prove impossible to give a genuinely eliminative account of necessity, then one could never explain that concept to someone who had not already grasped it. For the natural response to this is precisely to deny that any concept-user could ever be without a grasp of necessity. On the contrary, perhaps that concept must be implicit in a grasp of concepts from the start; perhaps it is a primitive concept, having to be introduced alongside the other basic concepts that a person learns. But on reflection this natural response turns out to be inadequate, and the line of thought suggested above can be seen to be a powerful one. The crucial consideration is that the concept of necessity is meta-linguistic (or better, meta-conceptual), thus requiring that some concepts have already been successfully introduced before it in turn can be explained.

Recall that for logical objectivists conceptually necessary truths reflect objective relations between concepts (senses). It is but a trivial step from this to the idea that a necessary truth is *about* (involving reference to) concepts. Then a truth such as 'Necessarily nothing can be simultaneously red and green all over' should properly be construed as saying something like 'The concepts *red* and *green* mutually exclude one another.' How then could someone come to possess the concept of necessity – involving as it does reference to concepts – unless they already possessed some concepts to refer to? It would surely be viciously circular to claim that a notion involving reference to concepts could itself be presupposed to a grasp of those concepts themselves. In which case some concepts at least must be apprehensible prior to any grasp of the notion of necessity; which is as much as to say that there has to be a class of mutually independent elementary propositions.

It might be objected against this line of thought that, powerful or not, it cannot be correct to attribute it to Wittgenstein. For of course the *TLP* view is that necessity is not a genuine (*Sinn*-determining) concept, but is rather a formal one. Since the status of a proposition as necessary is a feature of that proposition itself, his claim is that the attempt to assert its necessity will only result in nonsense (4.124, 4.125). How then can his main concern have been to provide a reductive account of necessity, if he believes that there is in reality no such concept? How can the point of the independence requirement have been to enable us to fix the sense of 'necessary' in a non-circular manner, if he thinks that the term is in fact nonsensical?

Although strictly correct, these points fail to undermine the interpretation. The official *TLP* doctrine of necessity-as-nonsense should no more prevent us from seeing Wittgenstein as trying to provide an account of the notion, than the official line that 'proposition', too, is a formal concept should stop us seeing him as trying to characterise the general propositional form (see 6). For the official doctrine merely reflects his account of what it is to say something, which is in fact violated systematically throughout *TLP* – and rightly so, as I argued briefly in Chapter 1.

(D) Doing without independence

We have now sketched two different arguments for the independence requirement. The first is that it must be possible to provide an articulation of that in virtue of which two incompatible concepts exclude one another, coupled with the plausible thought that such an account must in the end be truth-functional in form. The second is that it must be possible to provide a non-circular explanation of the notion of necessity, thus requiring us to generate a description of the set of all possible worlds without taking any modal notions for granted. Yet clearly there would have to be something wrong with each of these arguments if, as seems possible, the independence requirement cannot be complied with. Our immediate task is to find out what.

Consider first of all our second argument, from the possibility of reductive explanation. In fact this ultimately turns on the *TLP* account of the essence of communication, and of what it is to say something. For the only reason we have for denying that it is possible to explain the concept of necessity to someone on the basis of their grasp of a set of propositions which are not logically independent is that the idea of necessity is already presupposed in (entailed by) what they know. Recall that on the *TLP* account of semantic content 'Nothing is red and green all over' would say the very same as 'Necessarily: nothing is red and green all over' (because they are logically equivalent). That is why one could not explain the latter on the basis of an understanding of the former: they say the very same thing. But if we reject the ubiquity of this account of semantic content, as I urged in Chapter 1 that we should, then the argument collapses. We can allow that necessity is meta-conceptual, involving reference to some already-existing concepts, while still explaining it to someone on the basis of their grasp of concepts which necessarily exclude one another. For lacking as yet any explicit notion of necessity, they will not have realised that this is so. Indeed, it is precisely this that our explanation would bring them to see.[8]

What, then, of our first argument: the insistence that the grounds for any necessary truth be articulable? Here we need to consider what account might be given of the necessity of colour-exclusion, supposing that sentences such as 'This is red' and 'This is green' were genuinely elementary. As we mentioned earlier, on his return to philosophy in the late twenties Wittgenstein put forward an account according to which applying any one colour concept involves the application of all; individual colour concepts being like the marks on a ruler. Then in the same way that laying a ruler against an object and seeing that it is a particular length automatically implies that it is not any of the other lengths, so laying the whole colour system against an object, and judging that it is red, implies automatically that it is not green. Thus the idea is that by showing the colour concepts to be essentially part of a colour system, or colour space, we can exhibit the grounds for the necessity of colour-exclusion without having to subject the individual colour concepts to analysis.

Even if we grant Wittgenstein what is in fact far from obvious – that the understanding of any single colour concept presupposes an understanding of all[9] – the proposed solution will not work. For all it does is to explain colour-exclusion in terms of spatial-exclusion ('a boundary cannot be at two places on a ruler at once'). But this is equally problematic, if sentences ascribing spatial positions to objects are regarded as elementary. For in virtue of what is it necessary that an object cannot be in two distinct places at once? How are we to exhibit this necessity as flowing from the nature of the concepts involved? Of course one might reply that spatial position is the criterion for individuating physical objects; and this is no doubt correct. But then it is precisely to say that the concept of an individual object is analysable in such a way as to explain the necessity of 'a given object cannot be in two distinct places at once'. And there is no prospect of finding within that analysis a parallel principle for colours, since it is of course possible for a physical object to have no colour (to be transparent). So to say that the colour concepts are individually unanalysable, but are essentially members of a system of such concepts, is as yet to provide no explanation for why a surface cannot have two colours at once.

I can see no way for Wittgenstein to maintain both that there are no purely metaphysical necessities, and that necessity is objective, if it is allowed that there can be mutually inconsistent elementary propositions. Yet each is an essential ingredient in the philosophy of *TLP*. Moreover, the rejection of metaphysical intuition surely stands firm in any case. As already indicated in Chapter 3, I agree with Wittgenstein in finding the idea that our intellects might be such as to provide us with direct access to the metaphysical structure of reality wholly unintelligible. So it looks as if our only option is to give up the objectivity of conceptual necessity – in effect denying logical objectivism. Our account of the necessity of 'Nothing is red and green all over' could then take the sort of form we began to indicate at the end of Chapter 3, somewhat as follows. Having acquired the concepts *red* and *green*, we discover that we find it unimaginable how any surface could satisfy both concepts at once. Now so far this is merely a fact of psychology. But as a result of it we elevate, by convention, the proposition in question to the status of a necessary 'truth' (we 'put it in the archives'), employing it henceforward as a rule of description.[10]

Summary

We have found two distinct arguments for the independence requirement. One is premised on the reducibility, and one on the articulability, of necessity. Each may ultimately be unsound. But the reasons for their failure would lie deep within the structure of *TLP*: respectively, in its account of the identity-conditions for semantic content, and in its logical objectivism.

14 *Modelling elementary propositions*

Our task in this chapter is to provide a model for the elementary propositions of *TLP* which will meet as many as possible of the various constraints on their nature to have emerged from our previous discussions.

(A) Constraints on the model

We can distinguish three distinct kinds of constraint which a completely satisfactory model should meet. Firstly, there are Wittgenstein's explicit claims, which are so clear as to admit of no reinterpretation. No model could even begin to be adequate which did not respect them. We are told that Simples exist in all possible worlds (2.023), that elementary propositions consist only of names of Simples in immediate concatenation (3.2–3.21, 4.22), that elementary propositions are logically independent of one another (4.211, 5.134), and that an assignment of truth-values to all elementary propositions would constitute a complete description of the world (4.26). Many commentators have thought that nothing could even begin to satisfy all of these constraints. We shall show in the next section that they are wrong.

Secondly, there are the further developments of the above claims which are imposed upon us by some of the interpretations adopted earlier. We argued that the Simples of *TLP* are individuals, as opposed to universals (Chapter 1), which not only exist in all possible worlds but at all times in those worlds (Chapter 8). So the Simples in our model should be necessarily existing individuals. Moreover, since this narrow reading of 'object' requires an equally narrow reading of 'name', it will follow that elementary propositions consist only of proper names in immediate concatenation. So unless we were prepared to countenance Sellars' suggestion in his (1962a), that *TLP* allows monadic concatenations (propositions consisting of just a single name), it would be an advantage if our model were also to make clear why Wittgenstein should believe that all elementary propositions will be relational, with none being of subject/predicate form. These additional claims are of course open to reassessment. But since the arguments for attributing them to Wittgenstein are powerful, they too place constraints upon the adequacy of a model for elementary propositions. Only if it were to prove easy to provide a model for the explicit claims without these further developments, but difficult to provide a model which includes them, should we have any reason to look again at our earlier interpretations.

Thirdly, there is the specific problem I explained briefly in Chapter 1 above, concerning Wittgenstein's remark at 4.243 that one could not understand two names without knowing whether their reference was the same or different. This conflicts with my view that the names of *TLP* should be regarded as having senses, unless those names were to be introduced by means of some general rule which would enable a speaker to know *a priori* whether any given pair of names refer to the same or to distinct things. So the final constraint upon our model is that the names involved should be introduced (or be introducable) by means of just such a general rule. Otherwise I shall be forced either to discount 4.243 as an aberration, or to give up my doctrine that *TLP* names have senses.

We have already seen in Chapter 8 that there is a powerful case against taking Simples to be sense-data. For although it would be consistent with this that they should be constituents of all possible worlds, the cost would be to make the resulting doctrines absurd. Moreover, such an interpretation would leave us unable to meet the constraint of logical independence. For if elementary propositions consist of concatenations of names relating the corresponding sense-data to one another within the various sensory fields, then there can be no question of their being logically independent. However, we shall return to the question of phenomenalism in Section D below, showing that it is possible to provide a rather different sort of phenomenalist model for elementary propositions, which would satisfy many of the above constraints. This will then throw much of the weight of our rejection of a phenomenalist reading of *TLP* back on to claims about Wittgenstein's generally realist attitude to metaphysics and lack of interest in epistemology.

Another perennial temptation for interpreters of *TLP* is to picture Simples as being very small physical objects.[1] This is reinforced by the repeated use of the simple/complex contrast, which permeates Wittgenstein's thinking about them. Indeed, he seems, in *NB* at least, to have believed that the analysis of a term referring to a complex object like a table or a watch would be a description of the relations obtaining between its component parts (*NB* 62, 63, 67). Simples would then be physical components which do not themselves have components. But on such a view there could be no question of meeting the constraint of necessary existence. For as we observed in Chapter 9, there is no reason to think that any physical object, no matter how small, is a constituent of all possible worlds. Nor should we be able to meet the constraint of logical independence. For if Simples were physical objects, then some of the elementary propositions would have to describe spatial and temporal relations between them – otherwise there would be important facts left undescribed. But then such propositions could not be logically independent of one another, in virtue of the *a priori* principles that no physical object can be in two places at once, and that no two physical objects can be in the same place at the same time.

(B) The model[2]

Let the names out of which elementary propositions are to be constructed be names of planes of space and points of time, ordered discretely. The planes of space are named in relation to a point of origin, along three different axes at right angles to one another, their names being of three different kinds. Let 'a_{-3}', 'a_{-2}', 'a_0', 'a_1', 'a_2', 'a_3', etc. be names of planes in one axis. Let 'b_{-3}', 'b_{-2}', 'b_{-1}', 'b_0', 'b_1', 'b_2', 'b_3', etc. be names of planes at right angles to the first. And let 'c_{-3}', 'c_{-2}', 'c_{-1}', 'c_0', 'c_1', 'c_2', 'c_3', etc. be names of planes at right angles to each of the first two sorts. The points of time may also be named in relation to an arbitrarily chosen point of origin, taking the form 't_{-3}', 't_{-2}', 't_{-1}', 't_0', 't_1', 't_2', 't_3', and so on. Then let all elementary propositions take the form '$abct$', stating that a point-mass exists at the intersection of planes a, b and c at time t. For example, the proposition '$a_6 b_{-5} c_{16} t_4$' would say that there is a point-mass at the intersection of planes a_6, b_{-5} and c_{16} at time t_4.

Clearly this model stands at least some chance of meeting the requirement of necessary existence. For space and time could plausibly be thought to be constituents of all possible worlds. Moreover, planes of space do not consist of parts, or at least not in a way which would make it sensible to say 'Suppose those parts had never been combined in that way . . . '; for the lines and bands which make up any given plane of space belong to it necessarily. However, in order to meet this requirement in full we should have to take an absolute, as opposed to a relational, view of space and time. For consider the possible world in which there exists no matter whatever prior to time t_{-64}. On a relational theory of time there would be no times prior to t_{-64} in that world. In which case some points of time – for example t_{-66} – would fail to exist in all possible worlds. A similar thesis can be established concerning the contingent existence of planes of space, given a relational theory of space. Only if space and time are absolute, being able to exist in the absence of any material objects and of any change, can the requirement of necessary existence be fully met, on the above model.

The constraint that elementary propositions should consist of proper names in immediate concatenation is satisfied completely. The fact that three individual planes of space and a point of time are related to one another by way of intersecting at a point-mass is depicted by a relation – in this case a significant linear ordering – between their proper names. Indeed, we can even see why Wittgenstein might have been confident that no elementary proposition would be of subject/predicate form, if we suppose him to have had in mind something like our model. For there is nothing significant (contingent) that you can say about a plane of space or a point of time on its own that cannot also be said in terms of the propositions employed in our model.[3]

Most importantly, the model satisfies the requirement that elementary propositions be logically independent. For from the fact that there exists a point-mass at a certain point at a certain time, nothing at all follows about the existence or non-existence of point-masses anywhere else at that time. Nor is anything implied about the existence of point-masses at that or any other point of space at any other time. Indeed, since it is not a necessary truth that any given point-mass should continue to exist from one moment to the next, there are no restrictions whatever on assignments of truth-values to the class of elementary propositions.[4] Moreover, since no attempt is made to name point-masses or to treat them as individuals, there is no way to describe relations between them except by means of truth-functions of the elementary propositions stating their positions.

It might even be plausible to think that a complete assignment of truth-values to the set of elementary propositions would be a complete description of the world. For many have thought that all facts about the world must reduce, in the end, to facts about the distribution of matter in space and time. However, the model would face severe difficulties if we tried to regard it as the end-point of a programme of analysis. For remember that the touch-stone of an adequate analysis, on the *TLP* account, is analytic equivalence. And although there are many philosophers who are materialists, there are few who are analytic materialists.[5] Indeed, such a thesis appears wildly implausible. Although it is possible that such things as pains and sensations of red are, as a matter of fact, events occurring in the human brain, they do not seem to be so as a matter of conceptual necessity. And although it may be true that colours are physical properties of surfaces (capacities for the differential reflection of light), we could hardly have discovered such a thing by conceptual analysis alone. Yet it may be that these problems are not insuperable, only requiring that the model be extended rather than abandoned. We shall consider in Section D below whether our elementary propositions might be developed in such a way as to yield descriptions of colours and mental states without compromising their other features (logical independence, etc.).

Finally, in this catalogue of the virtues of our model, it can be seen how Wittgenstein might have thought that no one could understand two names of Simples without knowing whether their reference was the same or different. For consider the matter in the abstract: suppose there are two different systems of coordinates, in one of which (System A) the point of origin $(a_0b_0c_0t_0)$ is that which is designated as '$a_4b_8c_2t_{16}$' in the other (System B). Then someone who understands both systems of description, and who wishes to know whether or not 'a_{32}' in System A designates the very same plane of space as referred to by 'a_{28}' in System B, will be in a position to work out the answer *a priori*. However, the situation may be a little more complex when we consider how in any actual case a system of coordinates would have to be set up.

Even if space and time are absolute, we can surely only assign names to planes of space and points of time by relating them to the (contingent) positions of physical objects with which we are acquainted, or by relating them to ourselves. So in order to set up an actual system of coordinates we should have to say something like: 'Let the origin be here and now, with planes in the a-axis being in *that* direction, those in the b-axis being in *that* direction, and those in the c-axis being in *that* direction.' But then, of course, we should only be able to keep track of the referents of our names if we made contingent assumptions about the motions over time of ourselves and the physical items around us.[6] And we should only be able to work out whether a name from another system of coordinates – say one centred on the Post Office Tower in London – had the same reference as one of these names if we made assumptions about our own spatial position relative to London. Since we cannot know these motions and relative positions *a priori*, neither can we know *a priori* whether or not the names are co-referential. Our model is thus unable to make complete sense of Wittgenstein's commitment to the transparency of names at 4.243, unless we make the implausible assumption that there can be direct knowledge of planes of space and points of time irrespective of their relation to ourselves or to contingent distributions of matter.[7]

(C) The model and the text

There are two quite different ways of regarding our model. Firstly, we could see it as no more than that: a model, making no claims about what Wittgenstein may or may not have had in mind. It would then be merely an attempt to show that the various constraints which he places upon his elementary propositions are not wildly absurd or inconsistent. In this it succeeds admirably. But secondly, I have suggested that we could attempt to interpret *TLP* as involving our model, or at least something very like it. We might thus try claiming that Wittgenstein had such a model in mind when making his various pronouncements about the nature of elementary propositions. At any rate, it is worth asking whether our model can, in this second role, receive any textual support.

There is only one remark in *TLP* which can be construed as an explicit endorsement of our model. That is 2.0251, which says that space, time and colouredness are forms of objects. But even this is ambiguous. It could mean, as on our model, that space and time (and colour – see section D below) are themselves kinds of object. Or it could mean only that being in space and time and having colour are, necessarily, possible attributes of objects. The former reading is the more plausible, however. For as we have noted many times, there can be no question of physical particles having the sort of necessary existence required of Simples, or of elementary propositions describing spatial relations between such particles being logically independent of one another.

At various places in *NB* Wittgenstein considers the possibility of describing distributions of matter in space by means of a system of coordinates. For example, at *NB* 20–1 he supposes that we might express the fact that the material point P is to be found in place (ab), by means of a proposition of the form '$a_p b_p$'. (He is obviously thinking of descriptions of matter on a two-dimensional surface.) But it is not wholly clear whether he considers the sign '$_p$' here to be the proper name of a particular point-mass (which would immediately make '$a_p b_p$' incompatible with '$a_p c_p$'), or whether it is merely a (redundant) index of the names 'a' and 'b', signifying that there is some point-mass or other at the intersection of the lines they refer to (which would then be very close to our model). However, at least these remarks show that at a fairly early stage (1914) Wittgenstein was contemplating using spatial coordinates to describe the distribution of matter in the world.

A further strong argument for using our model in an interpretational role is that it does enable us to make sense of Wittgenstein's apparent confidence that there will be no elementary propositions of subject/predicate form,[8] as well as his claim that no one could understand two names for Simples without knowing whether their reference is the same or different. But then if he really did have our model in mind, the immediate challenge is to explain why he did not say so. Why, in that case, did he choose to remain silent on the crucial question of the nature of elementary propositions?

The most plausible answer lies in the difficulties with the model, some already noted. For Wittgenstein wants his Simples to have necessary existence, yet planes of space and points of time will only be necessary if space and time are absolute. But he would surely have been sufficiently aware of the debates within Physics at the time to realise that the absoluteness of space and time could not simply be taken for granted. Indeed, see *NB* 129, where he indicates as much. Moreover he seems to have been attracted towards some form of psychological dualism (see *NB* 85). In which case he would not have thought that our model as it stands could yield descriptions of all kinds of fact. Yet as we shall see in Section D below, we face severe problems in trying to extend the model to include descriptions of experiences. Naturally, then, if Wittgenstein's thinking about elementary propositions had been dominated by our model, he would presumably have been aware of the difficulties in the way of implementing it fully. And this would have been sufficient reason for him not to commit himself to it.[9]

One possible argument for thinking that Wittgenstein could not have had our model at the front of his mind would be this. Notice that not all systems of coordinates need name planes of space which have the same orientations. Instead of a system in which the a-planes are horizontal and parallel to due North–South, we could choose one in which they are some number of degrees off horizontal. Nor need the three axes be at right angles to one another. There would therefore be many more objects (planes of space) than we would actually need to name, and different complete descriptions of the physical world could name distinct sub-sets of them. And then the argument would be that there is no hint of this sort of optionality in *TLP*, where it seems to be assumed that all fully-analysed languages would employ names for the very same objects. Thus 3.25 asserts categorically that every proposition has one and only one analysis. Yet on our model there would apparently be many different ways of analysing it, each employing a distinct system of coordinates.

In fact it is not so obvious that different systems of coordinates must yield differing analyses of any given proposition. For remember that the criterion of correctness for an analysis is logical equivalence. And any two elementary propositions which both assign a point-mass to the very same place will be logically equivalent, despite the fact that they may employ names of different planes of space. For if the point of intersection of planes a, b and c is the very same as that of a*, b* and c* (where these are planes having a different orientation), then it will be logically necessary that this is so. Indeed, far from rejecting the kind of optionality involved in our model, Wittgenstein might be read as committing himself to it at 6.341, where he talks about the possibility of using alternative grids or 'meshes' to describe reality, it being an empirical matter how fine the grid would need to be – in our terms, the distances between neighbouring planes on an axis – in order to give a complete description of the world.

Since there are a number of good reasons for supposing Wittgenstein to have had our model in mind, and no good reasons against it, I propose that such an interpretation should be adopted.

(D) Colours and sense-data

Let us now consider whether our model could be extended to include descriptions of colours, without compromising the requirement of logical independence.[10] Suppose we impose a grid on the colour-spectrum, calling the left-hand end '0' and the right-hand end '1'. We then divide it in half, designating the left half '.0' and the right half '.1'. Dividing each of these in half again, we designate the left half of .0 by '.00', the right half by '.01', and the left half of .1 by '.10', the right half by '.11'. We then divide each of these quarters in half again, continuing our numbering system in the same way to produce a grid like that in Figure 2. Obviously we could go on to make the mesh of the grid as fine as we liked.

We now let the elementary propositions take the form 'abctn'. This states, as before, that a point-mass exists at the intersection of a, b and c at time t. But it now also states that the colour of the point-mass falls within one of the ranges which has a '1' in the nth decimal place on the grid. For example, the proposition '$a_4 b_8 c_{16} t_{32} 2$' would say that a point-mass exists at the intersection of planes a_4, b_8 and c_{16} at time t_{32}, whose colour falls either within the range .01 or the range .11. Similarly, the proposition '$a_4 b_8 c_{16} t_{32} 3$' would say that a point-mass exists at the same place and time, whose colour falls within either of the ranges .001, .011, .101 or .111. In order to say that a shade falls within one of the ranges ending with a '0', we should have to conjoin an elementary proposition of the form 'abct', stating that a given point-mass exists, with the negation of the same proposition extended to take the form 'abctn'. Thus, for example, '$a_1b_2c_3t_4$ & not $a_1b_2c_3t_42$' would say that there is a point-mass at the intersection of a_1, b_2 and c_3 at time t_4, having a shade of colour either from the range .00 or the range .10. Ascribing a particular shade of colour to the point-mass at abct might then look something like this: abct & not abct1 & not abct2 & abct3 & not abct4 . . . and so on, to the required degree of accuracy. We should, so to speak, have to 'zero in' on the shade of colour we want, by means of a whole series of elementary propositions and their negations.

This extended model goes some considerable distance towards complying with the requirement of logical independence. Since the proposition 'abct2' tells us that the colour of the point-mass falls either within the range .01 or the range .11, it is logically independent of the proposition 'abct1', which tells us that the colour falls within the range .1. And it neither implies nor is implied by 'abct3', which says that the colour falls within any one of the ranges .001, .011, .101 and .111. So all propositions of the form abctn are independent of one another. However, it is still the case that 'abctn' must entail 'abct'. For if there is no point-mass there, then it cannot have a colour. Moreover, 'abctn' and 'not abctn' can both be false together (that is, if 'abct' is false), thus debarring them from being genuinely elementary, on the *TLP* account.

Although the attempt to extend our materialist model to include descriptions of colour has failed, it does suggest how one might construct a system of logically independent elementary propositions for describing sense-data. We need only impose a grid on the 'spectrum' of the subject's colour sensations, rather than on the objective colour-spectrum as above.

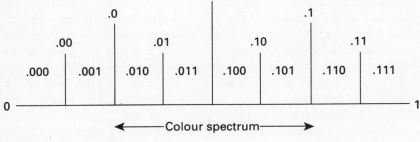

Figure 2

Then instead of using a system of three-dimensional objective spatial coordinates, we could use a two-dimensional system to map the visual field. An elementary proposition would then take the form 'detn', which would say that a colour sense-datum occurs in the visual field at the intersection of lines d and e at time t, where the quality of that experience falls within one of the ranges having a '1' in the nth decimal place on the grid. The propositions in such a system of description would be genuinely independent of one another (in particular, 'detn' and 'not detn' could not both be false), since any point in the visual field must have some colour (2.0131). We could then use a similar system (employing three 'spatial' dimensions once again) to describe the qualities of sense-data of touch and pain, giving their relative positions within the tactile field. And so on for the other senses.

Might one then conjoin such descriptions of sense-data with our earlier system for describing the distribution of matter in objective space and time, to provide a complete description of reality?) For example, we might attempt to give an analysis of colour-statements of the familiar disposition-to-cause-a-sense-datum sort.) Could this be how Wittgenstein might have hoped to accommodate his dualism?

He may indeed have had such hopes, but there would in fact be insuperable difficulties in the way of individuating the sense-data belonging to different persons. One could not, for example, ascribe them as properties of point-masses (an elementary proposition of the form 'abctden' saying that there is a point-mass at the intersection of a, b and c at time t, which has a colour sense-datum from one of the ranges having a '1' at the nth decimal place in the grid, occurring at the intersection of lines d and e in the visual field). For then precisely the sorts of problems would arise here as arose with our earlier attempt to find room for objective colours, since in order to ascribe sense-data from ranges having a '0' in their nth decimal place, we should have to conjoin a statement of the form 'abctde' with one of the form 'not abctden', hence losing logical independence. But then how else could we individuate sense-data? Since it is possible for two people to have sense-data which are qualitatively indistinguishable, what makes their sensations distinct can only be the fact that they are possessed by different subjects.[11] Yet Wittgenstein is adamant in rejecting the idea of a metaphysical subject, as we saw in Chapter 8. And as we have just seen, a system which ascribes sense-data to physical subjects cannot comply with the requirement of logical independence.

Although our model for describing the distribution of matter in space and time cannot be extended to include descriptions of colours or sense-data, what has emerged is that we have the materials for constructing quite a different model for the elementary propositions of *TLP*, which would be phenomenalist rather than realist. Names would not be names of sense-data, but rather of lines imposed upon the subject's various sense-fields, and of disjunctive ranges from the grids imposed upon the various sensation-kinds. So a phenomenalist interpretation of *TLP* is just as well able to cope with the requirement of logical independence as is a realist reading.

Nevertheless, the realist model remains the most plausible, quite apart from the considerations to do with Wittgenstein's attitudes towards metaphysics and epistemology. For it stands (or at least stood) a better chance of complying with the requirement that Simples should be constituents of all possible worlds. As we have seen, this would have been true on the realist model if space and time had turned out to be absolute. But on the phenomenalist model even cursory consideration shows it to be most unlikely. In particular, it seems obviously false that the lines of visual space and the planes of tactile space must exist in all possible worlds, since I might, for example, lose part or all of my visual or tactile fields – as when I go blind or lose feeling in my legs. Now, to this it might be replied that the names in the system are to refer to lines and planes in fields of possible rather than actual experience, since even if I am blind it remains possible that I should enjoy visual sense-data. Exactly so: if I had been blind from birth it would still have been possible that I should have had visual experiences. Yet I could not have learned names to refer to lines in the visual field, since I would have had no visual field. So even if the lines were to exist in all possible worlds, they would not be nameable in all of them. Indeed, there are many people in the actual world who cannot name them, but who are nevertheless capable of thinking (and so who are, for Wittgenstein, capable of representing all possible worlds).

Summary

We have provided two distinct models for the elementary propositions of *TLP*, each of which can meet some if not all of the constraints laid upon them, notably that of logical independence. It seems likely that Wittgenstein himself might have worked with the realist model, having it at the back of his mind (at least) in his thinking about elementary propositions.

15 Deconstruction: following a rule

In this chapter I argue against the logical objectivism of *TLP*, suggesting that this very critique may be found in the later Wittgenstein's discussion of rule-following.

(A) An argument in outline

The main argument against logical objectivism takes the form of a challenge to find something which can play the role of the sense of an expression, as logical objectivism conceives of it. In the next section we shall consider the various possible attempts to meet this challenge head-on. Here we shall consider the broad structure of the argument, supposing that the challenge cannot in fact be met.

Suppose then that logical objectivists can provide no answer to the question what it *is* to understand (to grasp the sense of) an expression. Indeed, suppose that they can find no object of awareness having the properties which they attribute to senses. What would follow from this? They might be tempted to claim that nothing follows, pointing out that it is precisely the fallacy sometimes labelled 'Socratic' to infer from the fact that speakers cannot say – cannot articulate – what their understanding consists in that they therefore possess no such understanding.[1] But in fact this line of defence is unpromising. For the standard way of explaining how the Socratic fallacy is indeed a fallacy is in terms of the distinction between knowing *how* and knowing *that*; the point being that speakers can know *how* to use a given expression correctly without knowing *that* the correct use of that expression is such-and-such. But this is not a distinction of which logical objectivists can avail themselves, in replying to our basic challenge.

The reason is that they cannot consistently equate understanding with a practical capacity: a matter of knowing *how*. For remember their idea is that the senses of our expressions are to reach out to the world and to one another in a wholly objective, mind-independent, manner. On this view sense is to *determine* what is to count as the correct use of an expression, rather than being *constituted by* it. (Meaning is not use, but rather determines use.) And so understanding – knowledge of sense – must consist in an intellectual grasp of that which determines correct use. Hence understanding cannot consist in a bare practical capacity, or at least not in the way that the Socratic-fallacy-defence requires. On the contrary, a person's capacity to use an expression correctly is to be *explained in terms of* their understanding of it, the explanation being that they are capable of deriving a knowledge of the correct use of the expression from their knowledge of its sense.

It follows that logical objectivists cannot brush aside our challenge by claiming that they simply have the capacity to use their expressions correctly, and to recognise internal relationships between them, without knowing what it is that makes their usage correct, or that in virtue of which those internal relationships hold. For this would be to concede that they do not, after all, understand (know the senses of) the expressions of their language. If understanding must involve, for logical objectivists, some sort of conscious awareness of whatever it is which is supposed to determine correct use, then they cannot intelligibly claim that they nevertheless have no idea what the senses of their expressions might be.

Nor can this difficulty be avoided by denying that understanding need involve conscious knowledge of sense, claiming rather that our grasp of that which determines correct usage and the internal relations between expressions is unconscious. For this would undercut the essential normativeness of sense. Speakers are supposed to be able to appeal to the senses of their expressions in justifying the use which they make of them, and in correcting the usage of others. Yet they could hardly do this if their knowledge of sense were unconscious. Indeed, on such an hypothesis an unbridgeable gap would open up, between both actual usage and the sorts of justifications we offer of it on the one hand, and what would really determine correctness or incorrectness on the other. Since we would not be supposed to have any conscious awareness of sense, we should be incapable of knowing whether or not our actual normative practice was appropriately justified. Indeed, it would be possible to doubt whether we really attached any senses to the expressions of our language at all. But this sort of scepticism must be wholly unacceptable. For whatever room there may be for doubts about other people's minds and meanings, I cannot doubt but that I, at any rate, mean something by the words that I use.

The upshot is that if it could be shown that we are none of us aware of anything which can play the role of the sense of an expression, as logical objectivism conceives of it, then it would follow (supposing logical objectivism to be true) that we none of us understand or mean anything by the expressions that we use. For understanding must, on such a conception, be essentially a matter of consciousness of senses. This would reduce logical objectivism to absurdity. We should then be faced with a choice of either rejecting the notion of sense altogether, or finding some alternative conception of it.

(B) Candidates for sense

Some suggestions can be ruled out straight away. We can discount mental images as being hopelessly implausible to account for the meanings of most words in an idiolect, let alone the meanings of sentences. And we can rule out thoughts as begging the question, since on the account of thinking which I (and Wittgenstein) believe to be correct, it is precisely one of those activities which needs explaining, on the logical objectivist account. For if thinking consists in the significant employment of sign-tokens, then we shall want to know how these signs are to reach out to reality in a manner independent of the dispositions of the thinking subject.[2] Fregean thoughts (*Gedanken*) can also be rejected as candidates since they fail to figure in the phenomenology of understanding. When I judge that an object is red I am certainly not aware of grasping a mind-independent abstract entity, nor is my use of the component terms in any way guided by awareness of such a thing.[3]

As I have noted at various points, *TLP* appears to be committed to a form of modified conventionalism, the sense of an expression being none other than the rules and conventions which determine (objectively, not conventionally) its use.[4] So we then need to ask how rules are present to consciousness. Some, of course, may take the form of explicit definitions. But this only pushes the enquiry further back, on to the sort of understanding we possess of the other terms involved. The most basic mode of explaining a rule must be by means of examples and training. But in fact it is clear that nothing we can give someone in the course of such training (or give ourselves by way of an exhibition of the rule) can determine by itself a unique pattern of application. In which case there is nothing here which can play the role of a logical objectivist sense.

For example, suppose that in explaining the rule for the use of the term 'red' to someone we exhibit a wide range of samples of shades of red, as well as samples of things that are not red. It is clear that a trainee could (at whatever stage) go on from this in a manner which we would consider perverse. For there will always be some shades of blue (for example) which have not been exhibited in the course of the training, and the trainee may naturally be inclined to respond to our explanations by classifying these together with red. And even if we were to go systematically through every distinguishable shade in the colour-spectrum, still our samples would have occupied some determinate position in space and time, and it would be possible that the trainee should cotton on to a rule which is some function of these – for example a rule which we might express by saying: 'is red' applies to an object if it is red in 1990, blue in 1991, yellow in 1992, and so on.[5] Since this must always remain a possibility, there can be nothing in the training which can reach out to determine a unique pattern of application in a manner independent of our dispositions.

Since nothing which can be exhibited in public use can play the role of a logical objectivist sense, we might be tempted to appeal to some object of private awareness, most plausibly an intention. It might be said that a speaker's understanding of a rule will consist in a certain intention, namely a commitment to employ the term in question in a particular manner. Indeed, this can seem quite a plausible line for logical objectivists to take.[6] For we not only appear to have non-inferential (perhaps even incorrigible) awareness of our own intentions, but we also seem incapable of error in judging whether or not an action accords with our intentions. For if I do not misapprehend what I am doing, and sincerely believe that I am doing what I am intending to do, then so I am. These facts might then be taken to show that intentions are objects of direct awareness which reach out to the world to determine what actions would or would not accord with them in such a way as to leave no room for misinterpretation – which is just what logical objectivism requires.

What gives the lie to this use for our ordinary notion of intention, however, is the phenomenology (or rather lack of it) of our awareness of our intentions. For to be conscious of an intention is often just a matter of finding oneself thinking about the intended action with one's mind made up. Perhaps I ask myself 'What was it that I intended to do today?' I may then recall having made up my mind to weed the garden, or I may simply think 'I shall weed the garden' in the knowledge that this is what I had made up my mind to do. Moreover, our awareness of an intention is quite unlike consciousness of a pain. For the former is wholly lacking in phenomenological content: it does not *feel like* anything to have the intention of weeding the garden.

There are of course cases where I have an intention, and am conscious of having it, without it being formulated in thought at the time. For example, while engaged in an argument I might know that I intend to hit my opponent if he says another word, without any thought of the form 'If he speaks again I shall hit him' going through my mind. But this in no way lends support to logical objectivism. For consider what occurs when I later recall such an intention. In one sense all I remember are the details of the whole situation – what was said, what I was thinking, and so on. Remembering my intention does not involve recall of a conscious state which existed alongside of these, but is rather a matter of having non-inferential knowledge, as I look back, that if another word had been said I would have turned to violence. I certainly do not have access to any conscious state which is capable of reaching out to the world in a manner independent of my capacities and dispositions, which is what the logical objectivist requires.

In fact the most plausible account of the features of intention to which the logical objectivist appeals is provided by a functionalist theory of the mind. An intention is a state apt to cause the intended action, conscious intentions also being apt to emerge in conscious thinkings with the same content, either at the time or later in memory. This is why knowledge of our intentions is non-inferential. It is also why we cannot in general be mistaken about whether or not an action accords with our intentions. For the intention which causes the action will also, if it is conscious, be apt to emerge in a thought which describes just such an act; so if I do not misapprehend what I am doing there is no further room for error. If this account is correct, then it follows immediately that intentions are not fit to serve as logical objectivist senses. For since they presuppose a notion of thought, just the same problems would arise about them. But I do not here need to rely upon the correctness of the account. It is sufficient to have established that knowledge of our own intentions is not a matter of awareness of a state which can reach out to the world in a mind-independent way.

We are then unaware of anything which can play the role of a logical objectivist sense.[7] But neither can it help to maintain that the notion of sense is *sui generis*, insisting that nothing further can be said about what I am aware of when I know the sense of an expression except that I am aware of its sense. For this is to forget that the challenge to the logical objectivist applies particularly in the first person singular. We are each of us invited to introspect: when I mean something by a word or sentence, is there anything in consciousness which can determine a unique pattern of use in a wholly objective mind-independent way? And the answer to this is clearly negative. In which case, since our challenge cannot be met, logical objectivism must be false. It turns out to be nothing more than a kind of mythology of symbolism. It is a picture of objectivity which, despite its attractiveness, vanishes from our grasp as soon as we try to render it concrete and substantial.

(C) The argument and *PI*

Readers familiar with *PI* will have noted in the above argument many echoes of Wittgenstein's famous discussion of rule-following. This is no accident, since the argument was constructed *via* reflection on that discussion, and since I take Wittgenstein's critical target to be none other than the logical objectivist conception of sense and relations between senses. Certainly that conception seems extremely close to the intended point of the metaphors of 'all the steps in the application of a rule having been taken in advance' (*PI* 188), 'a rule sending out infinitely long rails' (*PI* 218) and 'all the possible movements of a machine [as symbol] being already there in it in some mysterious way' (*PI* 193–4) which figure so prominently in the discussion. What Wittgenstein is wanting to criticise is the idea that in understanding one grasps something which is then able to reach out to the world in a mind-independent way, replacing this with the claim that understanding is a practical capacity: a matter of mastery of a technique (*PI* 182, 199).[8]

Not only is Wittgenstein concerned to attack logical objectivism, but the moves he makes closely parallel those of the argument above. Thus he criticises images as candidates for the meanings of words (*PI* 139–41), as well as arguing that no amount of training in the use of examples can determine independently of our reaction to it a unique pattern of application (*PI* 185–7). He also invites us to introspect, to consider whether there is anything in our consciousness which is able to reach out beyond the examples used in training (*PI* 208–9). He even tackles head-on the suggestion that a speaker's grasp of a rule might reside in their intention. This is covered rather briefly within the parts of *PI* most explicitly concerned with rule-following (*PI* 197 and 205), but he returns to the topic later, exploring it with great subtlety (*PI* 630–93). One clear theme of this later discussion is that intentions are not introspectable items in consciousness with a distinctive phenomenology; there is also a suggestion that conscious intentions are states which are apt to emerge in thinkings with the same content, either at the time or later in memory.[9] But in any case he clearly rejects any conception of intentions which might fit them to play the role of logical objectivist senses.

Another way of supporting my reading of the *PI* discussion of rule-following is to indicate how it is at least consistent with those interpretations which have recently attracted most attention. For example, note that it is closely related to the interpretation provided by Wright, who sees Wittgenstein's attack as being focussed on the objectivity of conceptual commitments.[10] But as will emerge shortly, I differ from Wright in thinking that it is far from clear that Wittgenstein must then be committed to rejecting the objectivity (let alone the investigation-independence) of truth. My interpretation also agrees in detail with the one provided by McGinn, except that he makes no attempt to motivate the arguments he attributes to Wittgenstein, never noticing that we can understand their point and significance if we see them as directed against logical objectivism.[11] My reading even agrees substantially with Kripke's, except that he sees the whole notion of meaning as being under attack. In fact Kripke himself, in expounding Wittgenstein, assumes that meaning must have indefinite significance as well as being available to consciousness – which are the distinctive marks of a commitment to logical objectivism, as we have seen. What he fails to notice is that by equating understanding with a practical capacity we can retain the normativity of meaning without being committed to the objectivity of semantic relations.[12]

If these remarks are sufficient to establish that logical objectivism is the intended target of the discussion which is generally recognised to constitute the very heart of *PI*, then we have finally found our way to a basic locus of conflict between Wittgenstein's early and late philosophies. For as we have seen, logical objectivism is crucially involved in many of the most controversial aspects of *TLP* – in its conception of metaphysics, in the idea of a programme of analysis, in the commitment to eradicate vagueness, in the argument to Simples, and in the requirement that elementary propositions be logically independent of one another. If the attack which is mounted on logical objectivism in the following-a-rule sections of *PI* is successful, as I have argued it is, then all of these strands in his earlier thinking must collapse.

(D) What price objectivity?

If logical objectivism is to be rejected, then what becomes of the arguments of Chapter 4 which were left standing in its support, premised upon the objectivity of contingent and of necessary truth? Must belief in these kinds of objectivity now be given up? If so, then our attack upon logical objectivism will have done a great deal more than undercut some of the more controversial doctrines of *TLP*, since a large part of common-sense belief will also have been undermined.

Consider first the objectivity of contingent truth. If we conceive understanding to be a practical capacity, rather than a grasp of something (a sense) which is able to reach out to determine a truth-value in a manner independent of us and our dispositions, then can there be determinate truths which outreach our capacity for verification? In fact it is by no means clear that a negative answer is forced on us. For the capacities held to be constitutive of understanding, which serve to project a sentence on to the world, are primarily those corresponding to its component words and their mode of combination. And these capacities may be such as to yield a determinate truth-value even in cases where we are incapable of verifying the sentence as a whole. In the same way, a subject may manifest their grasp of an objective truth-condition by manifesting the capacities which constitute understanding of the component words and their combination.[13]

For consider: according to anti-logical-objectivism, an understanding of a term is a multi-faceted capacity: namely to put that term together with others in such a way as to formulate sentences; to apply it to items in the world, employing as norms the various samples and training used in its explanation; and to hold oneself ultimately responsible to the use which other speakers make of it. This capacity presumably has some categorical basis in the mind, or more probably the brain, of the person whose capacity it is. We might think of this as a sort of mechanism. Now, it is surely reasonable to think that there are determinate truths about how this mechanism would react in regions of space and time that the person is incapable of reaching. For that mechanism, being part of the natural world, will be governed by causal laws whose operation is independent of space and time.[14] In which case it will be determinate whether I would be inclined to describe anything in my surroundings as 'living' were I positioned in the Andromeda galaxy, or were I situated on Earth in the year 64 million BC. (Strictly: 'Whether someone with the same conceptual capacities as me would be inclined to describe . . . ') This seems sufficient to imply that sentences such as 'There is life in the Andromeda galaxy' and 'There was life on Earth in 64 million BC' have determinate (though verification-transcendent) truth-values.

The account sketched here of the objectivity of contingent truth faces a number of problems and difficulties.[15] For example, someone might concede that it is determinate what would in fact be said were my capacity to be activated in remote regions of space or time, but object that this is insufficient to give the desired conclusion. For it needs also to be determinate that it would be *correct* for someone to say that. Yet does this not require that a norm of description can reach out to the world independently of my actual dispositions, which is just a return to logical objectivism? But this is to forget that the capacity in question is itself normative, in that it consists not only of dispositions to describe, but also of dispositions to correct and accept correction from others.[16] So what counts as the correct exercise of my capacity is not something independent of it (except in so far as it partly depends upon the capacities of other speakers), but is rather one ingredient within it.

Another difficulty is that there may be many circumstances in which the brain-mechanism constitutive of the capacity would fail to respond in such a way as to record truth. For example, if situated on the surface of the sun or in deep space it would vaporise. But the reply to this is straightforward. It is that the counterfactuals about the mechanism's operation must include the proviso that it be insulated from anything which would interfere with its normal functioning (that is, that the person instantiating the mechanism should be protected by a heat-proof suit, and so on), where the idea of 'normal operation' is defined relative to the judgements people make in normal circumstances here on Earth. Then on this account 'There is life somewhere in the Andromeda galaxy' comes out as objectively true or false, despite the facts (a) that we are incapable of getting there, and (b) that in most places in that galaxy we would be incapable of existing unprotected, because there are determinate facts about how the mechanisms constitutive of our understanding of 'living creature' would respond if positioned at any given point in that galaxy, provided that it were protected in such a way as to ensure that it operates as it does here on Earth.

A third problem is that there are cases in which realising the antecedent of the counterfactual would constitute a material change in the subject-matter of the judgement. For example, consider the statement 'There are no intelligent agents in the Andromeda galaxy.' Since the mechanisms constitutive of understanding would have to be instantiated in an intelligent agent, they would, if positioned in the Andromeda galaxy, render it false rather than true that the galaxy contains no intelligent agents. The obvious response is to require that in examples of this sort the consequent of the counterfactual be adjusted accordingly. In this case what confers objectivity is that if an agent with my conceptual capacities were positioned anywhere in the Andromeda galaxy, they would judge that there is no intelligent agent present *with the exception of themselves*.

Perhaps the most serious difficulty for the present defence of objectivity concerns theoretical statements in science. For in connection with a statement about sub-atomic particles, for instance, the idea of how the categorical bases of my conceptual capacities would respond if suitably placed can obviously get no grip. Now, one sort of response to this would be to point out that the objectivity of scientific truth is generally thought to be problematic in any case, quite apart from worries about the logical objectivist conception of meaning-to-world relations. We might then confine our account of objective truth to those domains where our pre-philosophical commitment to objectivity is strongest, namely truths about 'middle-sized' objects and processes, irrespective of their positions in space and time.

In fact it might be possible for us to make a more positive response, if it could be shown that there are limits to the thesis that scientific theories are underdetermined by their evidence. For suppose that the most that can be established is that there will always be more than one theory equally consistent with the data currently available to scientists, and that it would remain reasonable to believe that there would always be something to choose between theories assessed in the light of whatever criteria are accepted by scientists in good-making features of theories (simplicity, fecundity, etc.), in the face of all possible data. Then the existence of determinate truths about how the brain-mechanisms underlying a scientist's grasp of the concept *best theory* would react in the face of each item from the set of all possible data would be sufficient to confer objectivity on the claim that a given theory is better than any alternative.

The suggestion, then, is that my capacities and the state of the world may be said to settle all contingent truth-values between them, not independently of anything empirical (as logical objectivism requires), but in accordance with the laws of nature governing the operation of the mechanisms forming the categorical bases of the capacities. Since it is part of our ordinary world-view (of what we have reason to believe) that the universe consists of a wide range of mind-independent objects and events, some of which may be positioned beyond our cognitive access, and since it is also part of that world-view that capacities have categorical bases governed by laws which operate independently of spatial and temporal position, it then follows that we are committed to the objectivity of truth, believing all well-understood sentences to have determinate truth-values, quite apart from any commitment to logical objectivism.[17]

What, then, of the objectivity of conceptually necessary truth? Can this too survive the rejection of logical objectivism? In this case the situation is quite different; the argument to show it is presented best in the form of a dilemma. Firstly, suppose we are ontological realists about possible worlds. Then truths about all possible worlds will have to obtain in virtue of the operation of our conceptual capacities *within* each one of them. For our account of how a thought reaches out to another possible world to determine a truth value must surely be of the same kind as our account of how thought reaches out to different regions of the actual world: it will do so in virtue of the operation of our brain mechanisms in accordance with the laws of nature. But in that case it will follow that no statements are necessary, since the laws of nature vary across worlds. (In some worlds the laws of nature will be such that the mechanisms which are in fact constitutive of our understanding of 'red' and of 'coloured' respond in such a way that something can activate the first without activating the second.) So what emerges is that an ontological realist about possible worlds must be a logical objectivist about meaning-to-world relations, on pain of undermining one of the notions (conceptual necessity) that possible worlds were posited to explain. Or to put the point another way: in attacking logical objectivism we should have undermined the very notion of necessary truth, if we remained committed to the real existence of possible worlds.

Then suppose on the other hand that we are not ontological realists about possible worlds, regarding such talk as merely reflecting and 'objectifying' our discourse about what is and is not logically possible. In that case the closest that an appeal to the categorical bases of our conceptual capacities will get to vindicating the objectivity of a truth such as 'Necessarily anything red is coloured' is that the mechanisms constitutive of our understanding of 'red' and of 'coloured' are such that anything in the real world which activates the first would also activate the second. But there is nothing in this to distinguish the status of such a truth from a statement of natural necessity such as 'All mammals have hearts.' So if we have rejected logical objectivism, then the status as necessary of 'Anything red is coloured' must derive from something outside of it. For that status cannot be delivered by the idea of brain mechanisms operating in accordance with natural law alone. In which case, if 'Something is red but not coloured' is excluded from the domain, not only of actual but of possible truth, then this can only be because we have conventionally determined that it should be so.

If we deny both logical objectivism and ontological realism about possible worlds, then the necessity of 'Anything red is coloured' is best explained as follows.[18] Having acquired the capacities which constitute the understanding of 'red' and of 'coloured' respectively, and reflecting on our pattern of application of those terms, we realise that anything in the actual world which we should call red we would also call coloured. We also realise that we are unable, employing these capacities (and so in effect holding constant the causal laws which in fact govern their operation) to imagine circumstances where we should call an object red but be disinclined to describe it as coloured. As a result we elevate, by convention, the statement 'Anything red is coloured' to the status of necessity, using it from then on as an additional norm of description. We shall then say, if we are asked to consider worlds like the one imagined above where differences in the laws of nature mean that our capacities would operate differently, that in that case we should mean something different by the terms involved. But the status as such of a norm of description is not an objective, content-reflecting, feature of it, since someone could coherently accept that anything red will in fact be coloured (this is the most that is delivered by the underlying mechanisms) while remaining agnostic about its necessity. Conceptual necessity is thus not objective (mind-independent), but results from a combination of the limits of our imagination with a general convention requiring us to elevate the results of these limitations to the status of rules.

Either way, then (whether we are ontological realists about possible worlds or not), there is no place for the objectivity of necessary truth, given that the attack upon logical objectivism has been successful.

Summary

We have undermined the logical objectivism of *TLP*, using arguments gleaned from the later Wittgenstein's discussion of rule-following. The resulting identification of understanding with a practical capacity allows us to retain our belief in the objectivity of contingent truth, but requires us to give up our belief in the objectivity of conceptually necessary truth, embracing instead some form of radical conventionalism.[19]

16   Wittgenstein: early and late

Our task in this final chapter is to pull together some of the strands from our previous discussion, in order to locate and identify the real points of conflict between Wittgenstein's early and late philosophies.

(A) False contrasts

We can begin by noting how a number of recent commentators entirely misplace the nature of the contrast between *TLP* and *PI*. Firstly, and in emphatic denial of the position adopted by Baker & Hacker in their (1980), *TLP* should not be seen as exemplifying the 'Augustinian Picture of Language' which forms the target of attack of the opening sections of *PI*. That picture is, rather, their common enemy. Certainly *TLP* is not committed to the view that all words are names; quite the contrary, since the Picture Theory embodies a non-referential semantics for predicates, as we saw briefly in Chapter 1.[1] Nor is the *TLP* view that the logical grammar of a name has to be read off from our prior acquaintance with the necessities and possibilities in nature; quite the reverse: it holds that logic is epistemologically prior to metaphysics, as I argued in Chapters 2 and 3. Nor is *TLP* committed to a conception of thought as prior to language; on the contrary, it too holds that thought and language are closely intertwined, and essentially similar to one another, as I argued briefly in Chapter 1.[2] It would seem that, unless the later Wittgenstein wholly misunderstood *TLP*, the Augustinian Picture with which *PI* opens was used as a convenient focus to present (in his new idiom) points of agreement as well as disagreement with his earlier thought.

Secondly, it is quite wrong to see the contrast between *TLP* and *PI* as a dispute between phenomenalism or solipsism on the one hand and metaphysical realism on the other, as does Hacker (1972) and (1986), and also Hintikka & Hintikka (1986). In particular, there is nothing in *TLP* which renders it vulnerable to the later celebrated argument against the possibility of private language (*PI* 243ff.). For as we saw in Chapter 8, the *TLP* endorsement of 'solipsism' should not be seen as a commitment to solip- sistic phenomenalism. On the contrary, *TLP* is broadly realist, the simple objects which form the substance of the world existing necessarily, and independently of the human mind. Nor does the early Wittgenstein show any of the interest in epistemological questions which would be necessary to motivate his commitment to phenomenalism. (This is one of those places where an unargued assumption that Wittgenstein was heavily influenced by Russell has led many commentators astray.)

Thirdly, it is a mistake to see the contrast between *TLP* and *PI* in terms of differing attitudes to the relationship between thought and language, as do Malcolm (1986) and McDonough (1986). Certainly *TLP* is not com- mitted to the 'code-breaking conception' of language, according to which public signs get their life and significance from the private thoughts which accompany them. This was argued briefly in Chapter 1.[3] Nor, as we have noted a number of times, is the *TLP* view that all the complexity of a fully analysed proposition – including reference to Simples – is added in thought by the person who understands the proposition. Rather, Wittgenstein's view throughout was that thinking on the one hand, and the use of public language on the other, are essentially similar activities, similarly related to reality. And to say that our ordinary propositions are truth-functions of elementary ones is just to say that, in being analytically equivalent to such truth-functions, they possess the same semantic contents, and say the very same thing.

Finally, it is wrong to characterise the debate between *TLP* and *PI* as a dispute between Platonism and anti-Platonism, as does Pears (1987) and (1988). On the contrary, the early Wittgenstein was equally opposed to Platonism, whether about propositions or universals (as we saw briefly in Chapter 1), or about numbers (as we saw in Chapter 2).[4] It is true that *TLP* is committed to the existence of a class of necessarily existing objects, but this is not Platonism as it is usually understood – both because these objects are most plausibly thought of as planes of space and points of time (as we saw in Chapter 14), and because they do not constitute a realm of entities in contrast with the empirical world, but rather form its substance (2.021).

(B) Misplaced criticisms

Let us now briefly consider the various arguments in the early sections of *PI* which are generally taken to be criticisms of *TLP*. (I shall not attempt to judge whether Wittgenstein intended them as such. It is possible that he did, and that he is thereby shown to have misunderstood his earlier work: see my Preface.[5] Or it may be that his targets were somewhat different: perhaps Frege or Russell, or a general tendency of thought which he felt to be widespread.)

The points that Wittgenstein makes concerning ostensive definitions (*PI* 6, 9, 28–36), in particular that their success presupposes a background of language-mastery, altogether pass *TLP* by. For as we saw in Chapter 2, 3.263 should be seen as making an essentially similar point. Certainly the *TLP* view is not that there is any sort of simple hooking-up of language to the world. On the contrary, part of the significance of the *TLP* doctrine that logic is prior to metaphysics is that there can be no apprehension of the logical nature of an object in advance of acquiring some system of symbols in which it can be represented. And one of the consequences of the *TLP* endorsement of the Context Principle at 3.3 is that it must be some sort of training in the use of whole sentences which is foundational in language, not ostensive definition.

The point made at *PI* 40, alleging confusion between the meaning of a name and its bearer, is very naturally seen as directed at *TLP*, especially since *PI* 39 is a discussion of the idea that genuine proper names would have to be names of Simples. But the *TLP* semantics for names is not in fact vulnerable to such a charge. *TLP* does indeed hold that the distinctive semantic content of each particular name is its bearer,[6] so that it is sufficient to understand someone's use of a name that you know to which thing that name refers. But *TLP* also maintains that the logical grammar of names belonging to each sortal category will form part of their semantic content. So someone who understands a name for an historical individual will know that it makes sense to continue to use that name when its bearer has ceased to exist. Moreover, names have, in addition, idiolectic senses which determine their reference. So there is no question of *TLP* being confused between meaning and bearer.

The discussion of Simples and of analysis through *PI* 39–64 fails to get to grips with the real motivations and arguments of *TLP*, if the accounts provided in Chapters 7 and 12 above are correct. For there is nothing in these passages to challenge the idea that since the truth-conditions of a proposition must be determined in advance in all their particularity, it must be possible to display the particularised content of the proposition in the form of an analysis (a sentence logically equivalent to the original). Nor is there any hint of an argument to Simples premised only on logical objectivism, together with the claim that singular propositions are logically prior to general ones. So again, *TLP* has either been misunderstood or Wittgenstein is talking of something else.

We get closer to genuine conflict in the stress *PI* places on the multiplicity of language-games and the non-systematic nature of language (*PI* 21–7), as well as on the claim that our conceptions of language and propositions are non-unitary (family-resemblance) ones (*PI* 65, 92). For *TLP* does indeed take language to form a unity, both in its almost exclusive concentration upon factual discourse, and in its monolithic account of propositional content. But then these aspects of the philosophy of *PI* seem to me to be amongst its weakest. So if the fundamental point of conflict between *TLP* and *PI* were located here, then it is far from clear that *TLP* would not prove to be the outright victor. Let me briefly elaborate.

If the multiplicity of language-games is nothing more than the idea that there are a variety of uses (assertion, question, command and many others) to which a given propositional content can be put, then there is nothing here that need trouble *TLP*. It is true that the concentration of effort in *TLP* had been almost exclusively on the nature of propositional content, scant attention being paid to the various attitudes which one may take towards such content (belief, hope, desire, etc.), or to the various linguistic acts into which it may enter (assertion, question, command, etc.).[7] But there is nothing to prevent the semantics of *TLP* from being extended to take account of such matters. Certainly *TLP* is not committed to the view that all discourse is factual, or to the view that all propositional attitudes and linguistic acts are somehow covert assertions,[8] as *PI* 24 might be taken to suggest.

PI 23 claims (correctly) that there is no fixed limit to the number of different kinds of linguistic act, since new sorts of language-game are continually coming into existence. But there is nothing here to challenge the distinction between propositional content and linguistic act. We can still insist that in any language-game, including those that have not yet been invented, it will be possible to draw a distinction between the content of an utterance and the use to which that utterance is put. Indeed, there is nothing here to prevent us from providing a detailed theory of meaning for our language as it actually exists, giving an account of individual words in terms of their contribution to the semantic (propositional) content of sentences, and describing in detail the significance of the various forms of linguistic act currently in employment. All that follows is that we cannot provide a theory of meaning which will be complete, in the sense of covering every conceivable activity that we would be prepared to describe as 'language'. But then there is no reason to think that *TLP* is committed to giving the essence of language in *this* sense. Rather, what *TLP* attempts is to give the essence of propositional content; and this idea has not yet been undermined.

It does seem that *PI* 22 is intended to challenge the very existence of a distinction between propositional content and linguistic act. Here Wittgenstein objects, against Frege's view that the content of an assertion may be expressed in the form 'that such-and-such is the case', that this is so far not a move in a language-game. But this is a misunderstanding. Of course 'that such-and-such is the case' is not a move in a language-game, and the utterance of it does not effect any linguistic act; this is just Frege's point. The idea is not that assertion consists of two kinds of linguistic act; it is not that making an assertion is really to perform two distinct actions: assertion and assumption. It is rather that the meaning of any linguistic utterance has two distinct *aspects*, its content and the linguistic act effected through the use of that content on a given occasion. For the same reason the objection made later in *PI* 22, that you could equally well say that every assertion contains a question, because we can imagine a convention according to which one makes an assertion by asking oneself a question and answering it, misses the point as well. For to repeat: to distinguish between content and linguistic act is not to claim that an assertion consists of two distinct actions.

As Dummett points out in his (1981a), it is in any case hard to see how we could do without the distinction between propositional content and linguistic act, and the compositional conception of language-mastery that goes with it. For children do after all succeed in learning their native language on the basis of limited exposure, and become capable of understanding an unlimited number of unfamiliar sentences as a result. We cannot even begin to see how this takes place, except through the child learning the content of a limited vocabulary and the significance of various modes of combining that vocabulary, as well as the significance of the various things that can be done with the contents that result. Nor, so far as I can see, is there anything in the discussion of rule-following later in *PI* which need challenge this picture. For the compositional conception does not require us to believe that the rules governing the language fit together of themselves to determine the content of each possible sentence (that is, it does not commit us to logical objectivism). Rather, we can think of it in terms of the interaction of the various underlying capacities of the speaker, those capacities being exercised in any number of different possible combinations.[9]

Wittgenstein would appear to be on stronger ground in claiming that our concept of a proposition is a family-resemblance one (*PI* 65, 92). For as I argued in Chapter 1, the semantic contents of propositions in fact vary from one region of discourse to another.[10] This is because, our purposes being different within different contexts, the constraints placed upon successful communication (that is, the identity-conditions for semantic content) will vary also. But this need not mean that our concept of a proposition is a fragmentary one. For as I suggested, we can provide for unity in diversity by introducing a concept whose conditions of application are purpose-relative. And note, most importantly, there is nothing in the philosophy of *TLP* which need rule out such a move.[11]

(C) Retrospect

At this point let us review the manner in which the distinctive metaphysical theses of *TLP*, together with the *TLP* programme of analysis, depend upon a commitment to logical objectivism. I have tried to show that in each case the *TLP* view can be powerfully supported by argument, and that in only one of the cases is the conclusion of the argument obviously false (the rejection of vagueness); in all other respects a rational rejection of the *TLP* position has to wait upon an explicit attack upon logical objectivism itself, of the type outlined in Chapter 15.

As we saw in Chapter 6, the commitment to show the fuzziness of ordinary concepts to be illusory, while not explicitly stated in *TLP* itself, does seem to be imposed upon Wittgenstein by his programme of analysis, which in turn is motivated by the requirement of determinacy-in-advance (itself a form of logical objectivism). It is also arguably imposed upon him even more directly by his logical objectivism, in that only the sort of anti-logical-objectivist view which allows our understanding of vague terms to be equated with a simple recognitional capacity can provide an acceptable solution to the Sorites paradoxes. Yet the commitment in question is of course absurd: it is obvious that many of our ordinary thoughts and statements are indeed vague. The most charitable interpretation would be that by the time of writing *TLP* Wittgenstein was no longer explicitly considering the matter of vagueness at all.

The remaining consequences of logical objectivism were by no means so obviously false. First there was the belief in a set of objective metaphysical truths about the world, reflecting the determinate relations between concepts which are part-and-parcel of logical objectivism (see Chapter 3). Then second there was the programme of analysis itself, designed to reveal how language reaches right up to the world, the truth-conditions of ordinary propositions being determined in advance by their sense alone (logical objectivism) in all their possibly infinite particularity (see Chapter 7). Third was the commitment to Simples – necessarily existing individuals serving as possible objects of genuinely singular reference. This was entailed by a combination of logical objectivism with the very plausible thesis that there is a logical asymmetry between singular and general propositions (see Chapter 12). Even this strange claim was not obviously false, given that it is not being asserted that children have actually been referring to Simples in their private thoughts, prior to learning to designate ordinary contingent objects. Then finally there was the belief that analysis must terminate with a class of elementary propositions which will be logically independent of one another, at least one of the arguments for which was premised upon logical objectivism (see Chapter 13). Although it was by no means obvious that this demand could in fact be met, neither was it clear that it cannot (see Chapter 14).

The metaphysical system of *TLP* is, in general, both powerful and consistent. It can plausibly be held that we have no right to reject it, in the absence of a direct attack upon logical objectivism itself. In any case it emerges that those contemporary philosophers who remain tempted by a version of logical objectivism, or who think that they can hold on to the objectivity of conceptual necessity without it, are presented with a challenge: namely to show how they can consistently maintain their position without being committed to those of the early Wittgenstein's doctrines which would generally be regarded today as extraordinary.

(D) The true contrast

Since the metaphysics of *TLP* is ultimately premised upon logical objectivism, and since it is the latter which is the direct target of attack of the *PI* discussion of rule-following (as we argued in Chapter 15), it is here that the fundamental conflict between the two works is located. If, as I believe, the *PI* critique of logical objectivism is successful, then all of the above aspects of *TLP* must be swept away as a result. (We have already noted in Chapter 3 that the most plausible explanation of the later Wittgenstein's changed attitude towards the possibility of metaphysics lies in his rejection of the logical objectivism which had grounded his earlier view.) But the damage need not extend to the basic semantic system of *TLP*, sketched in Chapter 1 above and defended at length in *TS*. For this is in fact independent of any commitment to logical objectivism, and can stand largely unscathed by

Wittgenstein's later philosophy.[12] There is therefore no reason for us to reject Tractarian semantics – indeed, it is at least a distinct improvement on Fregean semantics, and is, in my view anyway, mostly correct – even though we may accept the consequences of the later Wittgenstein's discussion of rule-following.

Whether yet further damage must be inflicted upon the system of thought of *TLP* by the rejection of logical objectivism may be left as a matter for controversy. Here belong the questions whether anti-logical-objectivists can remain committed to Bivalence, and to two-valued logic generally, and whether they can continue to construct their semantic theory around the notion of truth-conditions, as opposed to assertability-conditions or criteria or some other substitute. Indeed, here belongs the question whether an anti-logical-objectivist can remain committed to the objectivity of truth. I am inclined to think that these questions can be answered affirmatively, as I indicated in the last chapter. But the issues are much in dispute, and go well beyond the scope of our investigation of the strengths and weaknesses of Wittgenstein's early philosophy.[13] Indeed, it is arguable that these issues even go beyond what would be required for consideration of Wittgenstein's *later* philosophy. For as I noted in the last chapter, there is little evidence that he himself saw the rejection of logical objectivism as having consequences outside of the *a priori* domains of philosophy and mathematics.

Conclusion

The metaphysics and associated programme of analysis of *TLP* is for the most part far from foolish, if ultimately unacceptable, resulting as it does from an endorsement of logical objectivism. The attack upon logical objectivism which Wittgenstein mounts in his *PI* discussion of rule-following constitutes the crux of the conflict between his earlier and later philosophies.

Notes

Preface

1 Baker and Hacker (1980) and Malcolm (1986) are particularly glaring examples of this tendency.

2 Consider the variety of interpretations offered in the five major studies recently published, namely Wright (1980), Kripke (1982), McGinn (1984), Baker & Hacker (1985) and Pears (1988).

3 This is most obviously true in the cases of Baker & Hacker and of Pears; but I believe it may also be true, at a rather deeper level, in the case of Kripke and McGinn. See the notes to Chs. 15 and 16 below.

4 Fogelin shows in his (1976) how Wittgenstein's account of the quantifiers is expressively inadequate, since there is no way in which the N-operator can be used to construct propositions of mixed multiple generality, such as '$\exists x \forall y F x y$'. (However, Geach in his (1981) shows how this defect could easily have been remedied.) Fogelin also argues convincingly that Wittgenstein's doctrines concerning the N-operator commit him to the existence of a decision procedure for predicate logic, whereas there is demonstrably no such thing.

5 Briefly, the problem was this. You cannot give a normal explicit definition of the negation-sign, for example, without first having introduced the quantifiers, since the negation-sign may take a quantifier within its scope. But then on the other hand you cannot give such a definition of a quantifier, either, without first having introduced the negation-sign. For a quantifier may be attached to propositional functions containing that sign. So it looks as if our only recourse, if we are not to employ just a single logical operator, will be piecemeal definition: we shall first have to define the logical connectives as they apply to elementary propositions and propositional functions, and then, on that basis, redefine them for contexts where they take other logical connectives within their scope. See 5.451, 5.46, 5.47.

6 See McGuinness (1988), pp. 245ff. Indeed, shortly after the completion of *TLP* Wittgenstein claimed in a letter to Ficker that the main point of the book was an ethical one – see Engelmann (1967), p. 143. But this was certainly an exaggeration, understandable in a letter to a prospective publisher. No one should be able to read *TLP* or the earlier *NB* without realising that Wittgen-

stein was fascinated by questions of semantics and metaphysics for their own sakes. All the same, there was, no doubt, an intended connection between the showing/saying doctrine as it applies to propositions of metaphysics and logic on the one hand (see *TS* 6) and the supposed inexpressibility of genuine value on the other. But my view is that there is, in truth, little more than an *analogy* between the two doctrines – though I do not propose to defend this here.

7 See Walt Disney's film *Bambi*. The advice is delivered to Thumper by his mother.

8 For more detailed exposition and defence of these principles, see *TS* 1.

9 Indeed, I once thought of calling this book *In Defence of a Dinosaur*. This was in deference to a remark of White's in his (1974), that the system of thought of the *Tractatus*, like the metaphysical systems of Leibniz and Spinoza, has to be regarded, in the end, as belonging amongst the prehistoric monsters of philosophy.

10 See von Wright's 'Historical Introduction' to *PTLP*. McGuinness conjectures (on the basis of rather slim evidence) that *PTLP* may have been written in the Autumn of 1917. See his (1988), p. 265.

11 These letters are collected together in Wittgenstein (1974).

12 For the conversations with Waismann, see Waismann (1979); for accounts of Wittgenstein's Cambridge lectures, see Ambrose (1979), Diamond (1976) and Lee (1980).

13 See the Editor's Preface to Wittgenstein (1973), pp. 12 and 15, and Wittgenstein (1974), pp. 114–18.

14 It is impossible to believe that the text of *TLP* is only the opaque, if highly polished, tip of an iceberg of explicitly articulated thoughts and arguments, most of which Wittgenstein chose to suppress for aesthetic or pedagogic effect – especially when we consider the equally opaque writing of *NB*, which was written purely for his own use. The truth is that he had difficulty expressing himself at all, and that his mode of thinking and arguing was always highly intuitive and inexplicit.

15 See *TS* 1, where this restriction is defended more fully.

16 See Blackwell (1981), p. 8.

17 Compare 4.116.

1 Semantic background

1 For further discussion of the directedness of *Sinn*, see *TS* 3.

2 For more detailed discussion of the textual evidence supporting the views presented here, see *TS* 3.

3 In *TS* 4 I note a number of ambiguities in the *TLP* use of both 'symbol' and 'proposition'. But I conclude that in general the terms are used to express the quasi-Fregean notions sketched in the text.

4 See *TS* 4 for a full defence of this interpretation of *TLP*.

5 Of course Russell held that all thought must concern entities with which we are immediately acquainted; in particular: sense-data and universals abstractable

from sense-data. See *TS* 2 for a brief account of Russell's views on semantics. As will emerge both from *TS* and from the present work, my view is that the extent of Russell's influence on *TLP* has been greatly exaggerated by most commentators.

6 Sameness of sense is sameness of cognitive content – two sentences possess the same cognitive content within a particular idiolect only if a speaker cannot take differing cognitive attitudes towards them; if a speaker believes the one they must believe the other, and if they doubt the one they must doubt the other. For a more detailed presentation of Frege's theory of sense, see *TS* 2.

7 In fact 5.141 actually says that all logically equivalent sentences express the same proposition. But see *TS* 4, where I argue that this is best understood elliptically, as saying that all such sentences, while expressing different propositions (having different senses), are *essentially* the same proposition, in that for the purposes of communication they are equivalent, in that they say the same thing.

8 In *TS* 5 I show how the *TLP* account of semantic content reflects the essential purpose of factual communication, namely to acquire rationally grounded beliefs from the assertions of other people. It is our need to share the same conception of a rational ground which requires the identity-conditions for semantic content to be expressed in conceptual rather than metaphysical terms.

9 See *TS* 5 for full development and defence of the ideas sketched here.

10 This is over-simple, since many philosophical terms, such as 'complex', may figure in contingent sentences by virtue of applying to things which exist only contingently. But they will make no contribution to the semantic content of such sentences over and above what is already contributed by the terms with which they are combined. See *TS* 6.

11 See *TS* 6, where this interpretation is expounded and defended in more detail.

12 For example, I argue in *TS* 7 that the condition for understanding the content of a command is mutual knowledge of causal equivalence – that exactly the same events would be necessary to bring about obedience to the command, on either interpretation of it.

13 See *TS* 7 for a full defence of a purpose-relative concept of semantic content, and of its consistency with the remaining doctrines of *TLP*.

14 See *TS* 11 for a full assessment of the evidence.

15 See *TS* 11 and 12, where this is shown in some detail.

16 See, for example, Stenius (1960), where such an interpretation is defended at length.

17 An alternative suggestion, made by Sellars in his (1962a), would be that Wittgenstein might have been happy to speak of monadic combinations of objects, just as Russell had been happy to speak of properties as monadic relations. See *TS* 11, where this interpretation is (tentatively) rejected.

18 For more extensive defence of this interpretation, see *TS* 4 and 12.

19 These views are defended more fully in *TS* 13.

20 See *TS* 12 for extensive discussion of the problems of interpretation and understanding which will be sketched briefly here.

21 This is especially plausible in connection with artefacts. Could a particular table ever have existed, for example, if the parts of which it is in fact made had never been brought together?

22 I also suggest that Wittgenstein employed a non-standard conception of knowledge, under which knowledge requires, not conscious belief, but merely the ability to deduce it *a priori* from what one does consciously believe. See *TS* 12.

23 See *TS* 15, where these ideas are developed more fully, and where I trace their genesis in Wittgenstein's early writings.

24 Property-tokens are spatio-temporal entities: the token of freckledness present in Mary moves around with her, and ceases to exist when she does. They may also have causal powers, it being the token of freckledness present in Mary which causes others to find her attractive.

25 See *TS* 15, where this interpretation of the mature Picture Theory is developed in detail.

26 See *TS* 16, where this is argued in some detail.

27 See *TS* 14 for examples and supporting argument.

28 This interpretation of *TLP* is defended in *TS* 8; and in *TS* 10 I argue that Wittgenstein's view of the matter is actually correct.

29 See *TS* 8, where the points which follow are substantiated in greater detail.

30 See *TS* 9 for supporting arguments.

31 See *TS* 8 for a defence of this interpretation.

2 The Context Principle

1 The principle is not intended to rule out all explicit definitions of individual words. For of course if it is only the meaning of a particular numeral – say '4' – which is not known, then there is no special problem: we can say that it refers to the successor of 3.

2 See *TS* 3 for further discussion.

3 In what follows I am heavily indebted to Wright. See his (1983), Ch. 1. See also Dummett (1973), pp. 495–8.

4 See Frege (1984), pp. 140 and 147 and (1979), p. 118. Currie argues in his (1984) that Frege's main reason for believing concepts to be incomplete is metaphysical rather than semantic. He bases his interpretation on remarks Frege made near the time of the publication of *Begriffsschrift*, when (prior to drawing the distinction between sense and reference) he seems to have thought of the content of a judgement as being something like a state of affairs. But this is insufficient to establish the resulting argument to be metaphysical, since even here Frege's views are driven by semantic considerations. (Thus whole contents are always contents of possible *assertion*, and the criterion of identity of content is given as sameness of logical consequences – see Frege (1972), pp. 112–13.) It is clear that for Frege throughout his career, the idea of incompleteness is introduced to explain the unity of *judgement*, rather than to underpin a prior metaphysical thesis about the unity of states of affairs.

5 Note that it does not follow from this that there is no independent reality

whose nature we come to discern, although McGuinness in his (1981) takes the Context Principle to undermine the realism of *TLP*. (Ishiguro, too, comes close to such a view in her (1969), suggesting that the names of *TLP* are mere 'dummy names'.) But there is an important distinction to be drawn here between two different versions of the thesis that the name/bearer relation is prior to propositions: a developmental thesis on the one hand (relating to the learning of language) and a semantic thesis on the other (relating to the nature of sentence-content). The Context Principle rules out the first of these, giving a central place to the use of sentences in the teaching of language. But the McGuinness view requires that it should also rule out the semantic thesis, entailing that for a name to refer is just a matter of how it functions in sentences. However, not only does this not follow, but it is of doubtful coherence. For the content of a sentence must surely be a function of the contents of its component words, since otherwise we should be incapable of understanding new sentences. So the content of a sentence must depend upon the objects to which its component names refer. This is the *TLP* view too – see 3.318, 4.026, 4.0311.

I agree with almost all of Pears' critique of McGuinness' interpretation, except that he too fails to draw the above distinction, apparently thinking the *TLP* view to be that one learns language by first having names attached to things 'like labels being attached to luggage'. See his (1987), pp. 102–3. We shall return to the issue of realism in the next chapter.

6 Frege comes to this doctrine through being impressed by an analogy between functions (such as *plus*) and concepts (such as *being freckled*). He thinks that both have to be regarded as essentially 'incomplete', and that both are rules of correlation: a functional expression introducing a rule mapping objects on to objects, and a concept-word expressing a rule for mapping objects on to truth-values. (See 'Function and Concept' and 'What is Function?' in his (1984).) But a close analogy provides no ground for an identification: it gives no reason for saying that the truth-values on to which concepts map objects are themselves objects, or for saying, in consequence, that sentences are complex names.

7 There is a remarkable similarity between 3.263 and Frege's discussion of indefinable signs in his 1906 essay 'On the Foundations of Geometry II'. There he writes: 'Since definitions are not possible for primitive elements, something else must enter in. I call it explication . . . Explications will generally be propositions that contain the expression in question.' (See Frege (1984), pp. 300–1.) This is surely too close for coincidence.

8 A thesis which receives striking empirical confirmation from studies of child language acquisition. See, for example, Ch. 18 in Ned Block (1981).

9 See Maslow (1961), pp. 63 and 73, and Baker & Hacker (1980), pp. 177 and 182.

10 This is another of those places where (as in the rejection both of pre-linguistic thinking and the idea that all words are names – see TS 8 and 15) I regard the early remarks in *PI* as expressing agreement with *TLP*, and not disagreement, as most commentators suggest.

11 See Baker and Hacker (1980), pp. 36–8 and 577–8. Pears too, although in general offering a more sensitive treatment of *TLP*, makes this mistake – see his (1987), pp. 10–17. He does so because he confuses the *TLP* commitment to the objectivity of logic and of meaning-to-world relations (on which see Chapter 4 below) with a commitment to Platonism. This in turn leads him to get the thrust of the later Wittgenstein's consideration of rule-following quite wrong (on which see Chapter 15 below).

12 This is explained briefly in *TS* 12. Of course on the interpretation of the Picture Theory defended in the final two chapters of *TS*, *no* relational expressions serve to refer to relations. The difference in the case of the identity-sign is that what renders an identity statement true is not a state of affairs, but an object; so not even relation-tokens need be introduced into its semantics.

13 For detailed development and defence of the argument sketched here, see Wright (1983).

14 *FA* 62. This was an important insight on Frege's part, with implications for many areas of philosophy. For example, if souls (non-physical subjects of consciousness) were to exist as genuine individuals, then there would have to be criteria of identity for them. Yet it proves impossible to provide such criteria. See my (1986), Ch. 3.

15 See *FA* 70–2. See also Wright (1983), Ch. 3.

16 See Wright (1983), Ch. 4 for a demonstration that the logicist programme can, in essence, be carried through using definitions of this sort.

17 An account not entirely unlike this is provided by Mounce in his (1981), Ch. 5. But he tries to elucidate the content of 'There are three eggs in the jar', not in terms of a 1–1 correlation between the eggs in the jar and the operations necessary to reach 'three' in the series of numerals, but rather in terms of the iterable operation of putting an egg into the jar. This is then vulnerable to Frege's crushing objection to Mill's similar account: 'What a mercy, then, that not everything in the world is nailed down!' (*FA* 7).

18 Frege appears to employ a maximising principle for objects: if an expression functioning as a name can be introduced and explained then (supposing it to figure in at least one truth) there exists a corresponding object. Reductionists like Wittgenstein, on the other hand, seemingly employ a minimising principle: if we can say what is said in a sentence containing an apparent name without using a referring expression, then there is no object referred to. Both principles are threatened with incoherence if, as Ramsey argued in 'Universals' (Ch. 1 of his (1978)), we can always transform names into predicates and predicates into names, for example using 'Wisdom carruthersises' to say the same as 'Carruthers is wise.' For in that case a minimiser will have to say that the latter sentence really refers to *no* object. Whereas a maximiser will be constrained to say that it in fact states a relation between *two* objects, and a vicious regress threatens ('Participation relates Wisdom and Carruthers'). In which case the only coherent strategy for constructing a semantic ontology would be to make use of the Principle of Semantic Relevance – see the discussion which follows in the text.

19 In *TS* 16 I deploy the principle on Wittgenstein's behalf in the course of arguing against the view that predicates refer to transcendent universals
   The argument which follows in the text is a development of the one given by Dummett in his (1973), pp. 499–500 and 509–10.

20 Note that the Principle of Semantic Relevance is not the same thing as Ideal Verificationism. The claim is not that understanding a sentence means knowing how an ideally situated intelligence would be able to verify it. Rather, the claim is that there must be a degree of isomorphism between the truth-condition of a sentence and the main features of what we count as evidence for its truth. For evidence for truth is, after all, evidence that the truth-condition is fulfilled.

3 The primacy of logic

1 Note that the 'great mirror' metaphor raises considerable problems for the sort of non-realist view of *TLP* adopted by McGuinness in his (1981).

2 I here assume the truth of the S4 axiom: $\Box A \rightarrow \Box\Box A$.

3 See *TS* 9 for a sketch of how such an account might go.

4 Notice that the 'great mirror' doctrine not only commits Wittgenstein to the view that to every possible or necessary representation in language there corresponds a real possibility or necessity in the world, but also to the reverse – that there can be no possibilities in the world which I am incapable of representing in language or thought. He must therefore hold that all natural languages are, in a certain sense, expressively adequate – maintaining that they are able to represent each one of the possibilities that there really are. This view seems plainly false. The addition of radically new concepts to a language (as often occurs in the course of scientific advance) will make it possible for us to represent things which we could not have represented before. So we have reason to think that there are possibilities which we are currently incapable of representing. This aspect of the 'great mirror' doctrine is imposed upon Wittgenstein by his view that all logical possibility must reduce to truth-functional contingency, where the elementary propositions out of which truth-functions may be constructed must be presupposed in any conceptual system whatever. On this see the discussion in Chapter 13.

5 Many commentators have argued for a connection between the doctrines of *TLP* and Kant's critical philosophy – see, for example, Maslow (1961), Stenius (1960) and Pears (1987). Just as Kant was concerned to draw limits to possible human knowledge, as well as maintaining that the structure of the human mind imposes a necessary structure upon experience, so Wittgenstein was concerned to draw limits to the possibility of thought, as well as maintaining that the structure of language imposes a necessary structure on the world of our apprehension. But one difference is that Kant held that we could still entertain thoughts about things outside of the possibility of experience (*Noumena*), whereas as I show in the text, for Wittgenstein we cannot even raise the ques-

tion what the world might be like, considered apart from its being an object of our thought. Another difference is that Wittgenstein takes no interest in questions of epistemology, his whole concern being focussed on the issue of thought and representation, as Anscombe argues in her (1959).

6 I here help myself to the assumption that dogs are not linguistically competent creatures. There are some who claim that all cognitive processing (including that of dogs) takes place in a language of thought – see, for example, Fodor (1981). I doubt whether this is true, but if it were it would only help my case.

7 Note that the usual sorts of response to scepticism are not available here. In particular, we cannot claim that belief in the accurate operation of our essence-sensitive faculty provides the best over-all explanation of the course of our experience. For the only 'experience' to be explained in this context is the class of our intuitively held beliefs about logical relationships.

In contrast there will, on the *TLP* view, be no special problem in explaining how we can have knowledge of the essence of language, since this need not be supposed to concern any mind-independent reality – rather it will be concerned with concepts (ideas) in our minds.

8 Hence making the counterfactual vacuously true.

9 Of course someone might say 'Numbers have colours' as an expression of a formalist position in the philosophy of arithmetic. But this would be a highly misleading way of putting their view, since for the formalist a number is not a numeral, but rather the abstract set of uses to which numerals are put – and these cannot have colours either.

10 I think such an account is consistent with the views of Kripke (see his (1980), pp. 128–9) and Putnam (see 'The Meaning of "Meaning"' in his (1973)).

To say that Wittgenstein's attitude to metaphysics is consistent with the recognition of metaphysical (as opposed to conceptual) necessity, however, is not to say the same for every aspect of his early thought. On the contrary, accepting that distinction would force him to give up the view that all necessity reduces to truth-functional tautology.

11 It might be suggested that such arguments may take the form: 'If it is possible that language (or such-and-such a feature of language) exists, then the world must be thus and so. But language (or such-and-such a feature of it) is possible. So the world must be thus and so.' Here the conclusion will be necessary because *both* premisses are. (If something is possible, then it is necessary that it should be possible.) But in fact there will generally be a suppressed third premiss of such arguments, since the only way of knowing, in general, that the existence of language, or of a certain feature of it, is *possible*, is by knowing that it is *actual*.

12 I have in mind an argument of the following general sort: I have a language for describing my sensations; if sensations were wholly private and unconnected with events in the physical world, then a language for describing them would be impossible; so sensations are not wholly private. See *PI* 243ff. See also my (1986), Ch. 6.

13 Of course Wittgenstein's view is that this contradiction will emerge, under

analysis, as truth-functional (6.3751). But this does not affect the point being made here.

On the issue of the world-referring nature of tautologies and contradictions McDonough goes seriously wrong. He correctly points out that the status of such propositions must, in Wittgenstein's view, be recognisable from the symbol alone, without consulting the real world. But he wrongly takes this to show that they are therefore not *about* the real world. (See his (1986), Ch. 11.) This makes it difficult to understand how Wittgenstein can think that tautologies nevertheless reveal the essence of the world to us (6.12).

14 In my previous publications I referred to this doctrine as 'logical realism', a title which now strikes me as somewhat unhappy.

15 See *TS* 9 for discussion of Frege's doctrine, and of the grounds of Wittgenstein's rejection of it.

16 Including, let me stress once again, Platonism about concepts. This is where Pears (1987) goes seriously wrong.

17 This account of logical objectivism needs to be made marginally more complicated to accommodate indexical statements. For the truth-condition of such a statement is not determined *a priori* by its sense, but rather by its sense together with the context of its present use. Nor does the sense of an indexical statement determine a truth-condition independently of literally everything contingent, since contexts of utterance are contingent. The crucial thing about the relationship between sense and truth-condition, for a logical objectivist, is that it should obtain independently of the capacities and dispositions of the judging subject: that it should be mind-independent.

4 Logical objectivism

1 See Russell (1921) and Ogden & Richards (1923).

2 See Frege (1984), p. 353.

3 For a demonstration of the innocuousness of the regress when deployed against theories of truth of other sorts, see my (1981).

4 See Frege (1979), pp. 128–9 and 134.

5 See Dummett (1973), pp. 661–2.

6 This is the argument I once thought decisive – see my (1981), pp. 28–9.

7 Frege's argument (or one of them) had been roughly this: (1) There are truths which are conceptually necessary – reflecting relations between our concepts (senses) and holding good for all times and possible worlds. (2) If senses existed only contingently, then there would be circumstances in which truths dependent upon them would fail to hold good (that is, worlds where those senses would not exist). (C) So senses in general and thoughts in particular (senses of complete sentences) must exist necessarily. The argument fails, since it turns on an equivocation between truth *in* a world (which is the notion involved in premiss (2)) and truth *about* a world (which is all that the truth of premiss (1) requires). See *TS* 9 for further discussion.

8 See the discussion in *TS* 9. Katz argues for the necessary existence of sentences on grounds very similar to those sketched in n. 7 above. See his (1981), Ch. 5.

9 Including Wittgenstein – see *TS* 8 and 9.

10 For discussion of this issue see Wright's chapter, 'Anti-Realism and Revisionism' in his (1986b).

5 Determinate *Sinn*

1 That the Simples of *TLP* are supposed to have necessary existence will be defended in Chapter 8 below.

2 This would receive some support from the fact that the previous remark is 2.03, which says that the objects in a state of affairs fit into one another like the links of a chain. For the relation of linkage is an all-or-nothing one. See also the discussion of 2.03 in *TS* 12.

3 It has been suggested to me that one might be able to fix a sharp boundary without discreteness thus: point at a surface of uniform colour and say 'This is green, but anything more yellow than this is yellow.' This might be formally adequate, but would mean importing a sample into the very sense of the word. For only if you can carry the sample around with you (and be confident that it has not changed) will the definition be usable.

4 There is only one other remark in *TLP* besides 3.23 where 'determinacy' occurs as a noun. This is 3.24, where it occurs as the contradictory noun, in the claim that there will be an indeterminacy in any proposition which contains a sign signifying a complex object. But there are two reasons why the notion involved here must be different. Firstly, because the requirement of determinacy could not be a genuine requirement of logic (as Wittgenstein plainly thinks it is) if any significant propositions failed to comply with it. (Illogical thought is impossible – 5.4731.) And secondly because it is propositions (i.e. symbols, sentences with sense) which are said at 3.24 to contain indeterminacy; whereas it is the truth-conditions (*Sinn*) of propositions which are required by 3.23 to be determinate.

In the light of this it is plain that Anscombe goes wrong in equating the requirement of determinacy with the demand that propositions admit of only one way of being true and one way of being false, which she bases on a reading of 3.24. (See her (1959), pp. 34–5.) For if this demand were placed upon propositions in general, then clearly it is one that none of the propositions of ordinary language in fact satisfy. Yet if it were only placed upon elementary propositions, then we would still await some account of why there have to be elementary propositions, and why they have to possess such a property. In which case the requirement of determinacy could not have the sort of foundational position which Wittgenstein plainly conceives it to have. We should have to consider separately what arguments might motivate a programme of analysis which would terminate with elementary propositions possessing such a property. On this see Chapters 7, 9, 10 and 12 below.

5 Translated by Anscombe as 'completely clear', thus missing the fact that

Wittgenstein is here running together the requirement of sharpness with the requirement that I shall shortly call 'the requirement of determinacy-in-advance'.

6 Note how the idea that the significant relation in a sentence must refer to a relation-token (and not a universal) is still dogging him at this stage in the development of his thought. (See the discussion of the Picture Theory in Chapter 1.)

7 There would also be a problem about the significance of false sentences, as we saw briefly in Chapter 1.

8 I say 'the Wittgenstein of *NB*' because we must remember that the passages under consideration were written in the Summer of 1915, three full years before the final drafting of *TLP*. We have as yet been given no reason for thinking that the concern with vagueness survives into the mature work.

9 See Wright (1975), from whom the examples which follow are derived. Note that the argument here is a conceptual pragmatist one – on which see my (1987b).

10 Most commentators simply assume without argument that the requirement of determinacy of *Sinn* may be equated with the principle of sharpness – see, for example, Fogelin (1976), p. 14, and Malcolm (1986), pp. 38–42. The one notable exception is Anscombe – see n. 4 above.

11 It may be this sloppiness of expression which explains why the passage in question never made it beyond *PTLP* into the text of *TLP* itself. For once cut loose from its context in *NB* it stands out as singularly ill expressed.

12 It is important not to confuse the requirement of determinacy-in-advance with the argument from describing in advance, discussed in Section A of Chapter 4. The former is none other than logical objectivism itself, applied to the particular case of the internal relationship between a proposition and its truth-condition. Whereas the latter is an (unsound) argument in support of logical objectivism, premised upon our ordinary notion of what it is to describe something in advance of knowing the fact described.

6 Vagueness

1 If every proposition must determinately possess one or other of the truth-values *true* or *false* (Bivalence), then plainly there can be no possibility of a proposition possessing *neither* of those truth-values (Excluded Third). However, the converse entailment does not necessarily hold. Those anti-realists who think that truth-values have to be epistemologically accessible to us will refuse to assert Bivalence, since some propositions may be neither verifiable nor falsifiable. Yet they may continue to endorse Excluded Third, maintaining that we cannot be in a position to assert *both* that a proposition is not true *and* that it is not false – claiming that to be in a position to assert that it is not true *is* to be able to assert that it is false. See Chapter 11 for further discussion.

2 See for example Frege (1984), p. 148.

3 I owe this point to Michael Dummett.

4 See *TS* 2 for further discussion of the criterion for sense-identity. The validity of the Same Sense Principle is not often noted, though it is in fact what Blackburn calls 'The Transparency Thesis' in his (1984), pp. 226f. Dummett defends what he calls 'The Equivalence Thesis', which is the claim that 'P' and 'It is true that P' are logically equivalent. (See his (1973), pp. 445–9 and 458–9.) He also notes the connections between truth and such notions as assertion and belief (ibid., p. 463), but without apparently realising that they warrant the stronger claim that 'P' and 'It is true that P' always share the same cognitive content (i.e. that they warrant the Same Sense Principle).

Note that the Same Sense Principle need not entail any form of Redundancy Theory of Truth. Someone endorsing it could consistently maintain, for example, that truth consists in some appropriate *correspondence* with reality. For while it is surely the case that 'P' and 'It is true that P' cannot have the same sense unless they at least have the same logical consequences, the Same Sense Principle can be preserved here, provided we are prepared to maintain that the very notion of a proposition implicitly contains the idea of such a correspondence within it. Indeed I take it that something like this is Wittgenstein's position in *TLP*.

5 The example is of course the one from 'Truth', in which Dummett first raised his anti-realist objection to verification-transcendent truth-values. See his (1978), p. 16.

6 I am in disagreement here with Wright, who asserts that there is no prospect of Bivalence being rendered consistent with the existence of vague statements. (See his (1986b), p. 4.) All we in fact require is a recognition that the Same Sense Principle governs the notion of truth (which renders vagueness consistent with Excluded Third), together with an insistence that 'determinately' in the expression of Bivalence means 'objectively' rather than 'clearly'.

7 Here, as before, the argument is a conceptual pragmatist one. See my (1987b) for a general exposition and defence of such arguments.

7 The programme of analysis

1 The idea of *Begriffsschrift* was explained briefly in *TS* 2. I agree with Griffin about its significance in *TLP*. See his (1964), pp. 135ff.

2 For a brief explanation and assessment of Wittgenstein's views on identity, see *TS* 12.

3 See *TS* 11 for a discussion of the *TLP* notion of logical form.

4 It is here that he makes the disastrous suggestion that 'I mean THIS.'

5 This is also what Wittgenstein means at 3.24, when he says that a proposition involving reference to a complex object will contain indeterminacy. The idea is that such a proposition will be both unspecific (containing no explicit mention of the individual parts of the complex) and general (being represented in the first stage of analysis by a proposition containing a definite description). Here again I agree with Griffin, whose work seems to me to have been unjustly neglected by most commentators. See his (1964), pp. 61–5.

Note that the 'indeterminacy' of 3.24, which relates to the surface-unspecificness (i.e. of cognitive content) of ordinary propositions, is not at all the same as the 'determinacy' required of us by 3.23, which relates to the manner in which the specific truth-conditions (*Sinn*) of such propositions are determined.

6 This is one aspect of the *TLP* requirement that propositions be articulate (4.032). The idea is that it must be possible to analyse a proposition in such a way that the *analysans* is just as complex, and just as detailed, as the truth-condition of the original. (See 4.04.)

7 I owe this phrase, and the insight into *TLP* which lies behind it, to Roger White.

8 It would appear to be in this final step of the argument that the slide between metaphysical and conceptual necessity occurs, giving rise to the criticism of the *TLP* programme of analysis noted at the outset of this chapter. For we might rather analyse 'That watch is on the table' as implying 'Most of the actual parts of that watch (whatever they are) are combined together in some manner appropriate to constitute a watch, and are lying on the table.' This would be sufficient to explain how the sentence can be true in the variety of circumstances mentioned in the text, but without the term 'that watch' itself disappearing under analysis; and without the actual parts of the watch having to be specified *a priori*.

Notice that on such an account, the truth of 'That watch is on the table' would not follow from a detailed description of an arrangement of the component parts on the table by itself, but only from this together with the statement that these are indeed the parts of that watch. So language would not 'reach right up to the world' by itself, but only in conjunction with a contingent fact; but still, apparently, in a manner which is consistent with the truth of logical objectivism. What therefore commits Wittgenstein to analysing ordinary names into descriptions of arrangements of component parts is not his desire to show how ordinary propositions can be made true by particular states of affairs (itself motivated by his logical objectivism). If there is really any important aspect of *TLP* which commits him to such an analysis, it will have to be the argument to Simples. We shall return to the issue in Chapter 12.

9 Malcolm takes just such a view of *TLP*. See his (1986), Ch. 7.

10 Note that this remark follows hard on the heels of 4, which tells us that a thought is a proposition with *Sinn*. So when 4.002 says 'Language disguises thought', this means 'Language disguises the forms implicit in sense, implicit in our use of symbols', and not 'Language disguises what goes on in private thinking.'

8 Sense-data and solipsism

1 Ayer, for example, always believed *TLP* to be phenomenalist, and more recently Favrholdt (1964) and Hintikka & Hintikka (1986) have defended the same position.

2 See, for example, many of the verificationist remarks in *PR*, as well as some of

the comments about *TLP* recorded in Waismann (1979). See also the evidence assembled by Hintikka & Hintikka in their (1966), Ch. 3.

3 The 'Lectures' may be found in Russell (1956).

4 Anscombe makes the same point, and to a similar end (see her (1959), pp. 14 and 27); as does Griffin (1964), pp. 4 and 149ff.

5 See Hintikka & Hintikka (1986), p. 46.

6 There is also the evidence of a letter written to Russell late in 1913 where he says: 'Your Theory of Descriptions is quite CERTAINLY correct, even though the individual primitive signs in it are not at all the ones you thought' (capitals in original). See Wittgenstein (1974), pp. 43–4.

7 In any case, it might be said in defence of a phenomenalist reading that it is a moot point whether any system of elementary propositions whatever can comply with this requirement. We shall take the matter up in Chapter 14.

8 This reading of 2.022–2.023 has recently been challenged in Bradley (1987). He argues that objects can provide the form which is common to all possible worlds (which is what 2.023 literally says) without themselves existing in all worlds. Rather, all possibilities reduce to possible combinations of objects, amongst which are combinations involving objects other than those which exist in the actual world. Now this produces an extremely strange reading of many of the remarks within the 2.0s. For example, the claim that objects subsist independently of what is the case (2.024) has to be interpreted as saying that the status of an object as a possible existent is independent of what is true about the world, which reduces it to the merest truism. Indeed, this interpretation makes nonsense of the argument at 2.021, that objects cannot be composite because they make up the substance of the world. If objects 'constituting the substance of the world' means only that in all worlds they are possible, as Bradley claims, then there is no reason whatever why they should not be composite.

9 This is the interpretation offered by Hintikka & Hintikka (1986), Ch. 3.

10 This is missed by Hintikka & Hintikka, who place great reliance on the passage (see their (1986), p. 58), as they do on a phenomenalist reading of Wittgenstein's 'solipsism' generally.

11 But only part, for this still does not find a role for the metaphysical subject, even as a limit to the world. So the account of Wittgenstein's 'solipsism' presented by Mounce in his (1981), Ch. 9, which thus far agrees with my own, is only partially adequate.

12 See Kant (1929), p. 152 (B 131). The connection is also noted by Maslow (1961), pp. 149–50.

13 This interpretation agrees substantially with that of Anscombe (1959), pp. 166–7. But she goes wrong in supposing that the idea has anything especially to do with the privacy (and hence uniqueness) of my own sensations, and in drawing a parallel with *PR* 58, where Wittgenstein imagines a notation in which we say 'There is a headache' when L.W. has a headache, but in all other cases we say 'A is behaving as L.W. behaves when there is a headache.' For these ideas only come to the fore with the shift to a verificationist concep-

tion of meaning, which makes it difficult to see how it can even be possible to think of someone else having sensations. But for the Wittgenstein of *TLP* there would be no particular problem about this, nor is there any hint of such an idea in the text. Rather, what is unique is my perspective on the world as a whole, including both physical objects and my own and other people's sensations. See the discussion which follows in the text.

The interpretation also partly agrees with that of Pears (1987) (see especially pp. 166ff.), who is similarly opposed to a phenomenalist reading of *TLP*. But Pears claims that the point of the discussion of solipsism is that it is one attempt to draw limits to the thinkable, the solipsist's idea being that I can only think about things with which I have been acquainted (ibid., pp. 34 and 162). This is to be rebutted by showing that in an important sense there is no self, thus undermining the attempt to use the self as a reference-point of all meaningful discourse. But it is hard to see how this can be right. For the thought that meaningful discourse is limited by the objects of actual acquaintance is available even to a Humean about the self, and so cannot be undermined merely by showing that there is nothing beyond the empirical self or 'bundle'.

14 Hacker, in the course of defending his phenomenalist reading of *TLP*, suggests that by the truth of realism Wittgenstein just means the truth (under an appropriate phenomenalist analysis) of many of our ordinary sentences involving apparent reference to physical objects (see his (1972), p. 80). But this is hardly very plausible, if only because 5.64 speaks of pure (or 'unadulterated') realism. Moreover, Wittgenstein does not go on to gloss his remark by saying that once the self of solipsism has shrunk to a point without extension there remains only the set of truths about experience, as one would expect if Hacker were correct, but rather by saying that there remains reality.

15 It is worth noting in passing that Wittgenstein certainly goes wrong in his analysis of reports of belief. For when I say what A is believing or thinking I do not need to specify what arrangement of signs is occurring in A's mind. (I can report the beliefs of a Japanese without mentioning any Japanese sentence.) So the quoted sentence in ' "P" says P' is certainly out of place. What he ought to have maintained is that 'A believes that P' may be analysed as follows: there occurs in the bundle of events which is A's mind some structured arrangement of signs representing that P. For this would then have been correct as an analysis of reports of (the contents of) belief from what I called in *TS* 'the belief-acquisitive perspective' (see *TS* 5 and 13). But of course Wittgenstein's primary purpose was not to present a polished analysis of reports of belief, but rather to block any account which would place the metaphysical subject within the world.

16 It is in fact extremely close to the position taken by Nagel. See his (1986), Ch. 4.

17 This is the standard functionalist account of self-knowledge. I do not mean to endorse it, but introduce it here simply to make the point that the 'myness' of an experience need not be an additional fact about it. For my own view, see my (1989a).

18 This is a rough outline of the account presented and defended with great subtlety by Evans in his (1982), Chs. 6 and 7.

9 Simples: weak arguments

1 I am aware that some philosophers disagree. For example Bennett, in his (1974), pp. 62–5, argues that given a Fregean conception of existence as a second-level attribute, there is no way of expressing the idea of an individual coming to exist out of nothing or going out of existence into nothing (what he calls 'an absolute existence-change'). But there are at least two possibilities which he does not consider, either one of which would be adequate to express such a change. The first is to employ second-order quantification over properties. Let 'Hx' be 'x is a hydrogen atom', and let 'Mxy' be 'x is the matter out of which y is made'. Then we could express the fact that a hydrogen atom goes clean out of existence between times t_1 and t_2 thus:

$\exists x \exists y ((Hy \ \& \ Mxy)$ at $t_1 \ \& \ \forall F(-Fy \ \& \ -Fx)$ at $t_2)$.

Alternatively, we could express the same fact by employing the notion of identity thus:

$\exists x \exists y ((Hy \ \& \ Mxy)$ at $t_1 \ \& \ -\exists z(z=x \lor z=y)$ at $t_2)$.

2 Indeed, I am told that some physicists have proposed that there are places distributed throughout the universe where hydrogen atoms are created out of nothing.

3 See the arguments of *TS* 8 and 9.

4 See the discussion in *TS* 12. Note that if I had adopted Sellars' (1982a) reading, which admits monadic 'configurations', then we should not be forced to see 2.0271 as committing Wittgenstein to the thesis that objects are changeless. For changing 'configurations of objects' could also cover changes in the monadic properties of objects. Objects would only be unalterable in the sense of being incapable of coming to be or ceasing to exist. But this in itself is an argument against Sellars, since it would be strange to describe this as 'unalterability' (see 2.027).

5 This fact is missed by most of those who attribute such an argument to Wittgenstein. See, for example, Malcolm (1986), pp. 37–43.

6 Yet precisely these moves are made by Hintikka & Hintikka in exposition of Wittgenstein, but without acknowledging how weak his position is rendered as a result. See their (1986), pp. 48–9, 61–2 and 68–70.

7 Malcolm, for example, attributes this argument to Wittgenstein (see his (1986), pp. 52 and 53–5); as does Griffin (1964), pp. 66–7.

8 Compare von Wright's essay 'Modal Logic and the *Tractatus*' in his (1982), where he argues on quite other grounds than those given here that the modal logic implicit in *TLP* is S5.

9 Malcolm recognises the argument from the fixed form of the world but seems to suggest, by implication, that the only way to avoid it is to give up the S5 axiom. See his (1986), p. 53.

10 Something like this argument seems to be advanced by McDonough (1986), pp. 108–13; but his presentation is far from clear. See also Griffin (1964), pp. 68–9, who also notes its unsoundness.

11 We might wonder whether the claimed reduction of all possibilities to the possible truth and falsity of elementary propositions can coherently be introduced into the argument at this stage. For must not this thesis presuppose that the existence of Simples has already been established? But in fact we saw in Chapter 7 that Wittgenstein has powerful reasons for thinking that it must be possible for all propositions to be analysed into completely detailed descriptions of their truth-conditions. And as we shall see in Chapter 10, he also has good reason for thinking that the terminal propositions of such an analysis must be genuinely singular (elementary). Indeed, as we shall see in Chapter 13, even his reasons for thinking that the elementary propositions must be logically independent of one another in no way presuppose that the existence of Simples has already been established.

10 Simples: stronger arguments

1 The possibility that the circle is not vicious but holistic will be discussed in Chapter 12.

2 Although 5.526 says that one can describe the world completely by means of fully generalised propositions without first correlating any name with an object, this should not be counted as contrary evidence. For it is clear that what Wittgenstein has in mind is that every state of affairs can in principle be described without employing any singular propositions, not that one can understand (grasp the concept of) generality prior to understanding singular reference. See Chapter 12 for discussion of some further contra-indications.

3 Here I have in mind the arguments of recent quasi-Russellians such as Evans (1982) and McDowell (1984), who believe (like Frege) that singular thoughts involve modes of presentation, but modes of presentation whose very existence is tied to the existence of the objects thought about. These arguments will be considered briefly in Chapter 12. But see also my (1987a).

4 Arguments essentially similar to this have been put forward, in exposition of Wittgenstein, by White (1974), pp. 19–21, and Kenny (1973), p. 78. See also Malcolm (1986), p. 52.

5 Precisely this conflation is made by White (1974), pp. 23–5, and lies at the heart of his account of the contrast between Wittgenstein's early and late philosophies.

6 See TS 9.

7 Provided, of course, that 'Fb' belongs to factual discourse. I leave to one side the issue of truth in fiction.

8 I here assume that 'exists' is not a predicate. I find the arguments for saying that it is (as presented, for example, in Mackie (1976) and Evans (1982), pp. 343ff.) unconvincing. But in fact even if this assumption is not granted the argument may still go through. For it seems plausible that a thesis of semantic hierarchy,

similar to the claim that understanding quantification presupposes a grasp of singular reference, applies to the existence-predicate. Surely no one could understand sentences of the form 'Eb' ('b exists') who did not already understand some sentences of the form 'Fb' ('b has such-and-such an attribute'). For someone only understands 'Eb' who understands its negation. And how is '–Eb' to be explained except in terms of the idea that no sentence of the form 'Fb' is currently true? Thinking of –Eb is certainly not just a matter of imagining b disappearing!

9 So it cannot strictly be said or asserted, given the *TLP* account of semantic content. McGuinness, curiously, takes this to be a reason for denying the *TLP* notion of a simple object to be a realist one. See his (1981), pp. 72–3. His reasoning is hard to understand. For from the fact that the existence of a Simple, being necessary, cannot be significantly stated, it does not even begin to follow that Simples therefore do not constitute a realm of entities independent of our minds.

11   The principles of logic

1 Notably Strawson. See 'On Referring' in his (1971).

2 It is also of course entailed by the Same Sense Principle, discussed briefly in Chapter 6. The weaker of the two principles is employed here because it is less controversial.

In this paragraph, as in much of the argument of this chapter, I am heavily indebted to Dummett's 'Truth' (see his (1978)).

3 On Russell's analysis, for example, it comes out as: One and only one thing is a father of Mary and that thing is not bald.

4 See his (1978), pp. 8–10.

5 Indeed, the issue is best seen as a conceptual pragmatist one. We can justify Excluded Third on another level if we can show that it reflects the concepts of truth and falsity which we ought to employ if those concepts are to be in accord with the purposes for which we draw a true/false distinction. See my (1987b) for further discussion of this style of argument.

6 See Dummett (1978), pp. 8–12 and 20. See also pp. xvii–xviii.

7 See Dummett (1973), pp. 354–5.

8 As Dummett argues ((1978), pp. 12–14), our interest in constructing a smoothly functioning semantics for the language might also motivate a distinction between different ways in which a proposition can fail to be true. But there are two points to be made about this. Firstly, this may not be the only way of achieving the intended effect (e.g. of explaining how 'The king of France is not bald' is false). We might be able to employ distinctions of scope instead, as Russell does; or we might distinguish between propositional and predicate negation. Secondly, this kind of motivation does not in any case derive from an interest in the truth, as such, of the propositions of our language. It comes rather from a second-order interest in semantic explanation. So even if the proposed distinction were accepted it would not justify rejection of Excluded

Third. Rather, as Dummett suggests, it would merely motivate distinguishing between two different types of falsehood.

9 More exactly, it gives rise to scepticism about the necessity of any system of representation whatever employing a concept of truth which would be such as to validate Excluded Third. It may be that Excluded Third is indeed necessary, given the nature of the true/false classification which we actually employ. But who is to say that all possible symbolic systems would have to employ precisely this way of drawing a true/false distinction?

12 Simples and logical objectivism

1 If the conceptual pragmatist argument with which we concluded Chapter 11 is correct, then what might be accidental is that we should have selected concepts of truth and falsity such that singular propositions are neither true nor false with respect to circumstances in which their objects of reference fail to exist. This much is consistent with logical objectivism – see my (1987b).

2 Note that there is nothing in this argument which entails the description-theory of names as it is usually understood, let alone the specific form of the theory to which Wittgenstein commits himself. For the claim that sentences containing ordinary names are not true with respect to the possible circumstances in which the bearers of those names would fail to exist is consistent with an analysis which takes an atomic sentence 'Fb' to have the form '$\exists x(Fx \& x = b)$'. Since this analysis still contains the name 'b', that name has not been analysed away into any sort of description. And since all ordinary names may be analysed in the same manner, we can still maintain that the distinctive contribution made by a particular name to the semantic content of sentences in which it occurs is exhausted by its bearer. Indeed, we could still maintain (as the semantic paradigm defended in *TS* requires) that a sentence containing a name which lacks a referent in the actual world is without semantic content.

Thus the plausible claim that sentences containing names are not true in the face of the possible non-existence of their objects of reference does not entail a description-theory of ordinary names. Moreover, even the claim that there have to be Simples does not entail that ordinary names are to be analysed into arrangements of Simples. For the argument only requires that there be some genuinely singular propositions which can be understood prior to acquiring the concept of generality, not that these propositions then have to be used to analyse the contents of all others.

What emerges from this is that the best way to understand Wittgenstein's commitment to a version of description-theory for ordinary names is in terms of the requirement of determinacy-in-advance, as we sketched in Chapter 7. For although that argument failed too, it had a degree of plausibility which is lacking here.

3 Further confirmation of the close connection between the argument to Simples and the requirement of determinacy-in-advance may be obtained from *PTLP*. There the equivalent of *TLP* 3.23 (namely 3.20101) is followed by two passages

expressing what is, in effect, that requirement. Thus *PTLP* 3.20102 tells us that the analysis of signs must come to an end somewhere, because if signs are to express anything at all then *Bedeutung* must belong to them in a way which is 'once and for all complete'. And *PTLP* 3.20103 is none other than the passage which when placed in its original context in *NB* formed our source for the very idea of the requirement of determinacy-in-advance (see Chapter 5).

4 It might be objected against this way of reading 2.0211, and in favour of the interpretation given in connection with the argument from Excluded Third in Chapter 10 (where the 'other proposition' is one asserting the existence of the object referred to), that it conflicts with the way in which Wittgenstein expresses the idea in the 'Notes Dictated to Moore' of 1914. There he says: 'The question whether a proposition has sense [*Sinn*] can never depend on the *truth* of another proposition about a constituent of the first.' (*NB* 116. Italics in original.) This certainly looks as if he is objecting to the possible contingency of the objects of reference, rather than the possible contingency of the relationship between a proposition and its truth-condition (as my interpretation would have it).

But there are two things which cast doubt on the connection between this passage and the otherwise similar-sounding 2.0211. The first is that there is some reason to think that he uses '*Sinn*', at this early stage, to mean 'sense', contrasting with its *TLP* usage to mean 'truth-condition'. See in particular *NB* 111. The second is that he is obviously not thinking of a situation in which an object of singular reference might fail to exist, since the passage continues by asserting that the sense of '$\forall x(x = x)$' cannot depend upon the truth of '$\exists x(x = x)$'. Indeed, the context makes clear that what he is attacking is the idea that the status, as such, of a necessary truth (which must be recognisable from the symbol alone) might depend upon some empirical fact. So if anything the passage quoted supports my own reading of 2.0211, since in both cases the 'other proposition' would describe a contingent condition for the obtaining of a conceptual relation – in the one case between symbols and reality, in the other case between the symbols in a tautology – thus conflicting with logical objectivism.

5 This view has gained increasing ground in recent years, with demonstratives being accorded the sort of detailed scrutiny which used to be reserved for proper names. See, for example, Perry (1977) and (1979) and Evans (1982). See also my (1987a).

6 See, for example, Evans (1982) and McDowell (1984), as well as many of the papers in Pettit & McDowell (1986).

7 So much, at least, follows from the Context Principle. See Chapter 2 above.

8 The image of the web is of course Quine's in 'Two Dogmas'. See his (1953), pp. 42ff.

9 Notice that a similar concession is forced on us from quite a different direction. For the truth-condition of an indexical statement also depends, not just upon its sense and the state of the world, but upon the context in which it is made; and this, too, is contingent. But to acknowledge that this is so is not in itself to

reject logical objectivism, since the manner in which sense reaches out, *via* a context, to determine a truth-condition can still be considered to be wholly objective. In order to deny logical objectivism one must hold that the manner in which truth-conditions are determined is some function of human dispositions and reactions.

10 I disagree. I find Wittgenstein's conception of philosophy – both early and late – excessively narrow. But this should not be allowed to get in the way of our appreciation of his positive contributions, including, in the present instance, the intellectual challenge presented by the argument to Simples.

11 Note, moreover, that Wittgenstein himself is only committed to the weaker claim about how it must be possible to acquire a grasp of language, since he speaks at 3.23 of the requirement that simple signs be *possible*, rather than the requirement that they be actual.

12 It ought at least to make many contemporary philosophers feel uneasy that they accept something like Wittgenstein's logical objectivism, and his hierarchical picture of language, while thinking that they can deny his conclusion.

13 Independent elementary propositions

1 The theory is as follows. Where A entails B it gives it a probability of 1. Where A and B are logically independent they give one another a probability of ½. And where A is inconsistent with B it gives it a probability of 0. Intermediate probabilities are arrived at thus: the probability which A gives to B is a ratio of the number of truth-grounds of B (lines containing a 'T' in its truth-table) which are also truth-grounds of A, against the total number of truth-grounds of A. For example, 'P ∨ Q' gives the proposition 'Q' a probability of ⅔, since 'Q' is true in two out of the three cases where 'P ∨ Q' would be true. Clearly this truth-tabular account is only workable if the atomic propositions are all logically independent.

2 Of course the text here is hard to disentangle, since his thesis is precisely that all logic reduces to logic in the narrow sense – that all logic is truth-functional.

3 Griffin, too, stresses this point, in the context of a similar account of the independence requirement to that given here. See his (1964), pp. 84–6.

4 The same can also be said of Russell, and indeed of axiomatic approaches to logic generally.

5 Note the parallel here with the arguments we used while expounding Wittgenstein's programme of analysis in Chapter 7. The focus there was on the internal relationship between a proposition and its truth-condition; the focus here is on internal relationships between propositions themselves. But the principle is the same: Wittgenstein's demand is that the contents of the propositions in question should be displayed in such a way that the internal relations will manifestly depend upon sense alone.

6 See, for example, Hughes & Cresswell (1968). In this and the next two paragraphs I have benefited from discussions with Jack Copeland.

7 Moreover, if 'necessary' were allowed to be a predicate of individuals, and if

we supposed predicates to refer, then on the *TLP* account necessity *would* be a genuine aspect of reality, since Simples exist necessarily.

8 The moves made here are essentially the same as those which, I argued, enable us to find a place for meaningful philosophical discourse; see Chapter 1 and *TS* 7. This is, of course, no accident, since 'necessary' is one of the crucial distinctively philosophical terms.

9 Is it really so very obvious that no one could grasp the concept *red* without as yet having any concept of the other individual colours?

10 Of course I am here intending to sketch the sort of account of conceptual necessity which is distinctive of the later Wittgenstein. We shall return to consider the issue in a little more detail in Chapter 15.

14 Modelling elementary propositions

1 See, for example, Griffin (1964), pp. 42–50 and 152.

2 I myself owe the model which follows to Roger White, though I have since discovered it in Keyt (1963), presented almost as an aside (see Copi & Beard (1966), p. 290). It also has some similarities with the very sophisticated models provided by Goddard & Judge in their (1982); but these are designed to meet a different set of constraints, the most important of which is that Simples should not only be unknown but unknowable. These constraints derive from an interpretation which is largely unargued, and they make no attempt to fit their reading of the metaphysics of *TLP* into the semantic doctrines of the work; though even cursory consideration shows that they have misplaced Wittgenstein's concerns. In particular, they are obviously mistaken in their contention that he belongs within the continental tradition in epistemology exemplified by Kant, Brentano, Meinong and Husserl (ibid., pp. 19–25).

3 For example 'There is a point-mass somewhere on plane a_1 at time t_2' will come out as: '$\exists y \exists z(a_1 y z t_2)$'.

4 In particular, an elementary proposition which states the existence of a point-mass at a given place and time does not entail the disjunction of the elementary propositions stating the existence of a point-mass at that or the surrounding places at the immediately succeeding time.

5 Moreover, even in the case of ordinary material objects, it is implausible that references to them are analytically equivalent to descriptions of the arrangement of their constitutive point-masses. See *TS* 12.

6 Not that these assumptions would necessarily have to be made explicitly. For a thinker's understanding of at least some of the names for planes of space might consist in an unarticulated recognitional capacity, acquired directly through immersion in the linguistic practice. But these capacities can only operate effectively if certain things are in fact true about the relative motions of the thinker and the physical items of their acquaintance.

7 We are nevertheless left with many interpretative options. For example, we might suppose Wittgenstein to have been working explicitly with our model, but to have failed to realise what would be required to set up and maintain a

system of coordinates, believing this to be of merely psychological interest. I therefore feel justified in continuing to maintain that *TLP* names have senses, despite the evidence of 4.243 – see *TS* 12.

8 In *TS* 11 I argued that Sellars' suggestion, that *TLP* admits of monadic concatenations, produces a reading of the text which, while possible, is far from natural.

9 Since Wittgenstein regards the full implementation of a programme of analysis as belonging to what he calls 'the application of logic', as opposed to logic proper (5.55–5.557), he feels that he can remain agnostic about its ultimate outcome. All the same he may have had firm ideas about the sort of direction in which a programme of analysis should go.

I take it that by the 'application of logic' Wittgenstein means the carrying-through of a programme of analysis for a particular natural language (as it exists in the world as we find it), as opposed to what can be said *a priori* about the form of all conceivable languages (logic proper).

10 Once again I owe the model which follows to Roger White.

11 This point is developed in my (1986), 2iii & 3iii. I believe it derives originally from Strawson's (1959), Ch. 4.

15 Deconstruction: following a rule

1 I have in mind Socrates' oft-repeated inference from someone's concession that they are unable to say what piety or courage or knowledge are, to the conclusion that they therefore do not know what they are.

2 See *TS* 10 for defence of the *TLP* view that thinkings consist in structured arrangements of sign-tokens. But notice that even if thinking could be explained in terms of non-language-involving beliefs there would remain a problem. For we should still want to know what it is about a belief which enables it to reach out to the world in a manner independent of the properties of the believer.

3 The same reasoning leads to the rejection of transcendent universals as candidates for senses. Thus Pears is quite correct that Platonism is a target of attack in Wittgenstein's discussion of rule-following (see his (1987), pp. 10–11, 15–16 and 59–60 and his (1988), Ch. 17). But this is true only in so far as Platonism is one form of logical objectivism. So it is wrong to characterise the main difference between *TLP* and *PI* in terms of acceptance or rejection of Platonism, as Pears does. On the contrary, Wittgenstein was opposed to any form of Platonism throughout. See *TS* 9 and 15.

4 I owe the distinction between modified and radical conventionalism to Dummett. See his (1978), pp. 169–80. See also Wright (1980), Chs. 18–20. The modified conventionalist holds that all internal relations are (objective) consequences of a base-class of conventions, whereas the radical conventionalist holds that each and every internal relation is a direct expression of a convention.

5 Nor is time by any means the only dimension along which possible misunder-

standings can occur. For the samples will also, for example, have been of particular shapes and sizes, and will have been viewed within a particular region of space.

6 This point is made by Wright in his (1984a).

7 The idea of a logical objectivist sense is very similar to what McDonough calls 'a meaning terminus' (see his (1986), Ch. 6) – that is, an object of awareness which both represents the world and somehow contains its own standard for interpreting itself. It is a further advantage of my way of reading *TLP* (where senses are functions of conventionally determined uses of signs) as against McDonough's (where meanings are acts of thinking) that it can partially explain how the early Wittgenstein never came to see the absurdity of his view. For he may never have raised the question what it *is* to know the sense of a sign, perhaps thinking this to be the business of psychology. Whereas if McDonough is right, the lack of candidates for meaning termini ought to have been patently obvious to him.

8 Here I agree with McGinn (1984) about Wittgenstein's positive views on meaning, particularly his denial that the latter takes meaning to be essentially communitarian (as Kripke (1982) and – in some moods – Wright (1980) believe).

9 Perhaps Wittgenstein would be more likely to say that my memory of an intention is a *criterion* for its existence. It is not often noticed that most of the benefits of a criterial theory for mental-kind terms can also be provided by functionalism – particularly loose logical connections between mental states and their behavioural manifestations (because the concepts take the form 'state whose normal causes and effects are . . . '). On the notion of a criterion, see Albritton (1959), and Chs. 7 and 8 of Wright (1986b).

10 See Wright (1980), Ch. 11.

11 See McGinn (1984), who thinks that in attacking the view that understanding must consist in something 'coming before the mind', Wittgenstein is focussing on an idea which is without any lasting philosophical appeal (ibid., pp. 95–6).

12 See Kripke (1982). We can distinguish four different constraints on the notion of meaning which are in play within Kripke's Sceptical Argument (the argument to show that there are no facts about meaning): (1) meaning is essentially normative, making room for a distinction between right and wrong use; (2) meaning provides unique justification, the meaning of 'plus', for example, justifying one and only one pattern of application; (3) meaning has infinite significance, justifying infinitely many possible applications; (4) meaning is non-inferentially accessible to consciousness, so that I do not have to form hypotheses about whether I mean *plus* or *quus* by 'plus'. He argues quite correctly that there is nothing which can meet all four constraints. But notice that the second and third are very close, at least, to logical objectivism. Once they have been dropped, there is no reason why a dispositional account of meaning should not be able to comply with the first and the fourth. What has to be given up is a myth about meaning, not the notion of meaning itself.

13 This is how I see Wittgenstein responding to Dummett's manifestation argu-

ment, which is a challenge to the believer in the objectivity of truth to say what a speaker could do to manifest a grasp of a verification-transcendent truth-condition (see, for example, Dummett (1976) and Wright (1986b), Introduction and Ch. 1). The answer is: by manifesting a capacity to employ the component terms in the sentence correctly. What the manifestation argument takes for granted is that a grasp of an objective truth-condition must, if it exists, be a separate capacity, not already accounted for by the thinker's capacity to use the component terms, as evidenced by their use of them in decidable sentences. But it is rather those capacities which *generate* the objectivity of truth, if the argument I give in the text is correct.

You could put the point like this: what a speaker grasps in understanding a sentence is not the objectivity of its truth-condition, but simply its truth-condition. Objectivity of truth is implied by the character of that understanding, rather than being a component idea within its scope. We can respond similarly to Wright's normativity argument (see his (1986b), pp. 23–6): the objectivity of truth need introduce no additional constraint on our linguistic practice, since it is something delivered by the capacities constitutive of our understanding, not a further normative component within the practice.

It might be replied that I am tacitly assuming that the understanding of words is prior to the understanding of sentences, whereas in fact it is secondary, having to be characterised in terms of the latter. But it is one thing to say that understanding a word is a matter of knowing how it will contribute to the content of sentences in which it occurs (with which I agree) and quite another thing to say that understanding a sentence must involve some capacity in addition to those which constitute the understanding of its component parts and their mode of combination (which seems to be what the manifestation and normativity arguments require).

14 I am grateful to Tim Fitzmaurice and A. D. Smith for helping me to appreciate this point.

15 Most of these difficulties were raised by Crispin Wright in correspondence.

16 Notice that this does not commit me to the sort of communitarian conception of meaning attributed to Wittgenstein by Kripke and others. To say that the norms of my language in fact involve reference to a community is not at all to say that the norms of any possible language must do so.

17 It is unclear to what extent Wittgenstein would have wished to endorse this anti-logical-objectivist defence of the objectivity of truth. For he appears to have been unwilling to accept that capacities have categorical bases in the brain (hence his view that there could not be just one occasion on which someone follows a rule, criticised soundly by McGinn in his (1984)). But on the other hand, he seems to have accepted that there are determinate counterfactual and hypothetical truths about my responses in various non-actualised circumstances (*PI* 187). In any case, it is striking that Wittgenstein does not in fact raise doubts concerning the objectivity of truths about remote regions of space and time (as do contemporary anti-realists like Dummett and Wright), his criticisms being confined to logic and mathematics. I suspect that there is a

deep tension within Wittgenstein's thought at this point. Dummett and Wright may be seen as defending one sort of rational reconstruction (extending the anti-realism), whereas I have been defending another (providing a categorical basis for determinate counterfactuals by dropping the opposition to physicalism).

18 Here I follow the account developed by Wright in his (1980), Part III.

19 The conventionalism is radical in the sense that necessary 'truths' are not thought to be genuine objects of discovery, but are rather the product of a general convention that we should elevate the results of our inability to imagine alternatives to the status of a rule of description. See Wright (1980), Ch. 23.

16 Wittgenstein: early and late

1 For full discussion, see *TS* 15.

2 For full defence, see *TS* 8.

3 See *TS* 8 for a defence of this claim.

4 For full discussion of Wittgenstein's opposition to Platonism in *TLP*, see *TS* 8, 9, 15 and 16.

5 For a more lengthy defence of the possibility that the later Wittgenstein may have misunderstood his earlier work, see *TS* 1.

6 Rightly, as I argue in *TS* 13.

7 Indeed, in one of the few passages in *TLP* where such matters are discussed (4.442), Wittgenstein assumes (wrongly) that Frege's assertion-sign is intended to contribute to the *content* of sentences to which it is attached.

8 Some commentators hold that the propositions of *TLP* are essentially assertoric, in that each *Satz* is an act of judging that such-and-such is the case. I argue against such an interpretation in *TS* 8.

9 What this then suggests is that the argument from determinacy of sentence-sense comes apart from the argument from the objectivity of conceptual necessity – see Chapter 4. Rather it, like the objectivity of contingent truth, can be accounted for adequately in terms of the operation of the categorical bases of our conceptual capacities in accordance with natural law.

10 See *TS* 7 for a full defence of this view.

11 That *TLP* overlooks the possibility of purpose-relative concepts is all-of-a-piece with the lack of attention it pays to context-dependent aspects of language generally. But so far as I can see there is nothing in *TLP* which necessitates this.

12 This is not to say, however, that the only aspects of the system of thought of *TLP* which need to be rejected are those that would be undermined by the attack on logical objectivism. On the contrary, the assumption that the identity-condition for semantic content is the same in all regions of discourse is also false, and could be corrected without surrendering logical objectivism. Moreover (and more surprisingly), the *TLP* idea that the principles of logic – in particular Excluded Third – must govern any system of representation what-ever, which we argued in Chapter 11 to be false, is also independent of logical

objectivism. Here all that was necessary was for Wittgenstein to recognise the truth of conceptual pragmatism, seeing that there may be a number of distinct but similar concepts in a given area of discourse from amongst which we are to select the one which best subserves our purposes. For as we saw in Chapter 11, our commitment to Excluded Third can only reflect the fact that within assertoric discourse our interest in truth is primary. Yet we can easily imagine circumstances in which our interests would be different, such that we should select a way of drawing the true/false distinction which would leave room for a third possibility. Yet so far as I can see, conceptual pragmatism would be consistent with all of Wittgenstein's other doctrines, including logical objectivism. On this see my (1987b), where I argue that conceptual pragmatism is not only consistent with both logical objectivism and its denial, but also with Platonism.

13 For discussion of these issues see many of the chapters in Dummett (1978) as well as his (1982), and Wright (1980) as well as the chapters in his (1986b).

References

Albritton, R. (1959). On Wittgenstein's Use of the Term 'Criterion'. *Journal of Philosophy* 56, 845–57.

Allaire, Edwin (1959). Tractatus 6.3751. *Analysis* 19, 100–5.

(1963). The Tractatus: Nominalistic or Realistic? in Copi & Beard (1966), 325–42.

Ambrose, Alice, ed. (1979). *Wittgenstein's Lectures, Cambridge 1932–35* (Oxford: Basil Blackwell).

Anscombe, G. E. M. (1959). *An Introduction to Wittgenstein's Tractatus* (London: Hutchinson).

Anscombe, G. E. M. & P. T. Geach (1961). *Three Philosophers* (Oxford: Blackwell).

Armstrong, D. M. (1978). *Universals and Scientific Realism* (Cambridge: Cambridge University Press).

(1983). *What is a Law of Nature?* (Cambridge: Cambridge University Press).

Ayer, A. J. (1936). *Language, Truth and Logic* (London: Gollancz).

(1985). *Wittgenstein* (Harmondsworth: Penguin).

Baker, G. P. (1981). Following Wittgenstein. In *Wittgenstein: To Follow a Rule*, ed. S. Holtzman and C. Leich (London: Routledge & Kegan Paul).

Baker, G. P. & P. M. S. Hacker (1980). *Wittgenstein: Understanding and Meaning* (Oxford: Blackwell).

(1984). *Frege: Logical Excavations* (Oxford: Blackwell).

(1985). *Wittgenstein: Rules, Grammar and Necessity* (Oxford: Blackwell).

Bell, David (1979). *Frege's Theory of Judgement* (Oxford: Oxford University Press).

Benacerraf, Paul (1965). What Numbers Could Not Be. *Philosophical Review* 74, 47–73.

(1973). Mathematical Truth. *Journal of Philosophy* 70, 661–80.

Bennett, J. (1975). *Kant's Dialectic* (Cambridge: Cambridge University Press).

Black, Max (1964). *A Companion to Wittgenstein's Tractatus* (Ithaca: Cornell University Press).

Blackburn, Simon (1984). *Spreading the Word* (Oxford: Oxford University Press).

Blackwell, Kenneth (1981). The Early Wittgenstein and the Middle Russell. In Irving Block (1981), 1–30.

195

Block, Irving, ed. (1981). *Perspectives on the Philosophy of Wittgenstein* (Oxford: Blackwell).

Block, Ned, ed. (1981). *Readings in Philosophy of Psychology*, Vol. II (London: Methuen).

Bogen, James (1972). *Wittgenstein's Philosophy of Language* (London: Routledge & Kegan Paul).

Bolton, Derek (1979). *An Approach to Wittgenstein's Philosophy* (London: Macmillan).

Bradley, Raymond (1987). Tractatus 2.022–2.023. *Canadian Journal of Philosophy* 17, 349–60.

Burge, Tyler (1979). Sinning against Frege. *Philosophical Review* 88, 389–432.

Butterfield, Jeremy, ed. (1986). *Language, Mind and Logic* (Cambridge, Cambridge University Press).

Carruthers, Peter (1981). Frege's Regress. *Aristotelian Society Proceedings* 82, 17–32.

  (1984). Baker and Hacker's Wittgenstein. *Synthese* 58, 451–79.

  (1985). Ruling-out Realism. *Philosophia* 15, 61–78.

  (1986). *Introducing Persons: Theories and Arguments in the Philosophy of Mind* (London: Croom Helm; Albany: SUNY).

  (1987a). Russellian Thoughts. *Mind* 96, 18–35.

  (1987b). Conceptual Pragmatism. *Synthese* 73, 205–24.

  (1989a). Brute Experience. *Journal of Philosophy* 86, 258–69.

  (1989b). *Tractarian Semantics: Finding Sense in Wittgenstein's Tractatus* (Oxford: Blackwell).

Coope, C., P. Geach, T. Potts & R. White (1971). *A Wittgenstein Workbook* (Oxford: Blackwell).

Copi, Irving (1958a). Tractatus 5.542. *Analysis* 18, 102–4.

  (1958b). Objects, Properties and Relations in the Tractatus. *Mind* 67, 145–65.

Copi, Irving & Robert Beard, eds. (1966). *Essays on Wittgenstein's Tractatus* (London: Routledge & Kegan Paul).

Currie, Gregory (1982a). *Frege: An Introduction to his Philosophy* (Brighton: Harvester).

  (1982b). Frege, Sense and Mathematical Knowledge. *Australasian Journal of Philosophy* 60, 5–19.

  (1984). Frege's Metaphysical Argument. In Wright (1984b), 144–57.

Davidson, Donald (1980). *Essays on Actions and Events* (Oxford: Oxford University Press).

  (1984). *Inquiries into Truth and Interpretation* (Oxford: Oxford University Press).

Davidson, Donald & Gilbert Harman, eds. (1972). *The Semantics of Natural Language* (Dordrecht: Reidel).

Diamond, Cora, ed. (1976). *Wittgenstein's Lectures on the Foundations of Mathematics* (Brighton: Harvester).

Donnellan, Keith (1966). Reference and Definite Descriptions. *Philosophical Review* 75, 281–304.

(1972). Proper Names and Identifying Descriptions. In Davidson & Harman (1972), 356–79.

(1974). Speaking of Nothing. *Philosophical Review* 83, 3–31.

Dummett, Michael (1973). *Frege: Philosophy of Language* (London: Duckworth).

(1975). What is a Theory of Meaning? (I). In Guttenplan (1975), 97–138.

(1976). What is a Theory of Meaning? (II). In Evans & McDowell (1976), 67–137.

(1978). *Truth and Other Enigmas* (London: Duckworth).

(1981a). Frege and Wittgenstein. In Irving Block (1981), 31–42.

(1981b). *The Interpretation of Frege's Philosophy* (London: Duckworth).

(1982). Realism. *Synthese* 52, 55–112.

(1984). An Unsuccessful Dig. In Wright (1984b), 194–226.

Engelmann, Paul (1967). *Letters from Ludwig Wittgenstein with a Memoir* (Oxford: Blackwell).

Evans, Gareth (1973). The Causal Theory of Names. *Aristotelian Society Proceedings* supp. vol. 47, 187–208.

(1982). *The Varieties of Reference* (Oxford: Oxford University Press).

Evans, Gareth & John McDowell, eds. (1976). *Truth and Meaning* (Oxford: Oxford University Press).

Favrholdt, David (1964). *An Interpretation and Critique of Wittgenstein's Tractatus* (Copenhagen: Munksgaard).

Finch, Henry (1971). *Wittgenstein: The Early Philosophy* (New Jersey: Humanities).

Fodor, Jerry (1981). *Representations* (Brighton: Harvester).

Fogelin, Robert (1976). *Wittgenstein* (London: Routledge & Kegan Paul).

(1982). Wittgenstein's Operator N. *Analysis* 42, 124–7.

Frege, Gottlob (1952). *Philosophical Writings*, trans. P. Geach and M. Black (Oxford: Blackwell).

(1964). *The Basic Laws of Arithmetic*, trans. M. Furth (California: California University Press).

(1968). *The Foundations of Arithmetic*, trans. J. Austin (Oxford: Blackwell).

(1972). *Conceptual Notation and Related Articles*, trans. T. Bynum (Oxford: Oxford University Press).

(1979). *Posthumous Writings*, trans. P. Long and R. White (Oxford: Blackwell).

(1980). *Philosophical and Mathematical Correspondence*, trans. B. McGuinness & H. Kaal (Oxford: Blackwell).

(1984). *Collected Papers*, trans. various (Oxford: Blackwell).

Geach, Peter (1951). Frege's Grundlagen. *Philosophical Review* 60, 535–44.

(1955). Class and Concept. *Philosophical Review* 64, 561–70.

(1957). *Mental Acts* (London: Routledge & Kegan Paul).

(1961). Frege. In Anscombe & Geach (1961), 127–62.

(1962). *Reference and Generality* (Ithaca: Cornell University Press).

(1974). Six Lectures on Wittgenstein's Tractatus. Unpublished typescript.

(1981). Wittgenstein's Operator N. *Analysis* 41, 168–70.

(1982). More on Wittgenstein's Operator N. *Analysis* 42, 127–8.

Goddard, Leonard & Brenda Judge (1982). *The Metaphysics of Wittgenstein's Tractatus* (Australasian Journal of Philosophy Monograph).

Goldstein, L. (1983). Scientific Scotism. *Australasian Journal of Philosophy* 61, 40–57.

(1986). The Development of Wittgenstein's Views on Contradiction. *History & Philosophy of Logic* 7, 43–56.

Grice, H. P. (1957). Meaning. *Philosophical Review* 66, 377–88.

(1969). Utterer's Meaning and Intention. *Philosophical Review* 78, 147–77.

Griffin, James (1964). *Wittgenstein's Logical Atomism* (Oxford: Oxford University Press).

Guttenplan, Samuel, ed. (1975). *Mind and Language* (Oxford: Oxford University Press).

Hacker, P. M. S. (1972). *Insight and Illusion* (Oxford: Oxford University Press).

(1986). *Insight and Illusion*, revised edition (Oxford: Oxford University Press).

Hintikka, Jaakko (1958). On Wittgenstein's 'Solipsism'. *Mind* 67, 88–91.

Hintikka, Merrill & Jaakko Hintikka (1986). *Investigating Wittgenstein* (Oxford: Blackwell).

Hughes, G. & M. Cresswell (1968). *An Introduction to Modal Logic* (London: Methuen).

Ishiguro, Hidé (1969). Use and Reference of Names. In Winch (1969), 20–50.

(1979). Subjects, Predicates, Isomorphic Representation and Language-Games. In *Essays in Honour of Jaakko Hintikka*, ed. E. Saarinen, R, Hilpinen, I. Niiniluoto and M. Hintikka (Dordrecht: Reidel), 351–64.

(1981). Wittgenstein and the Theory of Types. In Irving Block (1981), 43–59.

Kant, I. (1929). *Critique of Pure Reason*, trans. N. Kemp Smith (London: Macmillan).

Katz, Jerrold (1981). *Language and Other Abstract Objects* (Oxford, Blackwell).

Kenny, Anthony (1973). *Wittgenstein* (London: Penguin).

(1974). The Ghost of the Tractatus. *Royal Institute of Philosophy Lectures*, Vol. VII (London: Macmillan), 1–13.

(1981). Wittgenstein's Early Philosophy of Mind. In Irving Block (1981), 140–8.

Keyt, David (1963). Wittgenstein's Notion of an Object. *Philosophical Quarterly* 13, 3–15.

Klemke, E. D., ed. (1968). *Essays on Frege* (Chicago: Illinois University Press).

Kripke, Saul (1979). A Puzzle about Belief. In Margalit (1979), 239–83.

(1980). *Naming and Necessity* (Oxford: Blackwell).

(1982). *Wittgenstein on Rules and Private Language* (Oxford: Blackwell).

Lee, Desmond, ed. (1980). *Wittgenstein's Lectures, Cambridge 1930–32* (Oxford: Blackwell).

Lewis, David (1983). *Philosophical Papers*, Vol. I (Oxford: Oxford University Press).

Loar, Brian (1981). *Mind and Meaning* (Cambridge: Cambridge University Press).

Long, Peter (1969). Are Predicates and Relational Expressions Incomplete? *Philosophical Review* 78, 90–8.

(1982). Formal Relations. *Philosophical Quarterly* 32, 151–61.

McDonough, Richard (1986). *The Argument of the Tractatus* (Albany: SUNY).

McDowell, John (1977). On the Sense and Reference of a Proper Name. *Mind* 86, 159–85.

(1980). Meaning, Communication and Knowledge. In van Straaten (1980), 117–39.

(1984). *De Re* Senses. In Wright (1984b), 98–109.

(1986). Singular Thought and the Extent of Inner Space. In Pettit & McDowell (1986), 137–68.

McGinn, Colin (1982a). The Structure of Content. In Woodfield (1982), 207–58.

(1982b). *The Character of Mind* (Oxford: Oxford University Press).

(1984). *Wittgenstein on Meaning* (Oxford: Blackwell).

McGuinness, Brian (1974). The Grundgedenke of the Tractatus. *Royal Institute of Philosophy Lectures* Vol. VII (London: Macmillan), 49–61.

(1981). The So-called Realism of Wittgenstein's Tractatus. In Irving Block (1981), 60–73.

ed. (1982). *Wittgenstein and his Times* (Oxford: Blackwell).

(1988). *Wittgenstein: A Life*, Vol. I (London: Duckworth).

Mackie, J. L. (1976). The Riddle of Existence. *Aristotelian Society Proceedings* supp. vol. 50, 247–67.

Malcolm, Norman (1958). *Wittgenstein: A Memoir* (Oxford: Oxford University Press).

(1986). *Nothing is Hidden* (Oxford: Blackwell).

Margalit, A., ed. (1979). *Meaning and Use* (Dordrecht: Reidel).

Maslow, Alexander (1961). *A Study in Wittgenstein's Tractatus* (Los Angeles: California University Press).

Morris, Thomas (1984). *Understanding Identity Statements* (Aberdeen: Aberdeen University Press).

Mounce, H. O. (1981). *Wittgenstein's Tractatus: An Introduction* (Oxford: Blackwell).

Nagel, Thomas (1986). *The View from Nowhere* (Oxford: Oxford University Press).

Noonan, Harold (1979). Rigid Designation. *Analysis* 39, 174–82.

(1980). Names and Belief. *Aristotelian Society Proceedings* 81, 93–108.

(1984). Fregean Thoughts. *Philosophical Quarterly* 34, 205–25.

(1986). Russellian Thoughts and Methodological Solipsism. In Butterfield (1986), 67–90.

Ogden, C. K. & I. A. Richards (1923). *The Meaning of Meaning* (London: Routledge & Kegan Paul).

Pears, David (1971). *Wittgenstein* (London: Fontana).

(1981). The Logical Independence of Elementary Propositions. In Irving Block (1981), 74–84.

(1987). *The False Prison*, Vol. I (Oxford: Oxford University Press).

(1988). *The False Prison*, Vol. II (Oxford: Oxford University Press).

Perry, John (1977). Frege on Demonstratives. *Philosophical Review* 86, 474–97.
      (1979). The Problem of the Essential Indexical. *Nous* 13, 3–21.
Pettit, Philip & John McDowell, eds. (1986). *Subject, Thought and Context* (Oxford: Oxford University Press).
Putnam, Hilary (1973). *Mind, Language and Reality* (Cambridge: Cambridge University Press).
Quine, W. V. O. (1953). *From a Logical Point of View* (Cambridge, Mass.: Harvard University Press).
      (1960). *Word and Object* (Cambridge, Mass.: MIT Press).
Ramsey, F. P. (1923). Review of the Tractatus. *Mind* 32, 465–78.
      (1978). *Foundations* (London: Routledge & Kegan Paul).
Russell, Bertrand (1903). *The Principles of Mathematics* (London: Allen & Unwin).
      (1910a). *Philosophical Essays* (London: Allen & Unwin).
      (1910b). With A. N. Whitehead, *Principia Mathematica* (Cambridge: Cambridge University Press).
      (1912). *The Problems of Philosophy* (Oxford: Oxford University Press).
      (1914). *Our Knowledge of the External World* (London: Allen & Unwin).
      (1917). *Mysticism and Logic* (London: Allen & Unwin).
      (1921). *The Analysis of Mind* (London: Allen & Unwin).
      (1940). *An Inquiry into Meaning and Truth* (London: Allen & Unwin).
      (1956). *Logic and Knowledge*, ed. R. Marsh (London: Allen & Unwin).
      (1984). *The Collected Papers of Bertrand Russell*, Vol. VII, ed. E. Eames and K. Blackwell (London: Allen & Unwin).
Sainsbury, Mark (1979). *Russell* (London: Routledge & Kegan Paul).
Salmon, Nathan (1982). *Reference and Essence* (Oxford: Blackwell).
      (1986). *Frege's Puzzle* (Cambridge, Mass.: MIT Press).
Searle, John (1957). Russell's Objections to Frege's Theory of Sense and Reference. *Analysis* 18, 137–43.
      (1958). Proper Names. *Mind* 67, 166–73.
      (1983). *Intentionality* (Cambridge: Cambridge University Press).
Sellars, W. (1962a). Naming and Saying. In Copl & Beard (1966), 249–69.
      (1962b). Truth and 'Correspondence'. *Journal of Philosophy* 59, 29–56.
Shwayder, David (1963). On the Picture Theory of Language. *Mind*, 72, 275–88.
Sluga, Hans (1980). *Gottlob Frege* (London: Routledge & Kegan Paul).
Stalnaker, Robert (1976). Propositions. In *Issues in the Philosophy of Language*, ed. A. Mackay and D. Merrill (New Haven: Yale University Press), 79–91.
Stenius, Erik (1960). *Wittgenstein's Tractatus* (Oxford: Blackwell).
      (1975). Wittgenstein and Ogden. *Philosophical Quarterly* 25, 62–8.
Stock, Guy (1974). Wittgenstein on Russell's Theory of Judgement. *Royal Institute of Philosophy Lectures*, Vol. VII (London: Macmillan), 62–75.
Straaten, Zak van, ed. (1980). *Philosophical Subjects* (Oxford: Oxford University Press).

Strawson, P. F. (1959). *Individuals* (London: Methuen).

(1971). *Logico-Linguistic Papers* (London: Methuen).

Tugendhat, E. (1970). The Meaning of 'Bedeutung' in Frege. *Analysis* 30, 177–89.

von Wright, G. H. (1982). *Wittgenstein* (Oxford: Blackwell).

Waismann, F. (1965). *Principles of Linguistic Philosophy*, ed. R. Harré (London: Macmillan).

(1979). *Wittgenstein and the Vienna Circle*, trans. J. Schulte and B. McGuinness (Oxford: Blackwell).

White, R. M. (1973). Wittgenstein and the General Propositional Form. Unpublished manuscript.

(1974). Can Whether one Proposition Makes Sense Depend on the Truth of Another? *Royal Institute of Philosophy Lectures*, Vol. VII (London: Macmillan), 14–29.

(1978). Wittgenstein on Identity. *Aristotelian Society Proceedings* 78, 157–74.

Winch, Peter, ed. (1969). *Studies in the Philosophy of Wittgenstein* (London: Routledge & Kegan Paul).

Wittgenstein, Ludwig (1922). *Tractatus Logico-Philosophicus*, trans. C. Ogden (London: Routledge & Kegan Paul).

(1929). Some Remarks on Logical Form. *Aristotelian Society Proceedings* supp. vol. 9, 162–71.

(1953). *Philosophical Investigations*, trans. G. Anscombe (Oxford: Blackwell).

(1961a). *Tractatus Logico-Philosophicus*, trans. D. Pears and B. McGuinness (London: Routledge & Kegan Paul).

(1961b). *Notebooks 1914–18*, trans. G. Anscombe (Oxford: Blackwell).

(1971). *Prototractatus*, trans. D. Pears and B. McGuinness (London: Routledge & Kegan Paul).

(1973). *Letters to C. K. Ogden*, ed. G. von Wright (Oxford: Blackwell).

(1974). *Letters to Russell, Keynes and Moore*, ed. G. von Wright (Oxford: Blackwell).

(1975). *Philosophical Remarks*, trans. R. Hargreaves and R. White (Oxford: Blackwell).

(1978). *Remarks on the Foundations of Mathematics*, 3rd edn, trans. G. Anscombe (Oxford: Blackwell).

Woodfield, Andrew, ed. (1982). *Thought and Object* (Oxford: Oxford University Press).

Wright, Crispin (1975). On the Coherence of Vague Predicates. *Synthese* 30, 325–65.

(1980). *Wittgenstein on the Foundations of Mathematics* (London: Duckworth).

(1983). *Frege's Conception of Numbers as Objects* (Aberdeen: Aberdeen University Press).

(1984a). Kripke's Account of the Argument against Private Language. *Journal of Philosophy* 81, 759–77.

ed. (1984b). *Frege: Tradition and Influence* (Oxford: Blackwell).
(1986a). Inventing Logical Necessity. In Butterfield (1986), 187–209.
(1986b). *Realism, Meaning and Truth* (Oxford: Blackwell).
Young, Julian (1984). Wittgenstein, Kant, Schopenhauer and Critical Philosophy.
    Theoria 50, 73–105.

Index of references to the Tractatus

Index of names and subjects